Jizo
BODHISATTVA

南無大願地藏王菩薩

JIZO BODHISATTVA

*Guardian
of Children,
Travelers, and
Other Voyagers*

JAN CHOZEN BAYS

SHAMBHALA
Boston & London
2003

Shambhala Publications, Inc.
Horticultural Hall
300 Massachusetts Avenue
Boston, Massachusetts 02115
www.shambhala.com

Originally published under the title *Jizo Bodhisattva: Modern Healing and Traditional Buddhist Practice.*

Published by arrangement with Tuttle Publishing.

Permission acknowledgements for use of previously published material are set out on page 279.

Frontispiece art: Jizo Bodhisattva seated on a lotus, holding a ring staff and cintamani jewel. An offering to the Three Treasures by a Taiwanese artist.

9 8 7 6 5 4 3 2 1

First Shambhala Edition
Printed in the United States of America

⊛ This edition is printed on acid-free paper that meets the American National Standards Institute z39.48 Standard.

Distributed in the United States by Random House, Inc., and in Canada by Random House of Canada Ltd

Library of Congress Cataloging-in-Publication Data
Bays, Jan Chozen.
Jizo Bodhisattva: guardian of children, travelers, and other voyagers/ Jan Chozen Bays.
p.   cm.
Originally published: Boston: Tuttle Pub., 2002.
Includes bibliographical references and index.
ISBN 1-59030-080-7 (paperback)
1. Kṣitigarbha (Buddhist diety)—Cult. I. Title.
BQ4710.K73B39 2003
294.3'431—dc21
2003050415

At the time of his death the Buddha said, "I have worked hard for many kalpas to liberate obstinate living beings. Those who have not yet understood the Dharma will surely fall into states of suffering."

Kshitigarbha Bodhisattva said, "Even if their good deeds are as little as a hair, a drop of water, a grain of sand, a mote of dust, or a bit of down, I shall gradually help living beings to liberation. World Honored One, do not feel distressed over beings in generations to come." He repeated this vow three times.

Shakyamuni Buddha was delighted and said, "My blessings. I appreciate your strong vows and praise you for your efforts to heal the human world. When you fulfill this great vow after many kalpas, you will become a Buddha."

From the Sutra of the Past Vows of Earth Store Bodhisattva

DEDICATION

This book is dedicated to every reader. May your practice with Jizo Bodhisattva become a strong staff to support you in your pilgrimage through this life. May you awaken to the pure bright mind and open benevolent heart that have been yours since before you were born. May the benefit of your practice radiate to all whom you meet. May you live in happiness and at ease.

Contents

Foreword

THE *Earth Store Sutra*

JAPANESE BUDDHIST PILGRIMS, as Roshi Chozen Bays tells us in her remarkable book, brought Jizo Bosatsu, with his compassion and saving graces, back to Japan from China. Chinese Empress Wu Zetien (624–705), despite her reputation for ambition and ruthlessness, was nonetheless a devout Buddhist laywoman. Monks visiting the Tang Court from India spoke of a longer edition of a popular scripture, the *Flower Adornment (Avatamsaka) Sutra,* and she wanted to read it. She promised to reward any pilgrim who could deliver the text, in Chinese translation, into her hands. The Khotanese translator Master Shikshananda, "Joy Of Learning" (seventh century), did just that. He brought a palm-leaf manuscript of the *Flower Adornment Scripture* to the Tang Court where he skillfully turned the Sanskrit into Chinese. The empress assembled hundreds of scholar-monks and attended the translation sessions herself.

Before returning to Khotan, Shikshananda brought forth from his monk's bag a copy of the Sutra on the *Past Vows of Earth Store Bodhisattva* and asked permission to translate it as well. The stories of Earth Store (Jizo) Bodhisattva began in China with that text.

The narratives tell of great vows by heroic women; adventures of courageous children who make fearless sacrifices to repay their debt of kindness to their parents; graphic, gory accounts of the hells and sublime tales of the heavens. We find practical advice for the spiritual aspects of childbirth, interpretation of dreams, and guidelines for avoiding rebirth in the evil destinies of animals, ghosts, and the hells.

Now Jizo Bosatsu, along with this timeless epic narrative, has come to the West.

The Bodhisattva with the Greatest Vows

His name in Sanskrit is *Kshitigarbha*. The name "Earth Store" could also be translated into English as "Earth Treasury," or "Earth Store-house." Earth Store, like its Japanese equivalent, Jizo, and the Chinese Ti-tsang, is a quick two syllables, easy to chant in one breath, and easy to remember.

Earth Store, one of the four great bodhisattvas of the Mahayana, is known as "the bodhisattva with the greatest vows." His two unforgettable vows are

"Only after the Hells are empty will I become a Buddha"

and

"Only after all beings are taken across to Enlightenment will I myself realize Bodhi."

Implied in these vows is the assertion that although Earth Store has the wisdom and the virtue necessary to become a Buddha, he chooses instead to postpone his own liberation until all beings have been safely rescued from the evil destinies. Only when they reach nirvana, will Earth Store fulfill his vows. Since living beings are busy creating offenses nonstop, Earth Store's duties in the hells are likely to extend into the infinite future. Such unimaginable courage and compassion are what makes his vows particularly great.

Women's Relationships with Their Mothers

I was a graduate student when I first heard stories of Buddhist women heroes in the Mahayana tradition. I read the story of Gangadevi, "The Goddess of the Ganges," a Buddhist female saint. Gangadevi, like Kuan-yin Bodhisattva in the Lotus Sutra, had made a rich offering to the Buddha and in turn had received a prediction to enlightenment. Predictions to enlightenment mark a major turning point in one's cultivation of the bodhisattva path.

Gangadevi's prediction caused some of the less-accomplished Arhat disciples to grumble. "How could a mere maiden win the most sublime prize: a prediction to Buddhahood, when that goal has eluded us, the real disciples, for so long?" they complained.

The Buddha's "field of blessings," however, is impartial, compassionate, and nonjudgmental. He explained to the Arhats that whoever makes offerings to the Triple Jewel with a pure heart, seeking nothing from the act, gains a corresponding reward, regardless of gender, race, age, or social status. If the grumpy Arhats had made a similar offering with Gangadevi's sincerity, they too, along with the Goddess of the Ganges, might have gained their predictions to enlightenment.

Two of Earth Store Bodhisattva's epiphanies as a bodhisattva, came in the form of women: "the Brahmin Woman" and "Bright Eyes." Both women had found their strength by tapping into the roots of their lives; they were "filial daughters." While their mothers were alive, both women related to them with gratitude and honor. After their mothers died, the daughters extended their concern past the grave.

They sought the Buddha's instruction on how they might continue to care for their mothers into their next rebirth. The first time I read this account, I reflected on how shallowly I had explored my own relationship with my parents. Although the sutra was originally spoken in India of the sixth century B.C.E., it spoke directly to my present situation. I believe it will do so for others too; hence, this welcome new contribution by Roshi Chozen Bays.

SEEING INTO THE SHADOW SIDE OF LIFE

But Earth Store also talks of hells in nightmarish proportions. This is Buddhism with its eyes open, a religion that takes faith off the meditation cushion into the night of the soul, wide-eyed and open-handed into humanity's griefs, mistakes, broken hearts, and hurting wounds.

Earth Store's sutra takes us into the darker side of life's hidden but vital aspects. He reveals the tormented minds and spirits of beings who have lost the Way, and with therapeutic precision explains the causes for their grief. But the journey to the dark underside has a compassionate purpose: to light the way out. Earth Store extends a hand to pull us out of the cycle of negative karma driven by delusion that leads to more harmful deeds and even further painful retribution.

Anybody who criticizes Buddhism as an escapist religion for people who want to avoid reality simply hasn't heard about Jizo. The Buddha, in telling the story of Earth Store, paints humankind in its full spectrum of colors, from radiant to occluded. But this is not dour for dour's sake, nor is it intended to leave us with a one-sided description of an ugly reality. It serves a healing purpose. The Buddha Dharma, with its holistic vision, gives methods for transforming negative emotion, wrong perceptions, and harmful states of mind into wholesome views, kindness, and deep wisdom.

In the end, the Earth Store Sutra empowers us to fundamentally change our actions, words, and thoughts, and in so doing take charge of our lives. Thus, Jizo is in every way an epic hero.

We live in an age and a culture alienated from our roots as never before. In a time of broken families and when children turn guns on classmates, this sutra's wisdom has, though sadly, never been more relevant. Earth Store is medicine for the soul. It reminds us that our narrow focus on material things and sensory stimulation blinds us to the joy and satisfaction available on every side. A fullness of blessings lies beneath our feet and before our eyes, if only we take the time to look.

This scripture appeals to the rare individual who understands that the beauty of a rose depends entirely on the "invisible" parts: the stem, the leaves, the thorns, the stalk, the roots and the fertilizer, rain, sun, and the effort of the gardener. Our later years comprise the longer half of life; and in many ways the most valuable. Few, however, see anything but the blossom when they look at a rose. Our culture is fixated on youth. We neglect our elders like things stored in the attic and dread our own aging as a curse. Earth Store once again reminds us of the treasure trove right beneath our feet, right before our eyes.

I once asked my teacher in religion, Master Hsuan Hua, the monk who expounded Earth Store's Dharma to the West in 1971, this question: "If somebody wanted to repay parents' kindness while they are still in the world, what would be the best way to do it?"

Without skipping a beat Master Hua replied, "Explain the Earth Store Sutra for your mother. That would pretty much repay her kindness in raising you."

ENLIGHTENED CH'AN MASTERS LOOK FOR THEIR PARENTS

After years of perusing biographies of Buddhist masters and adepts, it has dawned on me how in the Chinese tradition, most Ch'an masters report that immediately after their experience of awakening, the first thing they did was find a way to repay their parents' kindness. From Mahamaudgalyayana (Moggalana), the Buddha's disciple who was foremost in psychic powers, to Ming dynasty Master Han Shan, all share a common thread: to repay the kindness of parents. Coming to terms with this the most fundamental of relationships seems to be a pressing priority for Ch'an masters when they view things through their newly enlightened eyes. The conclusion is inescapable: the child/parent relationship is in some crucial way essential to our spiritual journey.

Earth Store is the bodhisattva with the greatest filial regard. When he was born as a woman she valued her first relationship, her root connection with her mother and father. She thought to repay that debt of kindness for bringing her into the world and giving her start as a human. Now such sentiments seem hopelessly out of sync and unhip. To stay home with the folks, to ask after their contentment, and to work for their comfort, at best becomes duty, at worst a burden. One must wonder: why did the great Ch'an masters, enlightened monks and nuns, immediately upon awakening from ignorance and attachment, look for their parents, to see into which realm they had been reborn? What lessons are we to learn from them when they state, as they do in so many stories, that their purpose was to "repay the kindness of their parents for making it possible for them to hear the Dharma and realize liberation from lifetimes of birth and death?" I think it's more than metaphor.

SUE ELLEN'S REUNION WITH HER MOM AND ITS IMPACT ON HER MEDITATION

I proposed a project with the Vipassana group that meets each week at the Berkeley Monastery. I suggested that the eighty or so regular meditators were to spend three visits with a "significant elder" of their choice—either a parent, grandparent, teacher, neighbor, the closest elder in their life. The task was to ask the elder to speak on their wisdom regarding the "next step in the journey." I suggested that they say, "I'm aging, too, and I could use some good words from your current perspective about the journey into elder status. Would you please tell me how your spiritual path has developed?"

I said, "Visit them three times and listen carefully to the concerns and the advice the elder provides."

Three weeks later we gathered to hear the stories. One of the meditators, we'll call her Sue Ellen, explained her background:

> I hadn't talked with my mother for seven years. She and I always disagreed about my life and she had given me up as a lost cause. Something about this project you gave us hit the right spot at just at the right time. Since I've been meditating for six years, maybe I've gained a bit of stillness and composure. Anyway I called my mother after I got home from class and she started right in on me.
>
> I said, "Mom, you never change and I love you for it. I'm coming right over." I walked in her house, gave her a hug, and we didn't stop talking for eight hours. The next morning she asked me to teach her to meditate.
>
> Boy, was I ready to reconnect with my mother. And the strangest thing, this week when I went to meditate I discovered that my entire chest area from waist to shoulders was warm and flexible. Who would have thought that my estranged relationship with my mother had frozen my heart? I had been meditating with a block of ice in my chest. Now my sitting has come alive and I'm warm from toe to crown.

The urgings of Earth Store Bodhisattva, Jizo Bosatsu, to reconnect with our parents, still rings true and taps into our spiritual wellsprings. The ancients continue to remind us: the Tao is here in the world, in the careful and tender treatment of the things and people closest to us. Grafting our lives back into the network of humanity pumps tap water through our tree of wisdom. Read with joy and delight in this timeless story.

THE REVEREND HENG SURE
American Buddhist Bhikshu
Director, Berkeley Buddhist Monastery

Preface

WRITING THIS BOOK HAS been an activity of faith and thus of spiritual practice. It began when Michael Kerber of Tuttle Publishing called to say he had heard I made statues of Jizo Bodhisattva. Would I write a book about Jizo? His request caused a turning. I had always thought, no more books. Bookstores are full of Buddhist books; there are too many words already, like muddy boot prints all over the simple truth of the Dharma. But I answered yes. Why? Not because the book was needed by anyone else, but because it was an invitation for me to know Jizo more intimately.

Jizo Bodhisattva has appeared and disappeared many times during my twenty-five years of Zen training. I first encountered Jizo when I started Zen practice in the 1970s at the Zen Center of Los Angeles. My teacher Maezumi Roshi had placed a stone statue of Jizo next to the path leading to the zendo, under a small lemon tree. I was unexpectedly attracted to this statue and rose early each morning to place a stick of incense in the dirt in front of it and chant the Jizo mantra. I planted a small garden of moss around the statue. While watering the moss to keep it alive in the Los Angeles heat, I poured water over the statue as I had seen memorial stones washed in Japanese cemeteries.

My attraction to Jizo then made little sense to me. I had been raised Protestant and had been taught that Protestants never pray or bow to a "graven image." Maezumi Roshi then brought another statue of Jizo back from a trip to Japan. It was a slender golden figure with a staff in one hand, a round globe in the other, and two children at his feet, clutching his robe. He asked me to place it on an altar at the Zen Center's medical clinic where I worked as a pediatrician. Still I had little true feeling in my heart for this gilded statue. Probably it was more familiar and comforting to our poor Mexican patients, like a little golden saint for their sick children.

I did not encounter Jizo Bodhisattva again until I attended a mizuko led by Zen teacher Yvonne Rand. A *mizuko* is the ceremony for children who have died, which I describe later in this book. The mizuko opened my heart and mind to the ability of Jizo to intervene in the world of human suffering. As others experience the benefit of the Jizo ceremony, interest grows in Jizo Bodhisattva and the mizuko ceremony in America. There are Jizo sites in gardens and on altars around North America as well as Jizo sites on the unlocated space of the World Wide Web.

I hope this book will be of help to those who wish to know more about Jizo, to Buddhists and also to spiritual seekers who are not Buddhist.

In Buddhism we do not regard any being as outside of our own true self, no matter how small or repulsive—an earthworm or a tick—nor how large and lofty—an enlightened bodhisattva like Jizo. Our proper relationship then to an earthworm is not to withdraw in disgust from it; our proper relationship to a bodhisattva is not to admire or worship from afar. If we enter spiritual practice hoping to know ourselves completely, then our proper attitude toward all creation is one of curiosity and ultimately of communion. To know ourselves we must truly know all beings—from earthworms to bodhisattvas—intimately.

In this book we take up a particular form in which wisdom and compassion have manifested and continue to manifest in the many worlds. This is the form of Jizo Bodhisattva. In studying Jizo thoroughly, the separation between us and Jizo begins to disappear. Actually it is only the illusion of separation that disappears. Jizo Bodhisattva is never separate from us. In studying and practicing with Jizo, we do not actually become anything else; we only become more completely ourselves.

This practice of becoming a bodhisattva will be familiar to students of Vajrayana Buddhism whose training includes visualization. During a visualization, a student sees or, more accurately, uses all the senses to experience him- or herself as vividly as possible as a bodhisattva, with the beautifully colored raiment, ornaments, jewels, body postures, and attendants. This practice says, essentially, start pretending that you are a Buddha. Now go back to being a person. Now go back to being a Buddha. Now go back to pretending to be a human. If this practice is continued with great dedication and energy, we can drop the narrow awareness and outlook of a human and adopt the wide awareness and compassionate outlook of a Buddha any time we wish. Vajrayana practitioners could approach this book as a visualization practice with Kshitigarbha Bodhisattva, as Jizo is also known.

How can Theravadin or Vipassana practitioners relate to Jizo Bodhisattva? Students on these paths use concentration, or *samadhi*, to investigate the mind and its creation, the world. In this practice, the mind is concentrated by using a focusing object such as the breath. Once the mind is still and one pointed, it can be used to ponder a question. This is how the Buddha practiced before his enlightenment. He realized that:

> *Whatever a bhikkshu frequently thinks and ponders on that will become the inclination of his mind. If he frequently thinks and ponders on thoughts of sensual desire, ill will and cruelty, then he has abandoned the thought of renunciation to cultivate the thought of sensual desire, ill will and cruelty.*
>
> *For it is not by further hatred that hatred is ended. Hatred is only ended by the cultivation of loving kindness. This is a constant and unvarying law.*

The mind's attention is energy. Wherever the mind is directed, energy flows. If we direct the mind to thoughts of ill will, or think a lot about what makes us angry, then ill will and anger are nourished. We are thus actively turning away from the possibility of renouncing human suffering and becoming free from it. If we direct the mind toward compassion or wisdom, the aspects of a bodhisattva, we actually give energy to these qualities in ourselves and in the world around us. By using Jizo Bodhisattva as an object of meditation and investigation, we nourish the qualities of the bodhisattva in ourselves and in all that surrounds and supports us.

How can a Zen student relate to Jizo Bodhisattva? In Zen practice, meditation on breath is used to develop the ability of the mind to concentrate and see with clear insight. We also concentrate the mind through *koans*. Koans are questions that function as a sort of drill to penetrate the layers of confusion in the mind and to find the essential truth that dwells in each of us. We have collections of many hundreds of koans, some a thousand years old. Each one was a burning question for an earnest spiritual seeker and helped him or her open to the reality that underlies all existence. There are koans about aspects of Jizo Bodhisattva in this book. I have taken up several as a Zen student might, unfolding each aspect as a presentation of that One Truth. The Zen reader may wish to take up these koans, the non-Zen reader may learn something about how koans are used for self-excavation.

I hope this book gives non-Buddhists, no matter what your religious tradition, more understanding of your Buddhist companions and fellow spiritual pilgrims on this planet. I also hope it will enable you to probe more deeply into that great mystery that is your life.

I have tried to use a minimum of words that are specific to Zen or come from foreign languages. *Practice* refers to spiritual practice or discipline. In Zen the word practice includes not only meditation, both seated and walking, but also chanting, bowing, and eating. Ultimately practice becomes bringing the awakened mind to all activities of life and work. *Zazen* is the Japanese term for seated meditation. Zazen is a particularly potent tool for developing clarity of mind and heart. *Sesshin* is a silent Zen retreat, usually three to seven days in length. Unfamiliar words or concepts that are not defined in the text can be found in the glossary at the end of the book.

The bodhisattva called Jizo in Japan and America is known by different names in other countries. In India he is Kshitigarbha Bodhisattva, in China Ti-tsang Pusa, in Korea Ji-jang Bosal, in Tibet Sati-snin-po. Because I came to know her first as Jizo and because this is her name in Japan, the country where she is most revered, I have used the name Jizo throughout this book, except when discussing historical aspects unique to one country.

Because Jizo Bodhisattva has both male and female aspects, I have used masculine and feminine pronouns interchangeably. The energy of Jizo in this world is not limited to male or female bodies. It pervades all space and time. It is available to all in need.

Another source of potential confusion is the use of the term "the West" to refer to America and Europe. We say that the Dharma has been taken from Japan "to the West," even though America seems to be located to the *east* of Asia on our flat maps. This reflects an originally Eurocentric view, that Asia was the "Far East" thus making America "the West." Actually we are no direction from each other on this shining spinning sphere known as Earth—not up or down, east or west, only blue, green, brown, and white appearing and disappearing, half in darkness, half in light.

I explore four aspects of Jizo Bodhisattva in this book. The first is that of Jizo as a figure of history, a bodhisattva of Mahayana Buddhism who arose in India as Kshitigarbha Bodhisattva, and emigrated to the countries of northern Asia, becoming a deity that is popular and widely venerated. This traveler-saint has now arrived at a few Zen centers in America as the central figure in a particular ceremony for children who have died.

The second aspect is that of Jizo the protector and savior, who intervenes and helps those caught in places of suffering. That suffering may range from anxiety over passing a high school exam to terror over the possibility of falling into the vivid hells described by Chinese Buddhists. This is the Jizo who is fleshed out through myths and folk tales, the Jizo of the mundane world, to whom any small request can be brought. She acknowledges that we know what we need to alleviate our daily distress and that if she can provide relief, our faith will be rekindled and we will return to the path of practice.

The aspect of Jizo the rescuer is given life in the Jizo legends included in this book. Of course some of the miracle tales about Jizo Bodhisattva are inventions or colorful embroideries. As an example, in 1776 crowds of people went to hear a marvelous Jizo near Yedo who could be heard reciting the sutras continuously in a low voice. When the covering to protect the image against the rain was removed, however, a nest of bees was found to be making the humming sound! The stories of Jizo's powers and interventions in peoples' lives should not be just discarded by the skeptical mind as improbable or impossible. These legends speak to deeper truths: the power of faith and the possibility of transformation and redemption when our life has gone astray. These stories about Jizo tell of the kind of being we hope does exist. For if she does, we could become like her, a being of gentle benevolence, unquenchable optimism and unflagging energetic devotion to those who suffer. We tell and retell stories like these in order to envision the bodhisattva who moves among us today and thus to call forth the Jizo within us.

As Jizo became worshiped by both nobility and peasants, numerous legends arose about his intervention and assistance in the human world. Statues of Jizo Bodhisattva in temples often have one or more miracle stories associated with them. These stories can be divided into several general types: Jizo aids the weak, children, women or poor peasants; Jizo helps a person with physical labor; Jizo warns of and averts a disaster; Jizo intervenes and rescues from hell someone who has died; Jizo substitutes his body for someone and prevents his or her death; Jizo assists warriors; and Jizo heals illness. Often these themes are mingled in one tale, as you will see from the examples included in this book.

These legends have been preserved as part of historical records of towns or temples. It is hard for us to imagine, in a country that is just over two hundred years old, written records of events occurring fourteen hundred years ago. The caretakers of Japanese temples keep meticulous records. For example, my teacher Shodo Harada Roshi, abbot at Sogen-ji Temple in Okayama, keeps several diaries, writing each evening of the day's happenings, visitors, donations, and of those who came for sesshin and *sanzen* (private interview with the Zen master). If miracles occur, I am sure they also are logged. There are records at Sogen-ji, as at many other temples, dating back to its founding three hundred years ago.

Buddhist practice is new in America. History tells us that it takes several hundred years for Buddhism to adapt to a new culture. History can inform us about how those adaptations may occur. Jizo Bodhisattva is now almost unknown in America. As interest in Jizo and religious practices with Jizo are taken up in the West, I hope this book will help those who wish to know more of the history of this bodhisattva: how Jizo was born, where he has traveled, and how he has met the needs of suffering people, from Chinese and Japanese aristocrats of the sixth century who feared that their dying parents would fall into hell to twentieth-century women grieving after an abortion.

The third aspect of Jizo Bodhisattva I explore is that of practice. When spiritual practice is the foundation of our lives, we sometimes seem to be swimming upstream against the determined drive of our own ego and of society to accumulate material possessions and individual power. Jizo's unflagging optimism illuminates our nights of self-doubt. His endless vow shores up our flagging determination. His benevolence melts our harsh judgment of ignorance—both our own and that of others. His example inspires us to get up out of bed and to practice, and once practicing, we begin to experience benefit for ourselves and others.

Zen Master Dōgen has said that paintings of a rice cake will not satisfy our hunger. Just to read a history of Jizo Bodhisattva will not satisfy our deep longing to know personally the heart and mind of a bodhisattva. Thus to the history of Jizo I have added the fourth aspect, portions of Dharma talks I have given that were focused on practicing with this bodhisattva, his attributes and qualities. In addition, the Appendix is a collection of supplemental readings for those who treasure any bit or piece of extra information about this many-bodied bodhisattva.

I have selected poems to open each chapter. Most of these were written by Zen Master Ryōkan, who was a "living Jizo." He lived in Japan at the end of the eighteenth century. After twenty years of formal Zen practice in a temple, he retired to the mountains near his birthplace. Ryōkan lived in simple huts and supported himself by begging. He often forgot himself in the samadhi of games with children and of drinking with village friends, in addition to meditation. He brushed thousands of poems in a free-flowing calligraphic style.

A few poems are those of Dōgen Zenji, the most revered Soto Zen master in Japan. Ordained at age thirteen after both of his parents had died, he traveled to China at age twenty-three to study Zen. Upon returning to Japan, he began teaching Zen and established Eihei-ji, a large monastery in a remote mountainous area. His extensive writings include many poems, both in the formal classical Chinese style and also in Japanese in a more free-flowing form.

This book opens and closes with the ceremony of remembrance for children who have died, performed in the sacred space of a Jizo garden. In one Jizo garden in Japan, one thousand Jizo images are hidden among the trees. It is said that a person who looks long and carefully enough will find their own face on one of these Jizos. May this book help you to find your original face, to reveal yourself as a bodhisattva, and to continue to do whatever you can to help heal the suffering of the human world.

Introduction

IT TOOK TWENTY YEARS from the time I first encountered Jizo Bodhisattva before I awoke to the power of Jizo to ease human suffering. It took ten years of working as an expert in child abuse and accumulating the pain of thousands of children in the hidden places of my heart-mind before I called for help.

In 1993, thirty-two child-abuse deaths occurred in Oregon. I had known most of these children. I had examined their limp pale bodies in the pediatric intensive care unit. I had gently run my fingers through downy soft hair, turned back ear folds, opened unresisting mouths and eyelids, looking for subtle bruises. I had turned their bodies over, careful not to pull out tubes that pumped air into their lungs and infused intravenous fluid into their veins. I had talked as gently as I could to frightened and aggressive parents, parents whom I knew had smashed, shaken, and beaten these infants, and also to the nurses who were angry at these parents. When the nurses were busy and no one was looking, I held each baby's hand for a moment to pray for its transition out of suffering and into peace.

I had arranged for good-byes to be said, last kisses given. Then their bodies, still warm and only appearing to breathe (a respirator inflating their lungs), were taken away to surgery. Finally, those once warm and living bodies, now cold and lifeless, were transported to the morgue. Their organs, now in insulated boxes, were carried off into dark skies to be transplanted into other little bodies thousands of miles away, bodies from whom life was ebbing slowly, watched over by parents now filled with hope that their child might live.

I attended many of their autopsies. I carefully photographed their bruises, cigarette burns, rib fractures, and dark burgundy brain hemorrhages. I pried open cold lips and genitalia to swab for semen.

I meticulously labeled film and swabs so lawyers could not prevent valuable evidence from being presented at upcoming trials.

One part of me did all this with clinical efficiency, talking with the medical examiner and detectives about likely mechanisms of injury. Yet another part of my mind worked hard not to think of the horror of these children's last hours and days, their screams for help, their cries met with more kicks, curses, punches, and burns. I locked away the vivid scenes, the long bloody hair of the girl raped and drowned in the tub, the terrified blue eyes of the small boy photographed during the torture that finally killed him.

I dictated reports, testified in court, and used all the tools of my medical and meditative trades to keep the images at bay. For ten years, I had been successful. But finally there were simply too many, too close. There was not enough time to wipe the mind's eye clear between each battered child. I would suddenly find myself weeping in my dark car on the way home when a few lines of a soppy country-western song came on the radio. I became afraid that if I began to cry I might never stop. I had dammed up so much.

I called my Dharma sister Yvonne Rand. Could I come to the mizuko, the Buddhist ceremony of remembrance for children who had died, that she would be holding at Green Gulch Zen Center outside of San Francisco? Only as a participant, she said. No observers allowed. Fine. I was far beyond observer.

At the start of the ceremony, Yvonne's words defined a space that would be held in the deep intimacy of Noble Silence. It was a place and time made secure by her calm knowledge of this universal pain called grief. We sat in silence, sewing small garments of red material, to clothe the Jizo statues during the ceremony to come. Several people made capes, one a hat, another a scarf. I used red thread blessed by His Holiness the Dalai Lama to string a handful of gray-green eucalyptus leaves together by their stems, forming a little cape like the grass and leaf raincoats worn in Japan and Africa hundreds of years ago.

One leaf for each child battered to death. I said their names silently and willed my mind to open its locked places and bring up their images. I made myself look again into the horrified eyes and twisted mouth of the baby buried, perhaps still alive, in her father's backyard. When the medical examiner's deputy dug her body up, he had swaddled her completely in a blanket and carried her tenderly, as if she were only asleep, out into the darkened street. They were greeted by the harsh flash of cameras and newspaper photographers waiting to do their job. Tears dripped on my little leaves. A box of Kleenex was passed.

Only a few people spoke, and then only few quiet words about the child they had come to remember. A father talked of a baby taken by sudden infant death syndrome thirty years before. A young woman sobbed as she sewed. Her husband cut and stitched in silence, clumsily patting her knee as she spoke of a baby dying just before birth.

When we had finished sewing, we made a procession to carry the Jizo statues down to the garden. In a bamboo grove we chanted the *Heart Sutra* and offered incense. As we tied the red garments we had sewn on the weathered Jizo statues, Yvonne read the names of the children who were remembered and mourned.

Most of the parents stayed for awhile to walk silently in the garden. I had to leave to catch a ride to the airport. Later as I looked out the window of the plane heading back to Portland, I realized that my heart was palpably lighter. I hadn't realized how heavy the burden of sorrow was, accumulated over ten years of child-abuse work. Also relieved was the hidden sorrow of my own miscarriage twelve years before. I did not talk or think much about the miscarriage because people could not understand long-lasting grief over an eight-week-old fetus.

Until then I had discounted the power of an "invented" ceremony. When I realized how important this ceremony was, and how deep and long-lasting its effects could be, I conferred with Yvonne, and we began to offer the ceremony at our Zen center in Portland. A member of the Buddhist community, or *sangha*, who had experience in grief counseling in the perinatal loss unit at the university hospital helped plan the ceremonies, which are described in chapter thirteen.

For the first ceremony we needed a statue of Jizo Bodhisattva. Where to find one? When I called statuary and garden stores in Oregon, no one knew what I was talking about. My husband challenged me to make a statue myself. He had been collecting Buddha statues since the 1960s when he and Kapleau Roshi had rummaged through antique stores and junk shops for Buddhas to return to their rightful place—altars in homes or temples. I had been telling my husband we should not buy any more Buddhas, that our life practice was to make ourselves into Buddhas—into fully awakened beings. Now he returned those words to me with a box of Oregon carving stone. From it I made a first simple Jizo in time for the ceremony.

Thus began the making of Jizo images and the establishment of a Jizo garden at our Zen Center. After I gave a Jizo statue to Maezumi Roshi, he named our rural Zen center Jizo-in (temple of Jizo). As I witnessed the benefits of the Jizo ceremony to people moving through the death of children, I began to read about Jizo and to contemplate his aspects and attributes. I am writing this book to share with others what I have gathered and what has opened within my awareness of the living Jizo Bodhisattva. I hope it will help others to discover more about the Way that relieves all suffering.

THE POINT OF LEARNING about Jizo Bodhisattva is not to acquire knowledge that can be stored in a memory file for access during a gap in cocktail party blather. We seek to learn about Jizo Bodhisattva in order to become Jizo Bodhisattva. By means of this black ink on white paper; via the zap! of electricity and fit of neurotransmitter molecules in the retina, optic nerve, and optical areas in the brain; via the attraction to/curiosity about/hope for Jizo Bodhisattva, we can open our individual mind awareness and body experience to the universal bright mind and vast body awareness of Jizo Bodhisattva. This is not a process of gaining knowledge of Jizo Bodhisattva *out there* but of experiencing Jizo Bodhisattva *right here*. It is not a matter of worshiping or petitioning Jizo Bodhisattva on the altar, but of asking that the energy of Jizo fully awaken in us and manifest freely in the world.

In this book we will work together on Jizo Bodhisattva as a koan, entering each aspect—monk, child, jewel, staff, pilgrim, protector—and letting each aspect unfold, petal by petal, to the sweet nectar and fertile pollen heart of Jizo. That heart is the same heart that gives life abundantly to each one of us.

Jizo BODHISATTVA

Jizo in America

Your face so serene
Beggar's staff in your right hand,
Wish-fulfilling jewel in your left,
My brother, please escort him.
Give comfort to him, as today the sky is crying.

Jizo, guide my friend to Buddha's Western Paradise Playground.
He wants to run and play at last.
When I come, I will play tag with him, and hold him in my arms
once more
Mind him for me, gentle Jizo.

JOHN WENTZ

A JIZO GARDEN

A little man made of gray stone stands in the garden. His eyes are closed and his lips curve in a faint smile. A fern leaf arches over his head like an umbrella, holding a few bright drops of rain. Someone has made a small bonnet and cape of red cloth for him. A bit of paper peeks out of a pocket sewn on the cape. If you slip it out, you will find it is a message to a child, a dead child. *You had a sweet soul. In your short life you knew pain and love. I miss you.*

A small kite flutters on a low branch. It has a long tail made of twists of bright paper, each bearing a message. "*Uncle Jim remembers your wonderful laugh.*" "*Auntie Jean sends you butterfly kisses.*" "*Bye, bye, baby boy. Mommy loves you.*"

As you walk around the garden you find other stone figures standing among the slender trees and seated on cushions of green moss. Some have begun to crumble, their features softening, and the gray lichen has begun to creep over their patient bodies. There is something here that makes you fall silent, a tinge of sadness mixed with an embracing calm. You see several thin wooden plaques hanging from a tree and see that they bear names and dates of birth and death separated by only a few months or years. On some plaques are faded drawings, flowers, a teddy bear, a sprinkling of stars and on some, more prayers. *"You are loved and remembered my sweet baby girl. Conceived in love and desired. Died through medical mishap. Never far from our hearts and minds — one of God's smallest angels."*

There are messages to a seven-year-old boy who was killed when a soccer post fell on him during a pickup game and to twins conceived after many months of fertility treatments who died following a routine amniocentesis. There is a poem for an adult son who was irreversibly brain damaged when he was drunk and fell out of a tree. He had lost his house keys and was just trying to get in to go to sleep. There is a small statue of a turtle left by a man who cannot quite forgive his seven-year-old self for leaving a pet without water in the sun. At the base of a standing Jizo, there is a little blue doll. It was painstakingly cut and sewn from a favorite T-shirt by a man whose unborn son died when the mother was struck by a car. He had stuffed the doll with paper tissues wet with the tears of friends who came to mourn. There are notes and remembrance tokens from women recalling abortions many years past and from doctors and nurses who have assisted in abortions. A little card, beautifully decorated in an old-fashioned style is from a seventy-year-old mother who was bewildered to have survived her beautiful daughter, a young doctor and mother of two, who died of breast cancer only a few months after her diagnosis.

Under one statue there is a fringed miniature carpet. A note says, *"I came to remember the three miscarriages my wife had. They came so fast and I was afraid to feel then. I'm ready to remember now. Today I made a magic carpet because I always hoped to tell stories to my child about castles and magic carpets. Now we are divorced and I will have no children but these three who are gone."*

Today you are alone in this unusual garden. If you came on another day, you might witness a procession of men and women wending their way to the garden carrying tiny garments sewn from red cloth, wooden plaques, and pinwheels or other handmade toys. Led by a woman in a Zen priest's black robes, they chant together, offer incense, then place the remembrances they have made on the statues in the garden. The priest intones a dedication, a list of names of children including babies whose sex was unknown or who were never named. A few couples hold hands, tears run silently down cheeks, and one woman slips quietly into the trees for a few minutes to sob alone before joining the group for the final chant.

This is a Jizo garden, one of the first in America. In Japan there are many thousands of these sanctuaries, but in America as this book is written, only a few. Who are the figures of stone in these quiet gardens that embrace the fragility and brief happiness of a child's life? Where did this ceremony originate and how has it come to be celebrated in America?

Jizo statues with garments sewn in memory of children who have died. Pockets hold flowers, toys and messages for the children. Jizo garden in Oregon.

The ceremony in the Jizo garden has arisen to address a particular kind of suffering, the grief of those who have lost children. The statues are of Jizo Bodhisattva, a figure who is venerated in Japan as a benevolent protector of those who travel. There, stone figures of Jizo are frequently found along pathways between rice paddies in the country, beside city streets and busy highways, and particularly at crossroads. Jizo is there to help travelers on both the physical and spiritual plane, especially those who face a difficult decision about which path to take in life. Jizo is regarded as the especial guardian of those in difficult or potentially dangerous transitions such as pregnant women and young children. In the last three hundred years he has come to be seen as a particular caretaker of infants and children who have died.

Jizo Bodhisattva probably first entered America from Asia about one hundred to one hundred fifty years ago, carried as small images in the portable altars of Asian laborers and in the chants and devotional practices of Buddhist priests sent as missionaries to the new immigrants. The Buddhist religion, although new to the young American nation, was already almost twenty-five hundred years old, more than five hundred years older than Christianity. As the wave of Buddhism traveled across the Pacific, it carried with it many bodhisattvas, among them Jizo.

BODHISATTVAS AND SAINTS

What exactly is a bodhisattva? To begin to answer this question I will tell a story.

A few years ago I led a retreat in Alaska. It was held in a lodge on the shore of a frozen lake outside of Anchorage. We arranged our small altar between two big windows overlooking the lake. Behind it was the forest, dark with spruce, light with aspen, and behind the forest, great snowy mountain peaks. We had been meditating for three days and were sunk deep in silence by Friday night when suddenly cars began arriving at the adjacent lodge. Doors slamming, excited voices and shrill giggles . . . a flock of teenagers had descended for a weekend of silent retreat!

I went next door after evening zazen to find out who was brave enough to lead such an event. A lay leader told me it was a preconfirmation retreat for sixty-four Catholic teens from Alaska and a lone boy who had flown in from Samoa. He promised to send the two brothers in charge of the retreat to visit me the next day.

They arrived during our silent work period, a brother and a priest, both in the dark habit of the order of St. John. I showed them the meditation hall and began to explain our daily schedule. We arose at 5 A.M. for two hours of silent meditation. They nodded, eyes bright in recognition of a monastic schedule and discipline.

"Then we do chanting service," I said. They pounced on the chant book and started to read a seminal Zen scripture called the *Heart Sutra*, over my shoulder. I tried to think how to explain its words, "form is emptiness, emptiness is form," to the brothers in terms that might be understandable to a Christian.

No need. "Oh, emptiness," they said, "of course, all is empty except the Great Mystery!"

They pushed on, reading quickly. "Ah . . . Prajna Paramita . . . what is that?"

"Wisdom beyond wisdom," I replied. "Wisdom that is beyond intellectual knowledge and . . . "

"Oh, of course," they shot back. "Do you believe it has compassion too?"

"Yes, the two basic aspects, wisdom and compassion," I replied.

They nodded. "What else do you believe it has?" they asked.

"Well," I answered, "my experience is that it has a sense of humor . . . and a wicked one at that." We laughed in joy and mutual recognition.

Again they scanned the *Heart Sutra* and suddenly stopped. "A 'bodhisattva,' what is it?"

How to explain, I thought? "It's a person who is fully enlightened, completely awake to the Great Mystery, who could choose to merge with the Mystery forever, but looks back and sees others suffering and turns back from that merging to help the others." I looked into their eyes, a little worried it wouldn't translate.

"Ah, saints!" they exclaimed, "We know saints!"

Jizo Bodhisattva is in fact similar to the Christian apocryphal Saint Christopher. Both are revered as protectors of travelers, women, and children. Both have taken on the task of relieving human suffering in very practical ways. Both have a role as ferrymen who help in carrying people to the "other" shore. According to the fifteenth-century book *The Golden Legende*, Saint Christopher was a man of great stature and strength who declared in a straightforward way that fasting and praying were practices that were beyond him. A wise hermit then placed Christopher beside a dangerous river and instructed him to bear people over the flooding waters.

> *Christopher bore all manner of people over without ceasing and there he abode for many days. As he slept in his lodge he heard the voice of a child which called to him and said, "Christopher come out and bear me over." Then he awoke and went out but he found no one. And when he was again in his house he heard the same voice and ran out but found nobody. The third time he was called and came thither and found a child beside the ravage of the river who prayed him goodly to bear him over the water.*
>
> *Then Christopher lifted the child on his shoulders and took his staff and entered the river. The water of the river arose and swelled more and more. The child became as heavy as lead. As the man went further the water increased and the child grew more and more heavy until Christopher was in great anguish and was afraid he would drown.*
>
> *When he escaped with great pain and passed through the waters he set the child on the ground, saying "Child thou hast put me in great peril, thou weighest almost as much as if I had carried the burden of the whole world." And the child answered, "Christopher do not marvel for thou has borne not only all the world upon thee but thou hast borne him also that created and made the whole world upon thy shoulders. I am Jesus Christ the king whom thou servest in this work. And to give you cause to know that I speak the truth, set thy staff in the earth by thy house. And thou shalt see in the morn that it shall bear flowers and fruit. And anon he vanished from sight. And then Christopher set his staff in the earth and when he arose in the morn he found his staff like a palm bearing flowers, leaves and dates.*

There is similar legend from Japan about Jizo Bodhisattva ferrying a man across a river. In this legend Jizo appears as a child monk.

> *Once Governor Tagaya of Shimotsuma undertook a pilgrimage to a Jizo temple but the River Ki was flooded and he could not cross. A small boy monk appeared in a boat and ferried him across the waters. When he arrived at the Jizo-in temple, the governor ques-*

tioned the resident priest, asking who the boy might be, but the priest knew nothing about him. Then, as Tagaya prayed before the Jizo statue in the temple, he saw little muddy footprints crossing the chapel floor, leading right to the altar. He realized that it was Jizo himself who had rescued him. His faith became even stronger and he admonished the people of his province to believe in the power of Jizo Bodhisattva and to worship him.

A bodhisattva ("enlightenment being" in Sanskrit) is a sort of saint, one foot in the human realm and one in the realm of the divine, which in Buddhism is called *nirvana*. In Western or Christian terms this is the longed-for state of oneness with the source of all existence, the ground of being. As a bodhisattva is about to cross the threshold into that realm, she looks back and sees clearly all those left behind who suffer as she once did. With her wisdom eye she discerns the cause of their sorrow and harmful acts, which is ignorance. As compassion wells up in her heart she turns back, taking a vow not to merge with the wonder of the Great Mystery until every single being has also crossed over out of needless suffering and been brought to freedom.

There are many bodhisattvas who are revered in Buddhist countries. The most beloved is known in Japan as Kannon. She is called Avalokiteshvara in Sanskrit, Kuan-yin in China, Kwan-um Bosal in Korea and Chinrezi in Tibet. Like Jizo Bodhisattva, Kannon is an embodiment of compassion. Her name means "she who hears the cries of the world." She responds to these cries with her thousand arms, each of which holds a tool to help with yet another form of human suffering. Jizo and Kannon are often linked and venerated together as a sacred pair or as two of the eight great bodhisattvas. Both Jizo and Kannon have the ability to travel unharmed through the hell realms to rescue those who are trapped, unable to free themselves through their own efforts. Bodhisattvas are usually portrayed as masculine in form and energy, like Manjushri who rides a lion and carries an upright sword to sever all delusions. Jizo and Kannon both have strong feminine aspects. Thus I have chosen to refer to Jizo with both male and female pronouns in this book.

A person who is able to be aware and function simultaneously from both the huge awareness of the ground of being and also from the unique single body and mind they inhabit is called *awakened*.

Each bodhisattva represents a different aspect of the Awakened Mind, a different way in which beings are delivered from *dukkha*, from suffering, and are helped to awaken. Each bodhisattva points to energies that are in us, at times hidden, at times manifest. How can we believe that we have in us the aspects of a bodhisattva?

Who Is Not a Bodhisattva?

The Dharma, the law underlying the workings of the universe, is quite scientific, mathematically and physically precise. Our bodies and minds are like clay on a potter's wheel. Our bodies are formed from oxygen, nitrogen, carbon, hydrogen, and trace metals. These elements coalesce for a while into a body that moves and makes noise at both ends. Then it collapses, "dies," and falls apart. What then? The elements are recycled to form new existences. How old is the oxygen in us? The sodium? Where did the calcium in our bones come from? We say, oh, from the milk I drink. Before that? From the grass the cow ate. Before that? From the soil? Before that? Trace any small portion of us back and it has been part of countless other lives.

Our minds form the same way, from bits and pieces of thought energy, created by electrical and chemical signals in neurons. Certain patterns of electrical signals-thought-emotion are imprinted by heredity. Then the environment adds its shaping and we become more or less polite, feel more or less shame, anger, and joy.

But all these thoughts and emotions are just energy, coalesced for awhile, moving, and making noise. When we collapse and die, they also disperse. Like the carbon and calcium elements, the thought and emotion elements are still operating in the chain of cause and effect after we die. Thus we can ask the same questions we asked about the body elements. How old is the anger in us? How old is the jealousy, the joy? How many countless lives has it been a part of?

We are like clay formed into pots of different shapes and functions. When the pots wear out, they disintegrate into shards, into grains and eventually into clay again. They are picked up and kneaded again, then reformed into pots. If this happens over and over for millions of years, there is not one particle of "them" that is not "me." All parts belonged at one time and will belong again to what we call someone or something else. The Tibetans say that all beings have been or will be our mother and should be thus revered.

This is the reason a bodhisattva works to awaken all "other" beings before him- or herself: because all "other" beings are not other. Saving them is literally saving oneself. Saving oneself is literally saving others. "Like the foot before and the foot behind in walking," the sutra says. It is impossible to get anywhere by oneself because oneself is ONE SELF.

When we fall into thinking that we alone are practicing or that becoming enlightened is a race against others, we are like a person in a boat who believes that if they row faster they will beat the person on the plank seat in front of them to the other shore.

All energies are us. Any energy can be strengthened and enhanced. Any energy can be tamed and brought under control, if we have the tools and the determination to do the work. What are the tools? The tools of practice. What gives us the determination? Looking behind us at our wake and seeing what happens when we don't apply these tools with determination and vigor.

For it is not by further hatred that hatred is ended. Hatred is only ended by the cultivation of loving kindness. This is a constant and unvarying law.

The Buddha teaches that all energies make up who we are. We have a choice of what we do or do not cultivate, nourish, and act upon. We become free when we know what action, word, or thought will bear bitter fruit and we don't carry it out. This also means that we can cultivate the energies that enable human beings to become bodhisattvas. Bodhisattvas are not metal or wooden statues to be worshiped. They are living qualities that we all aspire to embody fully.

After the brothers of St. John visited me that bright day in Alaska, our retreats moved along in harmony. In one lodge sixty-five youth kept vigil through the night in front of the Blessed Sacrament, learning to find God in the silence of their hearts and minds. In twos they came, sitting before the altar for thirty minutes, then slipping out into the dark cold night to the cabins to quietly awaken the next pair to come and keep watch. In the lodge next door twenty-five adults sat in hours of silent meditation in a room with the small white Bud-dha in front of a window that opened to huge white mountains, opening themselves to the Great Truth in the silence of their minds and hearts.

A messenger arrived. The brothers had run out of incense. Could we lend them some for Mass? As we sat a little later I smiled to think of Japanese incense swinging in the Catholic censer in the lodge next door. During a break the teens spilled out onto the frozen lake to play ice hockey. Only one girl played with all the boys and a young priest as they slid around in their shoes. The other girls stood in a little clump on the shore and watched. The large Samoan boy stood immobile on the ice, roughly in the middle of the play-ing area, happily watching the others surge back and forth, parting around him. He told me later it was his first experience with ice. And maybe not yet to be trusted, I thought, the miracle of walking on a huge expanse of water, albeit currently frozen.

I had gone down to the shore in my black-and-white Zen robes to watch the game. "Sister, sister, come play with us!" the boys shouted. I tied up the sleeves of my black Japanese robes and slid out to join them. In a bit I looked behind to find all the girls had joined the game. Afterward the girl who had been the only girl in the game at the start came up to ask to have her photo taken with me. I'm not sure she knew I was a Zen priest, not a Catholic sister. What seemed to matter was that I was a visibly religious women, a player in the sacred game. It surprised and pleased me that perhaps just my appearing in robes inspired the girls to take themselves more seriously in the one great game that matters, spiritual inquiry and deep practice.

At the weekend's close the two groups joined in a large circle to sing a hymn and offer prayers for peace and understanding. The weekend taught me again that there is only one Truth. If not, it could not be the Truth. We only use different words to try to speak of it, and different rituals to celebrate our joy in being able to expe-rience it. Who at the retreat was a bodhisattva? The Catholic broth-ers so open to our Zen ritual? The lay leaders who had respect for the spiritual potential of the teens? The Buddhist adults who loaned their incense and sang a Taizé hymn? The Catholic youth who urged the American Zen teacher out onto the ice? Or the "sister" who led the way for the girls to join the game? If we encourage and delight each other as we travel together on the only journey that really matters, who then is not a bodhisattva?

How Jizo Came to the West

As this book is being written, Jizo Bodhisattva is found in a few places of Buddhist practice in the West. He appears in mandalas and teachings of esoteric schools of Buddhism, and is revered by the Jodo school. Recently Jizo has begun to fill a small but unique spiritual niche in America, honored as the central figure in ceremonies of remembrance for children who have died, in particular those lost through miscarriage and abortion. The first documented Jizo ceremony was held in this country thirty years ago at Tassajara Zen Center by Suzuki Roshi and a woman who is now a Zen teacher, Yvonne Jikai Rand. The ceremony is now held by the Zen Community of Oregon where I teach, and has spread through a network of second-generation American Zen teachers to several other Zen centers in this country.

This is Yvonne's story of the first Jizo ceremony:

I was introduced to the Jizo ceremony by my root teacher Suzuki Roshi. A dear friend of mine had died in the late 60s in a terrible train crash in Japan where he had been ordained and was studying as a Zen monk. I went to Suzuki Roshi to ask him to help me with my grief for my friend and also to deal with all of the belongings my friend had left with me before departing for Asia. Suzuki Roshi invited me to bring my friend's "leavings" to Tassajara Zen Mountain Center. In the rock garden that Suzuki Roshi had made there, he set a stone figure of Jizo on top of a boulder. He made a circle of rocks for a fire, and he and I piled up all of my friend's belongings that were appropriate to burn in a pile in the midst of the circle. Suzuki Roshi did a simple Buddhist funeral ceremony and then he and I burned everything. When the fire was out I placed the ashes in a hole in the garden and closed it with a stone. We used the Jizo figure as a marker. In his characteristically indirect way Suzuki Roshi taught me about Jizo through this ceremony.

Beginning in the early 1970s women began coming to me and asking for help with their grief following abortions and miscarriages. In one of the first ceremonies I walked with the woman to Muir Beach, a small beach on the north coast of California. There we searched and collected three particular stones. We climbed the hill overlooking the beach and found a place to pile the stones, one on top of another, to make a kind of Jizo figure. The woman placed a small bib she had sewn from a piece of red cloth on the figure and I offered a short funeral ceremony. Over the next several years I found myself doing other ceremonies like this. As women talked to each other about how these rites had provided solace for them, others began coming to me also asking for help. At the end of the Retreats for Women that I did, I began to offer to do the ceremony for anyone from the retreat who wanted to participate. For several years I did the ceremony for small groups of women, and then gradually began to do them including men as well.

At the second Conference for Celebrating Women in Buddhism, I put out a notice offering the ceremony on a Sunday morning at 9:00 A.M. I announced the ceremony for anyone who had experienced an abortion, a miscarriage, or who had a child die before it was grown. I set up a small wooden shrine with a stone Jizo in it in a secluded patio behind a meeting room. I waited to see who would come. To my surprise thirty-seven women gathered in the meeting room, sitting in a circle. For three hours they sat and sewed and one by one spoke about what had brought them to this gathering. The first woman who spoke was in her sixties. She spoke hesitantly at first about an abortion she had as a very young woman. She had never spoken of that experience before. Her speaking took the group deep and after her speaking everyone spoke, one by one. Her courage opened deep wells of sorrow. The entire spectrum of personal experience and political opinion about abortion was present that morning in that circle. Everyone listened. The container held what was common to each person in the group, their grief and sadness. After that experience I vowed to offer the ceremony as often as possible.

Later I learned from Robert Aitken Roshi that this funeral or memorial ceremony was done in Japan. There it is known as Mizuko Jizo Ceremony or water-baby ceremony. On a trip to

Japan in the early 1990s, I undertook a Jizo pilgrimage. I traveled by train all over the country, getting off to investigate any place that looked to be a likely Jizo site. I went to Tokyo to a temple where there was a crematorium built by a Buddhist nun who gathered the remains of aborted fetuses from four Tokyo hospitals. The nun cremated the fetuses and performed services for them, then buried the ashes in an old cemetery. I visited Jizo sites in Kyoto including Nembutsu-ji, where hundreds of old Jizo gravestones have been gathered from forgotten grave sites to make a small forest of Jizos. At Obon festival in the fall the site is illuminated by thousands of candles. At many Jizo temples and cemeteries I sat for hours, watching who came and what they did. I saw temples where the Jizo ceremony had been commercialized, an exploitation of people's fears and guilt to provide a source of income to support a failing temple. I saw temples where priests were quietly offering much-needed services and spiritual counseling.

I also walked for some days along the traditional pilgrimage route between Jizo temples on Shikoku Island. I sat for a long time one afternoon at a cemetery in Kyoto that was filled with Jizos where I meditated on the juxtaposition of happy children playing in the temple kindergarten just a few feet away from hundreds of Jizo statues for dead fetuses and babies. As I left, the day had gone to evening and rain. I saw a shop across from the temple gates with many Jizos in the window. When I crossed the street to look more closely at the figures, I discovered that in my pilgrim mind I had mistaken shelves of tennis shoes for rows of Jizos. I realize now how odd it must have been for the Japanese to see an American woman, shaved headed and in robes, out walking alone as a pilgrim. But I was so consumed with Jizo that I did not see the difficulty until after I returned home in California.

I came back from Japan with a renewed determination to offer the Jizo ceremony in America without allowing it to become commercialized. I do not charge for the ceremony, but I do accept donations. During that pilgrimage I also learned about the many other practices that can enhance the mizuko ceremony, including offering a book for written remembrances or prayers or messages that can be written and left anonymously. I saw the benefit of providing a quiet place for a cup of tea and quiet after the ceremony.

I have found that even people who are unacquainted with Jizo can see his image and understand that he is an expression of compassion. I feel strongly that the Jizo ceremony is much needed in the United States. It is needed both to help individuals who grieve, often for many years after an abortion or a miscarriage or after the loss of a baby, and also to help those with conflicting views regarding abortion find a way to work together in peace with the pain that surrounds this controversial and difficult issue. I have found that the ceremony helps caregivers as well.

If we wish to learn more about the origins of Jizo Bodhisattva and the mizuko ceremony, we must return, as Yvonne Rand did, to Japan.

chapter two

Jizo in Japan

When I see
The misery
Of those in this world
Their sadness
Becomes mine.

Oh that my monk's robe
Were wide enough
To gather up all
The suffering people
In this floating world.

Nothing makes me
More happy than
The vow
To save everyone.

AFTER RYŌKAN

IN JAPAN JIZO BODHISATTVA is a beloved bodhisattva, omnipresent and accessible. The other bodhisattvas sometimes have a fierce aspect and are housed in dark niches on altars at a distance from the people in the temples. Peering through a wire screen or wooden grate in the darkness of an old temple you catch a gleam of gold or a glimpse of a graceful arm or torso. In contrast, Jizo Bodhisattva resides in the open, among the people. His face is serene and gentle, with a hint of a smile. Even in city neighborhoods he can be found in small shrines every few blocks. The cities have grown up around him and the old altar houses that shelter him are sometimes notched into telephone poles or squeezed into a niche between modern buildings.

Jizo's presence helps maintain the palpable sense of orderliness and safety in the little neighborhoods that make up even the larger cities like Tokyo and Kyoto. One or two blocks off a busy commercial street you can enter a neighborhood that feels like a small village. A policeman notes your entry and exit from his ward, nodding politely from his small glass enclosed box as you pass. Mothers pedal bicycles serenely through heavy traffic with one or two children balancing in front or back seats. There is no graffiti. Vending machines are everywhere, with $30 bottles of whiskey behind intact glass. Children as young as three or four years play in groups, darting about, chattering happily. No adults seem anxious for their safety. No child whines or shrieks. No one yells at the children or smacks them. There is a palpable sense that everyone is watching over the children and the visitors . . . and Jizo Bodhisattva watches over all.

Jizo Bodhisattva is accessible. He can be found out among the activities of everyday life, at country crossroads, beside village paths, in many small altars on city street corners. These altars are maintained by people in the neighborhood. In the same way that everyone takes responsibility for the bit of street in front of their shops or houses, sweeping or washing it each morning, they also care for "their" Jizo. They keep the little altars clean and make offerings, a piece of candy, a golden tangerine, a few flowers in a washed jam jar, or even a cup of sake. In the larger shrines the offerings include children's clothing and sandals or shoes because Jizo travels far to comfort those who need his help.

If you need to ask Jizo for help, you probably won't have to go more than a few blocks. You could even duck into one of his temples during an errand or over lunch hour downtown. In Kyoto there are several small Jizo temples just off busy commercial streets. A steady stream of people enter these tiny oases all day long. There are grandmothers less than five feet tall, bent almost in two by the years, in their dark dresses or kimonos, pushing the strollers old people in Japan use to get around. There are business people in suits and parents carrying infants or holding children by the hand.

Jizo statue at the Kugi Nuki Temple in Kyoto. The brocade-covered baton at the base is used to stroke the statue in areas where a person is in pain. The fingers, cintamani jewel and lacquer covering the statue have been worn away by the countless touch-prayers of those seeking relief of suffering.

Entering the temple courtyard they take water from a stone trough in a bamboo dipper to rinse hands and mouth in ritual of purification. Parents help the smaller children. Then they light and offer a candle or stick of incense, ringing a bell to attract Jizo Bodhisattva's attention. They may circumambulate the Jizo image or pour water over it. Some stand, palms pressed together, whispering earnest prayers.

THE JIZO WHO PULLS OUT NAILS

One busy temple in Kyoto is the Kugi Nuki or Nail Pulling Jizo Temple. You enter through a passage lined with red lanterns. It opens into a courtyard with an ancient twisted pine and a small carpet-covered and roofed dais where old people sit and talk quietly. In the course of a Jizo pilgrimage we visited this temple and sat for a while on the platform to watch what was proper to do here. We saw that after praying to the large half-hidden image on the main altar many people move to a smaller image with a large brocade-covered baton on its lap. They strike a bell and use the baton to touch the statue and then stroke their own bodies in the same areas, those afflicted by pain or disease. Elderly people most often touch the head, the neck, the shoulders, the stomach, and the legs. This Jizo is unusual, made of bare wood with large open glass eyes. His face has the look of a Western saint, patient and life-worn. The fingers of his right hand are half gone and his cintamani jewel has been reduced to a small mound in his palm. If you look closely, you find this Jizo was originally covered with red lacquer, now worn away by the countless strokes of the brocade baton in the hands of those who suffer. (In Japan a statue that is called a Jizo and revered as Jizo may have begun its life as another deity. This statue, for example, is actually of one of the Buddha's disciples, Pindola.)

A young priest sells sticks of incense. People circle the main building to offer incense at several smaller shelters housing old and new Jizos. One is a beautiful modern bronze statue. In an open-faced shed at the back there are many stone Jizos from a few inches to four feet tall. Some are new with sharply carved features. Some are ancient, almost formless and dark-stained from centuries of incense and candle smoke. Legend says the bodhisattva is singed with smoke from nightly trips to hell to rescue sinners. Red capes adorn even the oldest headless torsos. Many little baby bibs in gay colors are strung as offerings along the wooden slats of the small Jizo shrines. Plastic toys, infant clothing, baby blankets, and tiny sneakers lay at the feet of the statues, placed there in memory of children who have died.

The outside walls of the main building at Kugi Nuki Temple are covered with curious wooden plaques. To each are affixed two long iron nails and a pliers. The plaques bear dedications to individuals in black calligraphy and requests for afflictions to be removed. In the courtyard of the temple is a sculpture of a huge metal pliers and two nails.

A pamphlet explains that the Nail Pulling Temple originated with Kobo-Daishi, the founder of the Shingon sect. Kobo-Daishi

Plaques with pliers and nails covering the walls of Kugi Nuki ("Nail Pulling") Jizo Temple in Kyoto. Each bears a written petition for relief of pain.

returned from China to Japan in the ninth century with a large stone from which he carved a statue of Kshitigarbha Bodhisattva (Jizo). He prayed to this image for the relief of people's suffering and sickness. Seven centuries later in Kyoto a well-known merchant named Dorin had a sudden onset of severe pain in his hands. He tried many remedies with no relief. Finally he undertook a religious retreat in hopes of ending his pain. On the last night of the retreat he dreamed of Kshitigarbha Bodhisattva who told him that his pain was due, not to sickness, but to evil deeds committed in a previous life, when in anger he had driven nails into a straw figure of an enemy, a kind of voodoo. Kshitigarbha told Dorin that because of his recent devoted practice the pain that afflicted him would be cured by divine intervention.

When Dorin awakened he was astonished to find that his pain had vanished. He hurried to the statue of Kshitigarbha and found that two long red nails had appeared in front of it. In gratitude for the "pulling out of the nails of pain," Dorin worshiped at the temple for one hundred days. This Jizo became known as the Nail Pulling Jizo.

THE JIZO WHO HEALS EYE DISEASE

A second popular Jizo temple in downtown Kyoto houses the Ameyami or Meyami Jizo. The entrance to Chugen-ji Temple, lined with white lanterns, is off a busy street in the old Gion district. At the left in the small courtyard is a simple Jizo of smooth black stone about five feet tall. Here, after purifying their hands, people take a dipper full of water and dash it energetically at the statue rather than pouring it gently over. Its primitive style and wet gleam make this Jizo not cheerful but somewhat dark and mysterious.

In the main shrine is a beautiful sixteen-foot Jizo carved of wood with eyes of glass. In a side shrine is a beautiful old many-armed Kannon. *Ame* means "rain" in Japanese and Ameyami means the "Rain Stopping Jizo." Kyoto was once the capital of Japan, a beautiful and fragile city of paper and wood houses always under the double threat of flood and fire. It is situated on a floodplain and its buildings are kept from sinking by a series of drainage canals that course their way through the city. The Ameyami Temple was founded in 1228 in an effort, fortunately successful, to stanch rising floodwaters. The name also may signify the shelter the temple offered to people caught in downpour. Now the name has become Meyame Jizo, meaning the Jizo who miraculously heals eye (or *me*, in Japanese) disease.

This transformation in Jizo's function to meet the needs of the times is not uncommon. In ancient times Jizo's protection was invoked for floods, fires, and epidemics. In modern times people have gained relative freedom from large-scale disasters and ask Jizo for help with individual needs such as cataracts, passing exams, or securing a certain boyfriend. Some prayers to Jizo, like those for successful conception and easy childbirth, are timeless.

THE WHEEL-TRACK JIZO

A third small and quiet Jizo temple is tucked under high-rise hotels only a few blocks from the huge Kyoto train station. It houses the Wagata or Wheel-Track Jizo. In the old days the main trade items between Kyoto and Nara were rice and salt, carried on carriages by horses and cows. To lighten the burden of the animals on the rough and rutted road, people laid stone tracks with chiseled grooves for cart wheels to run in smoothly.

Three hundred years after these stone pavers were laid, a local man had a dream. A priest appeared to him saying, "I have been practicing under the ground to save the souls of hard-working horses and cows. Now their hardship is less. I would like to save people instead. Please dig me out of the ground." When the man looked at the road the next morning one of the stones was shining. The villagers worked together to dig the paving stone up and found it was a statue of Jizo lying face down with the wheel groove running right down its back. They built a small shrine for the statue, and later a temple. It became a well-known guardian of travelers and a

Wheel-Track Jizo, who protects travelers. Found under a paving stone.

protector of the health of horses and cows. People came from near and far to petition for safety in travel, the smooth delivery of a baby, or freedom from suffering.

In Japan Jizo Bodhisattva is like a comfortable, country-style general practitioner. This doctor is always in, available to everyone for any pain, fear, or worry, large and small. He provides solace to all who ask his help and to infants and other creatures who suffer and cannot speak. In modern times there are bodhisattvas for the protection of the elderly from senility and Alzheimer's disease. A doctor's wife whom I met at one temple told me of the Yo-mei irazu Jizo and Kannon. She explained, "Our religion is very practical. *Yo-mei* means 'bright' and also 'daughter-in-law.' *Irazu* means 'without.' Older people pray to these bodhisattvas to prevent their having to be cared for by their daughters-in-law." She said this is for two reasons: first, those who have cared for their own in-laws in the past know what a trial it can be, and second, they do not want to become indebted to their daughters-in-law. She also mentioned the Pokkuri Jizos and Kannons who receive prayers for a quick and painless death. *Pokkuri* is an onomatopoeic word for the sound of—what we would call in English—suddenly dropping dead. Old people do not want to linger in illness and become a burden to the next generation.

THE HISTORY OF JIZO IN JAPAN

How and when did Jizo Bodhisattva become so popular in Japan? Jizo probably entered Japan when Buddhism did, in the fifth or sixth century, from China via Korea. The early history of Jizo in Japan consists of many colorful legends embroidering a thin fabric of fact. The oldest known statue of Jizo is a standing figure, made of sandalwood, with empty hands in the *mudras* (sacred hand gestures) of fearlessness and blessings. This image is said to have been given to Emperor Bidatsu in 577 C.E.

Buddhism and its bodhisattvas did not enter Japan to fill a religious void. They encountered indigenous religious beliefs, animism and Shinto. Shinto had existed for over five hundred years, as the worship of the divine in nature. This essential force manifested as a multiplicity of *kami*, or spirits. They were petitioned to help fulfill the basic human need for fertility of person and crop, and to avert disaster related to natural forces, flood, drought, and fire. Rocks, oceans, groves of trees and cascading waterfalls were themselves held sacred. There were no statues to represent the kami. The only images were fertility symbols such as phallic stone rods and primitive female fecundity figures of unglazed clay.

When Chinese and Korean Buddhists entered Japan in the fifth century, they found a people less sophisticated than they, and by comparison, uncultured. Perhaps these traits survived longer in Japan because of the frequency and fury of earthquakes, volcanic eruptions, and tsunami. The Japanese people lived in simple huts clustered in villages ruled by local chiefs, subject to the upheaval of frequent wars. They had no cities, no money, little commerce, no written language, no science, little knowledge of other lands, no formal schools, and no temples or complex religious rites. The Chinese brought to Japan all the manifestations of a civilization already old, a religion that had developed beyond the magical and animistic, and with these, a literal age of enlightenment.

Imagine a retinue of cultured men, women, and priests in beautiful silken robes, riding on groomed and ornamented horses or carried in decorated palanquins, entering a nondescript fishing village on the coast of Japan. The strangers bring scrolls, paintings, fine jewelry, poetry, and musical instruments. They unwrap a beautiful image, which they call a bodhisattva. It is exquisitely carved, quite lifelike, with benevolent features and eyes of shining crystal that seem to follow the onlooker, and flowing robes painted in bright colors, trimmed in gold. The strangers offer fragrant incense and chant melodiously in praise of this lovely god. Who would not wish to worship this wondrous being who seems to grant its believers these riches, such heavenly delights?

The villagers suddenly become aware of the possibility of a life filled with luxury and pleasure—in comparison with their lives, a heavenly realm. If a realm so far above is possible, it is a logical step to imagine a realm below, an existence filled with terror, unending pain and hunger. Some historians believe that the early Shinto view was life affirming and did not concern itself with what occurred after death. Human effort was directed toward staying alive and reproducing both people and food. Death is a simple, necessary fact to people who hunt and grow crops. Beings are alive until they die, when they decay and disappear. Through Buddhism, the Japanese were introduced to a more complex cosmology including belief in an afterlife with various potential destinations, either wonderful or terrible.

This same awakening occurs in the life of each human. We are happy in childhood with our life just as it is until we develop a mind that compares. Then, when we see another child being treated differently, in our own or in a different family, or even on TV, we realize that things could be much worse or much better. We crave the better, are afraid of the worse. The very treasure that makes us civilized, our discursive minds, becomes the source of our suffering. We compare ourselves to others and the present to the past. We are worried about what will occur tomorrow or after we die. Thus are born hope and anxiety, clinging and avoiding.

Historians speak of the Japanese as eminently practical, adopting new ideas from China but adapting them to serve the basic realities of daily life. The Chinese worshiped Jizo because he could intercede with the fearsome Lords of Death and mitigate their sentences. To the Japanese it was fine to have a Jizo who helped after death, but couldn't he also help with everyday worries like planting rice and having babies?

Jizo's designation as the Earth Store or Earth Womb Bodhisattva was understandable to the Japanese, very much like the familiar kami of mountains and rivers. Jizo could easily blend with old beliefs, becoming a more personal sort of kami. The Sai no kami were ancient phallic stone images placed at crossroads to represent the gods of the way and of fertility. Stone Jizos and wayside Jizo shrines gradually replaced these. As Jizo statues age, they often lose their heads due to accidents, earthquakes, or by being defaced during times of persecution. Over time they weather to featureless lumps noticeably phallic in shape, just like the stone rods of old Shinto. Old and headless, they are almost unrecognizable today as Jizos, but are still adorned with red capes and offered pieces of fruit or bits of candy.

From China and Korea, the Japanese adapted Buddhist, Taoist, and Confucian ideas, developing more sophisticated systems of legislation, jurisprudence, and education. The Shinto religion evolved into a more complex belief system, incorporating ethical codes and

the practice of veneration of ancestors from Confucianism, and a sophisticated cosmology, philosophy and ceremonial rite derived
from Buddhism. The aristocracy was the first to take up Buddhism
and with it the worship of bodhisattvas like Jizo. The ruling class had
a vested interest in maintaining the power of their feudal families
over generations, an interest supported by Chinese Buddhist rituals
in which ancestors were honored and enshrined. They used their
wealth to build temples and commission religious works of art, leaving a legacy that continues to inspire us over a thousand years later.

Jizo Bodhisattva also had popular appeal. He was incorporated
into the indigenous Shinto religion and eventually adopted by all
the foundational schools of Japanese Buddhism including Shingon, Tendai, Jodo, and Soto and Rinzai Zen. For several centuries
there was relative peace in Japan, but in the twelfth century Japan
entered five hundred years of bitter strife. Monasteries became
citadels and battlegrounds, monks trained and fought as soldiers,
and Jizo Bodhisattva became the guardian of those at war. He was
also a savior for hapless victims of the conflicts. As conditions in society deteriorated, people became convinced that they lived in the
time of the *mappo*, an era when the truth of Dharma would be lost.
Buddhism became a religion to comfort those who suffered and
were most helpless: the oppressed, aged, and poor. Jizo Bodhisattva
emerged as a benevolent savior for a degenerate age, a bodhisattva
who helped those who were unable to raise themselves out of misery, a bodhisattva who descended into hellish realms that were to
those unhappy people not allegorical but real.

During this time people were anxious to confess their sins and
atone before death. Repentance rites were commonly held in honor
of Jizo and other bodhisattvas. The founder of the Pure Land school
of Buddhism, Shonin Shinran, taught that a Buddha called Amida
would save devotees at the moment of their death if they had recited
his name. Shinran said that Jizo's mercy, however, was universal and
not dependent upon the sinner's readiness, prior spiritual practice,
or even upon any prior belief in Jizo.

Japanese religion is characteristically inclusive and syncretic,
adapting to the needs and sophistication of the people. Jizo Bodhisattva fit this flexible form of spiritual belief, taking on whatever
form necessary to help rescue beings from misfortune and pain. For

aristocrats he was a bodhisattva in royal jewels and fine raiment, sitting in a posture of ease. For peasants he was a humble priest with smoky face and muddy toes acquired, like theirs, from hard work helping people in simple and practical ways. These are the two iconographic forms of Jizo in Japan, regal bodhisattva and rustic priest. These are the two forms of Japanese Buddhism. It is simultaneously a religion of the state, supported by the aristocracy, manifest in great temples and beautiful works of art, and a folk religion that offers a doctrine of compassion to the poor and oppressed. These two forms were personified in two Japanese men who promoted Buddhism soon after it entered Japan and who became venerated as "living bodhisattvas." They were Prince Shōtoku, who spread Buddhism among the elite, and Gyōgi Bosatsu, who brought Buddhism to the common people.

Prince Shōtoku (573–621 C.E.) was born just as Buddhism was being introduced into Japan. Tutored by Korean monks, he became a devout Buddhist, building temples and monasteries and giving his own lectures on the sutras. Although he promoted Buddhism as the "final resort of all beings," he supported a multi-religious state, issuing edicts invoking Confucian principles of propriety in government and asking all ministers to pay homage to the Shinto kami in order to maintain the natural order of the world. He wrote Japan's first constitution in 604 C.E. as a moral guide for government officials. It begins with these words: "Harmony is to be esteemed above anything else." Later it asks, "Who is wise enough to judge which of us is good or bad? We are all wise and foolish by turns, like a ring without an end." After his death, Prince Shōtoku was worshiped as an incarnation of Kannon Bodhisattva. His name is linked with several Jizo images, and he is said to have built a Jizo chapel, but little is known, fifteen hundred years later, about what devotional relationship Shōtoku had with Jizo.

The name of Gyōgi Bosatsu (670–749 C.E.) is often associated with Jizo Bodhisattva. Gyōgi was a monk from a Korean family, ordained at age fifteen in the Hosso sect. He spread Buddhism to the common people by charismatic preaching and social welfare projects. His followers numbered in the thousands and whole villages would empty when he was speaking nearby. He traveled through Japan preaching and is credited with drawing the first map of Japan and conducting the first census. He undertook many public works projects, mobilizing large numbers of believers to build a major road, six bridges, three aqueducts, fifteen reservoirs, forty-nine chapels, and nine charity houses. The government became uneasy with his popularity and in 717 C.E. issued edicts against him. He was charged with leading people astray by ordaining people without government permission and of encouraging so many farmers to leave their farms to do social welfare work that tax revenues from farms decreased.

About twenty years later, however, Japan suffered from a fresh series of natural disasters: famines and epidemics. Shinto prayers could not save the four sons of the Fujiwara regent; all four died of smallpox. Hoping to turn the fortunes of the nation around, Emperor Shomu ordered the construction of the Great Buddha statue at Todai-ji in Nara and turned to Gyōgi, who helped raise the necessary funds and labor. Because there was concern that the Shinto deities might be offended by the projects, Gyōgi, now age seventy-two, was sent to the shrine of the Sun Goddess at Ise, carrying with him a holy Buddhist relic. After he had prayed for a week, the oracle proclaimed that the emperor's project was agreeable. The emperor then had a felicitous dream in which the Sun Goddess proclaimed that the sun and the Buddha were the same. Gyōgi thus helped prevent conflict by mitigating the resistance of Shinto adherents against the immigrant Buddhist religion. He was proclaimed a living bodhisattva (bosatsu in Japanese) and worshiped by the masses. He died at age eighty-one soon after conferring the bodhisattva precepts upon the emperor.

Several stone, wood, and earthen Jizo statues are said to have been carved by Gyōgi Bosatsu. One was credited with saving the life of a priest. The priest had been attacked by robbers wielding swords. A blade descended on his neck and as he collapsed, he prayed to Jizo for help. When he awoke the robbers were gone and his body was miraculously unharmed. The next day the priest went to give thanks to Jizo. He found the head of the statue lying on the ground with blood flowing from its neck. This Jizo was named the "Jizo whose head was cut off."

While on a Jizo pilgrimage in Japan, I asked Shodo Harada Roshi about Jizo Bodhisattva. He elaborated on the connection between Gyōgi Bosatsu and Jizo, saying that Gyōgi Bosatsu was a great philanthropist who raised money for the casting of the great Buddha statue in Nara, an effort that gave employment to poor people at a time when economic and social conditions were very difficult. The building of a huge Buddha helped them find both financial security and also increased faith and hope. Thus Gyōgi Bosatsu himself became worshiped during his lifetime as a "living bodhisattva" who had rescued many people from the hell realms of starvation and disease. Because he was a special protector of the weak, particularly children, the poor, and slaves, he was linked with Jizo Bodhisattva. Jizo Bodhisattva had become popular among the poor and powerless because they were better able to relate to a simple and homey Jizo in a weathered wayside shrine than to a huge golden image of an enlightened Buddha on the high altar of a fancy temple, a temple they might not even be allowed to enter.

JIZO BODHISATTVA IN TENDAI AND SHINGON BUDDHISM

The founders of two schools of esoteric Buddhism that remain important in Japan today, the Shingon and Tendai sects, both venerate Jizo Bodhisattva. Shingon practice emphasized recitation of *dharanis* and the representation of the truths of the universe as mandalas. The two basic mandala forms, the *vajradhatu* (diamond realm) and the *garbhadhatu* (womb), both contain Kshitigarbha (Jizo) as one of the great Bodhisattvas. Shingon believers can select one bodhisattva to practice with, the choice being made by casting a flower on a mandala while blindfolded. If the flower lands upon Jizo (Kshitigarbha), then special practices related to Jizo are undertaken for a period of time.

THE SIX JIZOS

Statues of six Jizos (Japanese: *Roku Jizo*) are often found at the entrance to cemeteries in Japan. The Six Jizos likely came from China, as the *Sutra of the Ten Kings* describes six figures of Ti-tsang. The Six Jizos may also come from the division of Jizo into six bodies, one to take care of suffering living beings in each of the six realms (see chapter ten). The Six Jizos became very popular and

were worshiped even by non-Buddhist Shinto priests, as documented in this story.

> *Koretaka was a priest at a tenth-century shrine. Although he was
> Shinto, he also believed in Jizo and constantly recited the bod-
> hisattva's name. One day he was taken ill and quickly died. Three
> days later he suddenly came back to life. He related that after
> death he found himself alone and lost in a desolate wasteland. As
> he cried out for help, he saw six handsome boys coming toward
> him, each carrying a different object: an incense burner, a rosary,
> a pearl, a six ringed staff, a flower basket, and a jeweled banner.
> They said to Koretaka, "Don't you know us? You worshiped us
> when you were alive. Because beings who dwell in the six realms
> are affected by different causes and conditions and each suffers dif-
> ferently, we manifest a hundred thousand forms, each to benefit a
> specific being according to his suffering. Please return home and
> make six statues of Jizo." Koretaka later erected a Buddhist temple
> with six statues of Jizo as he had seen them in the afterworld. He
> lived past age seventy, dying with the name of Jizo on his lips.*

Because of Jizo's vow to protect travelers, images of the Roku Jizo
were placed on the six entrance roads to Kyoto in the twelfth century. In the seventeenth century similar statues were erected around
Tokyo. People began to undertake a pilgrimage in late August to
worship each of the Jizos, a custom that has continued for many centuries. It was said that those who completed a pilgrimage to a series
of temples devoted to a bodhisattva like Kannon or Jizo would have
feet that "shone with sanctity." Thus their merit then would be recognized when they arrived in the dark judgment halls of hell.

Shogun Jizo

About three centuries after Jizo Bodhisattva entered Japan, the cult
of the Shogun Jizo arose among the warrior class. It was a mystic
cult based upon secret practices, with elements of Shingon Buddhism as well as Taoism. The Shogun Jizo was worshiped as a special protector of the military class, helped by a Sanskrit reading of
the term "shogun" as *prasenajit*, or "conqueror of armies."

The cult of Shogun Jizo originated with the priest Enchin, who
in 798 built a beautiful Temple, Kiyomizu-dera (Clear Spring) on

a hill overlooking Kyoto. Construction of the temple was funded by General Sakanoue Tamuramaro. The emperor had ordered the general to lead troops to quell a rebellion in the north. Before embarking on his journey, he visited Enchin and asked the priest to assist him through the power of the Buddha Dharma. Enchin promised to do this. The general was confident of victory, but in the first battle the enemy overwhelmed his troops and he was forced to flee. In a second encounter, when another defeat seemed inevitable, suddenly a little Buddhist priest appeared on the battlefield accompanied by a small boy. They picked up the many spent arrows lying on the ground and gave them to Tamuramaro. With these gleaned arrows, the general killed the enemy leader and quelled the rebellion. Returning in triumph, he hastened to Kiyomizu-dera where he asked Enchin how the miracle had occurred. The priest replied, "Among my practices there is one devoted to Shogun Jizo (Army Conquering Jizo) and to Shoteki Bishamon (Enemy Conquering Vaisramana). I made images of these two deities and made offerings and prayed to them." The general realized who the priest and boy had been. As he entered the temple to give thanks, he found that both images had wounds apparently inflicted by swords and arrows, and their feet were covered with mud! Struck with wonder, Tamuramaro reported this miracle to the emperor, who was deeply impressed.

The Shogun Jizo is portrayed as a soldier monk, riding on horseback, wearing armor and a warrior's helmet. He carries Jizo's staff and jewel or pearl in his hands, with his armor covered by a priest's robe! His face is gentle, not fierce. The Chinese had sometimes shown Ti-tsang Bodhisattva riding or leading a horse in hell but not in armor. The Chinese saw Jizo more as a public defender than a soldier. During five hundred years of warfare, the Japanese adapted the gentle Jizo to their needs. He literally became a god of battle. The Japanese strategically placed him at the gates of castles and erected his image in their battle camps to support their cause. Warriors must have taken solace in the belief that, although killing was forbidden by the Buddhist precepts, Jizo would accept sincere atonement and help save those condemned to hell for their sins.

A document from the seventeenth century praises the Shogun Jizo:

*Shogun Jizo in armor,
with two swords and
a banner.*

*Shogun Jizo . . . resides on Mount Atago in the west of the capital
and is the tutelary god of the gentry. Going to the battlefields he
kills the wicked and gives peace to the world. Moreover he removes
calamities and fires, and gives many generations and felicity to
families and he bestows easy birth upon women. Oh! Who would
not praise the blessed power of this Bodhisattva!*

Sometimes Jizo led people to abandon a life dedicated to war. In
1340 a rebellion was led by Nitta Yoshisuke. One of the rebels, fleeing from soldiers, took refuge in a temple where he prayed for help.
A priest approached him and quickly gave him a rosary in trade for
his sword. When the soldiers arrived they found an innocent-look-
ing man with a rosary reading a sutra. Searching outside they found
the priest holding a bloody sword. The bound him with thick ropes
and cast him into prison. The next morning they were astonished to

find that although the cell was still locked, the priest had vanished. A lovely fragrance, called a "divine odor" in Japanese, permeated the empty cell. The soldiers, angry that the priest had escaped, ran back to the temple. When they threw open the shrine they found a Jizo statue that was bound with their very ropes. A brilliant light emanated from the statue. Filled with awe they all knelt before Jizo. Overcome with repentance for their many acts of killing, they cut off their hair with their swords, took vows, and entered the monastic life. The Jizo statue still retains the marks of the bonds of rope.

JIZO LEGENDS

There are many folk legends of Jizo helping poor or desperate people with simple tasks. One of the Six Jizos on Mount Koya was called the *Kotsumi no Jizo*, or "Jizo who piled up wood." In 1270 the chief of a village at the foot of Mount Katsuragi ordered his people to cut wood to be burned in the making of salt. One old woman was ill and unable to do the work. On the altar in her small hut was a simple wooden Jizo. No matter how little food she had, every morning and evening she had made offerings to this Jizo. That night the old woman complained to Jizo asking why, if she had been so devoted to him, he did not help her with the work she had to do. In her dreams that night she saw a small priest leaving her house. When he returned he said, "Old mother, I have done the work for you." The next morning she went outside to find freshly split firewood piled as high as the roof eaves. She ran to make an offering to the Jizo and saw that the feet of the statue were covered with mud. She realized that he had cut and piled the wood for her during the night.

Another of the Mount Koya Roku Jizo performed a miracle for an elderly caretaker. Each winter the abbot of Jurin ordered the temple servants to rake the snow from the garden paths in front of the Jizo shrine. He told them that Jizo might need to rise early to go about helping living beings. One serving man did this work faithfully, year after year. One winter evening as he was working in a heavy snowfall, sweeping the walk in front of the hall where the statue stood, the old man grumbled, "You go out every night to help people who are suffering. Raking snow is hard work for an old man. Why don't you take a turn?" At daybreak when the servant arose, he was astonished to see that the night's snowfall had already been cleared from the garden. Snowy footprints led to the porch of the hall where the Jizo image stood. This Jizo became known as *Yuki-kaki Jizo*, or "Snow Raking Jizo."

A letter-delivering Jizo is mentioned in the history of the largest wooden building in the world, Todai-ji Temple in Nara. The temple was rebuilt after a fire in 1195 by Yukitaka, a devoted believer in Jizo Bodhsattva, who died while his daughter was still young. The grieving girl wrote a letter to her father and tied it to the hand of the Jizo statue in the main shrine. She wept night and day before the image praying, "Jizo-sama, you save those in the six realms and are sure to know where my father is now. Please give him this letter and bring me his answer." On the morning of the seventh day her letter had disappeared from Jizo's hand and in its place she found a response from her father. Historical records showed that in 1675 the letter was still preserved at the temple.

The Many Forms of Jizo

As these legends illustrate, Jizo is a very adaptable bodhisattva. He is able to fly, speak, to do chores, exchange his body for those in danger, and to cure illnesses. Here is a partial list of the many forms of Jizo found in Japan:

ABURAKAKE JIZO — Jizo that worshipers paint with oil

AMAGOI JIZO — asks the sky for rain

ASHI-ARAI JIZO — washes his feet after helping peasants in the rice paddies

ATAGO JIZO — a warrior Jizo on horseback who rescues warriors in difficulty and puts enemies to flight

DORO-ASHI JIZO — Jizo who gets his feet muddy helping in the fields

EMMEI OR ENMEI JIZO — the Jizo who prolongs life and provides many benefits including watching over children, curing illness, preventing accidents, and granting success in business and school

HANATORI JIZO — leads horses and cattle

HARA OBI JIZO — stomach-wrapper Jizo who protects women during pregnancy

HIKESHI JIZO — protects houses and harvests from fire

HOSHU JIZO—jewel-holding Jizo

HOSHU SHAKUJO JIZO—jewel- and staff-holding Jizo

HOYAKE JIZO—Jizo who burned his cheeks rescuing someone in hell

INDO JIZO—saves humans after death and leads them to enlightenment

KARA TE JIZO—empty-handed Jizo

KOSAZUKE JIZO—child-granting Jizo

KOSODATE JIZO—Jizo who helps with successful rearing of children

KOYASU JIZO—easy-childbirth Jizo

KUGI NUKI JIZO—Jizo who pulls out pain

MEYAME JIZO—restores eyesight

MIGAWARI JIZO—surrogate or body-exchange Jizo who helps peasants in their work and substitutes for someone in danger

MIWARI JIZO—protects villages

MIZUHIKI JIZO—brings water to the rice paddies

MIZUKO JIZO—water-child Jizo who protects aborted and miscarried fetuses

NEKO JIZO—cat Jizo

NURI KOBE JIZO—Jizo who cures dental problems

OMUKAI JIZO—Jizo who comes to greet you when you die and leads you to Amida's heaven

OTSUKIYARE JIZO—"inspired" oracle Jizo to whom questions are posed

ROKU JIZO—six Jizos, one for each realm of existence, usually shown in a group with different objects in the hands of each

SENTAI JIZO—one thousand bodies of Jizo, sometimes represented as one thousand statues of Jizo

TACHIYAMA JIZO—a Jizo who takes the place of a woman devotee so she can rest once a month

TAGENUKI JIZO—removes splinters and thorns

TAI-SAN JIZO—prosperous-birth Jizo

TAUE JIZO—helps farmers plant rice

TOGE NUKI JIZO—pulls thorns out

TSUNBO JIZO—deaf Jizo to whom letters must be written

YUME JIZO—dream or sleep Jizo

THERE ARE MANY UNUSUAL Jizos and customs surrounding these Jizos in Japan. The "Oil Painted Jizo" got its name when an oil merchant stumbled and spilled almost all the oil he was carrying. What little oil remained he gave to Jizo by pouring it over his statue. The man's business grew and he became very prosperous and for the last five hundred years worshipers have anointed this statue with oil. An "Asekaki Jizo" sweats white sweat during times of good fortune and black sweat in times of calamity when he is bearing the pain of the people. Devotees believe that if they wipe the white beads of moisture that form on his stone body with special paper and carry this home they will have good fortune. There is a Jizo named Gacha Gacha after the sound he made when people removed him from his mountain home and placed him in the middle of their village. He began to rattle ("gacha gacha") to let them know that he was homesick and wanted to be returned. There is a "Threaded Stone" Jizo who heard the prayers of a poor couple and cured their infant daughter of deafness. The parents were overjoyed when the child was awakened by the sound of a rooster crowing. They could not afford the usual offerings to Jizo and gave instead an odd stone with a hole in it that they had found and threaded with string. Now the statue is surrounded by piles of threaded stones.

To retain its vitality a religion has to adapt to the needs of the people. These adaptations are mirrored in the changes that have occurred to Jizo Bodhisattva over the past one and a half millennia in Japan. Once a religion becomes well established and interwoven with bureaucracy, it begins to serve the fears of those who cling to power. Empty pomp and ceremony becomes a substitute for an experience of the deep Mystery. A few moments of silent prayer are mistaken for the deep inner silence in which the voice of that Mystery can be heard. As the religion loses its connection with the source of spiritual life and the needs of the common folk, it begins to die. Then it is the "heathen" and the "barbarians" who can see it with fresh eyes, ask and discover how this religion can help this very day, and thus bring it back to life. A religion that allows this to occur will survive.

Compared to our pubescent American society, the Japanese culture seems ancient, subtle, and refined. It is a surprise to discover that when Buddhism entered from China, it was the Japanese who were the "eastern barbarians." Now it is the Americans and

Europeans to whom the beauty and benefits of Buddhism have appeared. We are the new eastern barbarians. Jizo Bodhisattva has been transported to America by priests bearing the gift of the pain-relieving truths discovered by the Buddha. Jizo has come as a quiet stowaway. In twenty years of practice with Maezumi Roshi, the only contacts we had with Jizo Bodhisattva were the two statues in the garden and clinic at the Los Angeles Zen Center and a service for the center children held on Jizo Bodhisattva Day each August. We were not taught anything directly about Jizo. We had to discover him for ourselves when the need arose.

For twentieth-first-century Americans, the notion of enlightenment introduced by our Japanese teachers may seem as distant and unimaginable as the notion of the Chinese Buddhist heaven once was to the fifth-century Japanese. We, like the early Japanese, want a religion that can help with the problems, fears, and sadness of our daily life. The goal of rebirth in heaven or enlightenment seems far away when we are suffering now. The early Japanese wanted a Jizo who could avert floods, help crops grow, ease the pain of childbirth, and cure eye disease. Now we have huge dams engineered to control floods and medical technology to ease birth pangs and prevent blindness. Some forms of suffering have been softened over the last fourteen hundred years, but what has not changed is the fact that whether we are Chinese, Japanese, Korean, or American, we are still humans, and thus can never escape the fundamental suffering that the Buddha described. We and those we love will inevitably become ill, grow old, and die. Having found their natal religions somehow opaque and inaccessible, many have turned to Buddhism for answers.

A hundred years after the introduction of Buddhism to the West, there are American Buddhist teachers who have found that Jizo Bodhisattva offers solace to those with a particular kind of poignant suffering, grief over the death of a child. The Mizuko Jizo, who helps children who have died, is the Jizo of the ceremony described in the introduction, the most popular Jizo in Japan today, and the Jizo who has begun to be found at Zen temples in America. In the next chapter we look at the role the Mizuko Jizo has played in Japan and consider how and why she of all the many Jizos in Japan has found her way to America.

chapter three

THE *Water-Baby Jizo*

For Children Killed in a Smallpox Epidemic

When spring arrives
From every tree tip
Flowers will bloom,
But those children
Who fell with last autumn's leaves
Will never return.

RYOKAN

THE MIZUKO JIZO AND THE MIZUKO CEREMONY IN JAPAN

The most common form of Jizo made in Japan today is the Mizuko Jizo. The Mizuko Jizo often is portrayed as a monk with an infant in his arms and another child or two at his feet, clutching the skirt of his robe. The Mizuko Jizo is the central figure in a popular but somewhat controversial ceremony called the mizuko kuyo.

The word *ku-yo* is composed of two Chinese characters with the literal meaning "to offer" and "to nourish." The underlying meaning is to offer what is needed to nourish life energy after it is no longer perceptible in the form of a human or occupying a body we can touch. In actual use kuyo refers to a memorial service and mizuko kuyo to a memorial service for infants who have died either before birth or within the first few years of life. An image of the Mizuko Jizo usually is the central figure on the altar at such a ceremony. Grieving parents may buy a small statue of Mizuko Jizo to place on the family altar or in a cemetery as a memorial for their child.

The two Chinese characters in the word *mizu-ko* are literally translated "water" and "baby." It is a description of the unborn, beings who float in a watery world awaiting birth. The Japanese perceived that all life originated from the sea long before evolutionary theory proposed this. Their island home and all its inhabitants float in the ocean, which is the source of much of their nutrition. In actual use, the term "mizuko" includes not only fetuses and the newly born, but also infants up to one or two years of age whose hold on life in the human realm is still tenuous.

In Japan young children are regarded as "other worldly" and not fully anchored in human life. Fetuses are still referred to as *kami no ko* or "child of the gods" and also as "Buddha." Before the twentieth century, the probability that a child would survive to age five or seven was often less than 50 percent. Only after that age were they "counted" in a census and could they be "counted upon" to participate in the adult world. Children were thought of as mysterious beings in a liminal world between the realm of humans and gods. Because of this the gods could speak through them. For centuries prepubescent children in Japan have been chosen as *chigo*, or "divine children," who do divination and function as oracles. Even today children below school age still are allowed a somewhat heavenly existence, indulged and protected without many expectations or pressures. They often sleep in bed with their parents and younger siblings until age seven. School entry and displacement from the parental bed can come as a rude shock.

Although people in America and Europe have only recently become acquainted with Jizo Bodhisattva, mistaken beliefs among Westerners about Jizo already exist. The Mizuko Jizo, although currently popular, revered, and omnipresent in Japan, is not an ancient Jizo. Nor is it the only form of Jizo, as the list of types of Jizos at the end of the last chapter demonstrates. The term "mizuko" does not appear in Buddhist or Shinto scriptures. The mizuko kuyo is not an ancient rite nor was it originally a Buddhist ceremony. Both the Mizuko Jizo and the mizuko ceremony arose in Japan in the 1960s in response to a human need, to relieve the suffering emerging from the experience of the large number of women who had undergone abortions after World War II.

To understand the origins and current popularity of the mizuko ceremony in Japan we have to review some pertinent history.

A Brief History of Abortion in Japan

Abortion and infanticide (*mabiki*) were practiced widely in Japan in premodern times, as they were in Europe. In societies where all life energy is devoted to mere survival, where famine and epidemic are common, early death becomes a fact of life. When infants and children die frequently and when religious beliefs hold death either as the simple but inescapable return of all that lives to the earth, or as a restoration to a pleasant heavenly abode, it can be less—or not at all—a source of sorrow compared to modern societies where we are uncertain as to our destiny and meet early death with anger, indignation, and a sense that somehow we have been betrayed.

In early times in Japan a first pregnancy was a young woman's initiation into adult life. She was not recognized as pregnant until a ceremony held in the fourth or fifth month of gestation when the midwife tied a special belly band containing charms on her. New life thus was not recognized until the time of quickening. This was natural at a time when people lacked knowledge of the biology of conception, when irregular menstrual periods could have many causes such as disease and poor nutrition, when early miscarriage was common, and when the outcome of any pregnancy was uncertain. Midwives were responsible for ushering new life into the world. In some areas of Japan they maintained a lifelong relationship to the children they delivered. They made the baby's first clothing and attended celebrations during the children's lives. Midwives also made herbal preparations for contraception and abortion. At a birth the midwife could ask if the infant was to be kept or should be sent back to the realm of the gods. The decision was made jointly by the husband and in-laws, not by the woman alone. *Mabiki* (infanticide) was accomplished by strangulation or by suffocation, sometimes between the legs of the midwife. The infant, newly emerged from between its mother's legs, thus could be returned between the legs of the midwife to its original dwelling place.

There is no evidence that there were any prescribed religious ceremonies around pregnancy and birth in old Japan. In fact pregnant women were not allowed to enter Shinto shrines between the time of tying on the pregnancy sash until about one month after birth, an interval when they might pollute the sacred site. Midwives sometimes acted as intermediaries for the gods, praying for the sake of women under their care. Infants could be brought to Shinto shrines to be recognized by the kami—(the gods) and placed under their protection. The Shinto religion was concerned with purity and enhancing the life force and had nothing to do with funeral or memorial rites. People prayed to the kami both for fertility for their crops and for themselves. Children were desired and a source of joy but also provided needed labor in the fields and were counted on as social security, caretakers for their aging parents.

Although the gods could end the sorrow of infertility by granting children, another kind of suffering could be the result of the birth of too many children. A poor family might be able to feed and raise two or three children, but everyone's life was at risk if they had eight. The Japanese practiced abortion and mabiki as a practical means of ensuring the health and well-being of the entire family. Some historians suggest that this straightforward attitude developed over many centuries of cultivating rice, an awareness that rice plants have to be thinned to thrive. Too many plants, like too many children, overtax the available resources. If some are not culled, all will be weakened or die.

Buddhism entered Japan flavored with a particularly Chinese preoccupation—what was one's fate after death? This was not a Shinto concern. Funerals thus became the responsibility of Buddhist priests and temples. Buddhist rites for aborted fetuses and dead babies were uncommon in premodern times in Japan, and, when performed, differed from those held for adults. In fact, the term mizuko was not found in Buddhist or Shinto scripture. A central aspect of funerals for adults was transfer of merit to help the person attain Buddhahood. The Soto and Rinzai Zen sects had ceremonies for women who died in childbirth. The purpose of the ceremonies was to help the mother avoid a particular hell, the Pool of Blood Hell, and to help her become a Buddha. The concern for the fetus or baby was to help it toward a speedy rebirth. In some areas of Japan, in fact, babies were buried with a dead fish so that the bad smell would keep the Buddhas away. Often dead infants

were put in rivers or the ocean to be carried away with other unwanted items. A priest's wife explained to me that the term mizuko
came from the last resort of a poor woman—to starve herself and
stand chest high in freezing river water for long periods to induce
abortion. The fetus, afterbirth, and blood would be washed away in
the river, eventually returning to the ocean. There were no marked
graves or periodic memorial services for children dying before birth.
If a child died in the first few years of life, the family could hold memorial services and place a tablet on the family altar.

In fifteenth-century Japan, abortions were common. The government asked physicians not to advertise this service openly. Although
child abandonment was prohibited in 1687, it was a common practice among the poor in Japan as it was in Europe throughout the
nineteenth century. One priest revered in Japan as a "living Jizo"
gathered abandoned and orphaned children and raised them in his
temple. While on a pilgrimage in 1684 the poet Bashō encountered
a deserted child and was moved to write a poem. His diary also reflects the belief that a fetus or child has its own karma.

*As I was plodding along the River Fuji, I saw a small child, hardly
three years of age, crying pitifully on the bank, obviously abandoned by his parents. They must have thought this child was unable to ride through the stormy waters of life which run as wild as
the rapid river itself, and that he was destined to have a life even
shorter than that of the morning dew. The child looked as fragile
as the flowers of bush-clover that scatter at the slightest stir of the
autumn wind, and it was so pitiful that I gave him what little food
I had with me.*

> *The ancient poet*
> *Who pitied monkeys for their cries,*
> *What would he say if he saw*
> *This child crying in the autumn wind?*

*How is it indeed that this child has been reduced to this state of
utter misery? Is it because of his mother who ignored him, or because of his father who abandoned him? Alas, it seems to me that
this child's undeserved suffering has been caused by something far
greater and more massive—by what one might call the irresistible*

will of heaven. If it is so, child, you must raise your voice to heaven, and I must pass on, leaving you behind.

In the mid-1800s Japan, isolated for two hundred years, opened its doors and allowed Europeans and Christianity to enter again. With them came new Western perspectives on life and death that began inevitably to alter indigenous views. In 1873 infanticide was made illegal, punishable as homicide. In the 1920s a law was passed to license midwives as medical professionals and their role in the community changed as a result. They no longer delivered infants in just their own communities but traveled outside to families with whom they had no long-term relationship. Pregnancy and child-birth became medical events and lost their ritual context. In the two decades before World War II, the government became aggressively pronatal and abortion became stigmatized as scandalous, shameful, and also unpatriotic. Margaret Sanger, the birth-control crusader, was prohibited from lecturing publicly in Japan. Surreptitious birth-control clinics opened only to be shut down by the government in the 1940s.

Economic conditions were very poor after the war. Food and other basic necessities were scarce and resources became further strained when tens of thousands of Japanese soldiers returned from occupied countries. During the war, conditions in Japan had been so severe that thousands of civilians had migrated to places like Manchuria to settle and grow food for their families. When Japan was defeated, the occupied countries no longer welcomed these immigrants and all were forced to return to a devastated Japan.

After Japan lost the war, the government reversed its policy and both birth control and abortion became legal. Abortions were legalized in Japan in 1948 under the Eugenics Protection Act, later renamed the Law for Protection of Mothers' Bodies. Illegitimacy was not tolerated in Japanese society. Abortion was openly advocated as necessary and inevitable in light of dire economic conditions. The ideal of the two-child family was promoted; large families were stigmatized. Hospital births became the norm and professional midwives disappeared. At the same time, the technology of X rays and ultrasound created visual images that changed notions of the fetus as a mysterious and ethereal being into that of an unborn and concrete individual with an existence already separate from the life of the mother.

The Eugenics Act was passed at that time to allow abortion for reasons of economic hardship. Other effective methods of birth control were not available. The primary means of family planning were the rhythm method and condoms. The former was unreliable even when understood, and condoms were expensive and unavailable to most people. Even today, the oral contraceptive, IUD, and diaphragm are not in widespread use due to fear of side effects, modesty, reluctance to handle one's genitalia, as well as lack of education about sex and reproduction. A significant portion of the income of gynecologists is derived from performing abortions, an economic fact that further embeds abortion within a matrix of social acceptance. Thus abortion became and still remains a primary form of birth control in Japan. The majority of women marry in their early twenties and soon give birth to the current ideal, two children. Because birth control is not used or is not effective, unwanted pregnancies are common. One in three pregnancies ended in abortion in 1989. In 1960 it was two in three. As a consequence it is not uncommon for women ages forty to fifty to have had two or more abortions.

While modern medical technology made the procedure safe and efficient, and poverty and legislative sanction made it common, the effect of abortion upon the psyche of the women was overlooked. The ritual context, which in earlier times had addressed the spiritual aspects of a life transition such as abortion, had been lost.

The Recent Development of the Mizuko Ceremony

Small wonder that the women and men who were caught up in the government's abrupt reversal of policy toward contraception, abortion, and family size, and who had no ethical and spiritual rudder to steady them as they entered these rapidly changing times had difficulty with psychic whiplash. People may do what has to be done to survive in desperate circumstances, but it does not mean they escape without emotional pain. Once abortion was perceived as the ending of an individual life and once economic conditions became

less severe, then abortion could no longer be held as a compassionate act, an act that would return a child destined for a life of suffering back to a heavenly realm. Abortion then became a difficult
decision, fraught with conflicted and repressed emotions—sadness
and resignation, shame and relief. Women began to request help.
They wrote letters to advice columns in newspapers and magazines
asking for guidance and approached their religious leaders to appeal for help in their distress.

When people are under stress and feel that their lives are influenced by unseen forces, religions based on superstition and magic
flourish. In the context of rapid social change, some of the new religions that emerged after the war returned to old beliefs in ancestral spirits who could be protective or malevolent, depending upon
whether and how they were honored. These churches were called
spiritualist. They offered the services of a medium, who, if life
brought misfortune, could contact the spirits to see why they were
upset and find how to propitiate them.

If there is a demand to relieve a particular kind of distress, sympathetic people of compassion and integrity will try to develop a
spiritual context to meet the need. People with less integrity will
seize the opportunity to make money. Both responses have occurred in Japan. With many women and some men feeling guilt
and grief over previous abortions, it is natural that a ceremony such
as mizuko kuyo arose.

In its best form, the mizuko kuyo is performed by Buddhist and
Shinto priests only upon request. The ceremonies are private and
infrequent, and the priest also may provide counseling to the
woman or couple. At its worst, the mizuko kuyo has become a vehicle for deliberately enhancing and exploiting the feelings of guilt
people have after abortion. Certain spiritualists and priests tout the
ceremony as a cure-all for every type of physical problem from joint
pain to poor vision to cancer. It is the solution for an array of difficulties including traffic accidents, rejection from arranged mar-
riages, and delinquency in surviving children. Advertisements from
these "mizuko specialists" and lurid stories in tabloids illustrated
with images of fetuses tell of terrifying tatari, or "spirit attacks," in
which unborn infants haunt people and cause a long list of problems. The lists are of ills common to all who are human and espe-

cially to menopausal women, that is, the current age of women who were fertile during the time when abortions were most frequent.

Once the ceremony was offered, requests for mizuko rites increased. Between 1965 and 1984 the number of religious organizations offering mizuko ceremonies rose from 15 percent to 42 percent. However, almost half of religious organizations reported in 1986 that they took a negative view of these ceremonies and did not believe in the existence of spirit attacks. The mizuko ritual is offered most often by spiritualist groups, called Spirit Rappers, and "new" religions. About 10 percent of Shinto shrines do mizuko rituals. Among the Buddhist schools, the Shingon sect performs mizuko ceremonies most often (about one-quarter of temples) followed by the Soto Zen, Jodo, and Tendai sects. Rinzai Zen temples are least likely to offer mizuko kuyo (4 percent in one survey). Only the Jodo Shinshu sect has prohibited mizuko kuyo officially, although some Jodo Shinshu temples will do the ceremony quietly if requested.

A central belief of the Jodo Shinshu school is salvation by faith alone. No ritual is necessary beyond this understanding. Any death, at any age after conception, should be treated in the same way without singling out fetuses. Jodo Shinshu publications describe the mizuko ritual as a magical practice that exploits people's superstitious tendencies. Buddhist priests of other sects agree with this view and also object to mizuko on other grounds: it is a vulgarization of Buddhist practice; it is a rite that has no scriptural basis; it is an activity that allows people to be relieved of guilt without a sincere review of their behavior and subsequent repentance; it is a practice that can tarnish a temple's image, causing it to be seen as cheap or moneygrubbing. Rinzai Zen priests in a 1989 survey also commented that mizuko do not cause spirit attacks because the souls of unborn babies are originally pure and innocent.

It is clear from the testimonial letters sent to temples performing mizuko kuyo that people try the ritual in hopes of relieving all manner of suffering in their lives, from chronic pain to infidelity by a spouse. People write that the memory of the abortion has weighed on their minds for years. People are aware that, all rhetoric aside, abortion extinguishes the spark of a potential new life and violates the commandment or precept against killing. They want to acknowledge and atone for what they wish they could have done in a different way. They wish to purify themselves and start afresh, with new wisdom and compassion gained from their suffering.

Of the people who ask for mizuko rites or who can be seen praying to a Mizuko Jizo at a temple, most are women. They fall into three categories: those who have had abortions recently, middle-aged women who would have been reproductive during the peak in abortion procedures in the 1950s to 1970s, and a new category of young people. Although the rate of abortion in teenage girls is rising, most of the last group often has had no experience with abortion. They are moved to pray for the well-being of aborted fetuses and hope to temper any malevolent influences the spirits might exert.*

To preserve anonymity, people desiring mizuko kuyo often go not to their home temple but to a temple in another district or town specializing in mizuko kuyo. Although abortion is common, most people keep it a secret. They may be advised by the priest not to tell a marriage prospect or partner about a premarital abortion that occurred with another man or woman. This secrecy tends to enhance existing feelings of shame and guilt.

Hundreds of temples in postwar Japan have closed for lack of membership and contributions. Some temples that were in danger of closing have found a new and welcome source of income in the mizuko rites. A few have become quite prosperous as a result. Temples may begin offering the ceremony after an approach from a stone masonry company promoting the sale of a huge Jizo statue costing tens of thousands of dollars. The masons point out that if the

---

* The Japanese tolerate an unusual degree of ambiguity in religious beliefs. The Buddha originally taught that there is no permanent and unchanging thing like a soul that continues after death. All forms of energy—physical, emotional and mental—"unbind" at death. However, the Buddha refused to say that nothing continued after death. He said that the craving for existence will ignite another flame of life. As Buddhism entered China, it picked up Taoist beliefs in the individual's existence after death and the possibility of good and bad subsequent destinations. As Buddhism entered Japan, it further incorporated folk beliefs in spirits that could be helpful or cause mischief and also Shinto beliefs in the essential purity of all existence into what one author calls a "bricolage" of spiritual beliefs. Hence the use of the terms "soul" and "spirit" above.

temple installs a large Jizo and becomes known as a Mizuko Jizo site, the income derived from people on pilgrimage and those seeking mizuko kuyo will cover and soon exceed the cost of the new statue. Temples charge between one hundred and three hundred dollars for a mizuko ceremony, and some temples recommend repeating the ceremony each month for several months or each year indefinitely. In one survey, temples reported performing ten to one hundred ceremonies a month. A stone Jizo statue placed in a Jizo cemetery as a memorial can cost a family over one thousand dollars. A large four-day mizuko festival held annually at one temple was estimated to bring in sixty thousand dollars.

The Form of the Mizuko Ceremony in Japan

The simplest form of mizuko ceremony occurs thousands of times a day all over Japan as people enter the many neighborhood temples that have an altar for Mizuko Jizo on their grounds. They purify

Mizuko ("water baby") Jizo in a cemetery in Japan, holding a baby in place of the cintamani jewel.

their hands with a dipper full of water from a stone basin, light a small candle or stick of pungent incense, make an offering of a toy or sweet, and pray. If the Jizo image is of stone or bronze and accessible, they may dash water over it three times. The ritual is usually brief.

The form of a more formal mizuko ceremony varies with many factors including the type of temple (Buddhist sects, Shinto, or new religion), the priest who officiates, and whether the ceremony is held privately for one woman or family, or is a large public event attended by many people. There are elements that are common to most ceremonies. The central figure is almost always a Mizuko Jizo. Occasionally it is a Mizuko Kannon or Jizo and Kannon together. On the altar are the traditional five offerings: flowers, candlelight, incense, water or tea, and food. There may be offerings of children's toys, bibs, and other clothing, and food and drink such as juice, milk, candy, or a piece of fruit. A wooden rack for mizuko offerings

OFFERINGS TO JIZO

Small felt Jizos that are purchased, inscribed with a message, and hung on a rack at a small temple in a shopping arcade. They serve as both a prayer and an offering.

Jizo with offerings of small coins and, at left, a bird's nest.

*Author with hundreds
of hand-made bibs and
wooden plaques at a
Jizo temple.*

*Jizo with red crocheted hat, bib, and
pinwheel.*

*Mizuko Jizo with offerings of pinwheels (on
post), water in a coffee mug, flowers and stuffed
toys. On the wooden slats (ihai) behind the Jizo
is calligraphy with names of those who have died.*

at a Kyoto temple, for example, includes plastic toys, stuffed animals, and cartons of milk with plastic straws inserted, ready for the infant to drink. A woman at one temple told me of a friend who had a miscarriage. Every year on the anniversary date, she carefully prepares a meal for the child whom she believes was a girl. She offers the food on her home altar and talks to her daughter about what the family has been doing in the last year. She chooses the food appropriate to the child's age. This year, when the girl would have been fifteen, the mother offered a McDonald's hamburger and french fries.

The liturgy for a Buddhist mizuko service includes chants such as the *Heart Sutra*, the sutra to Kannon, and specific songs or short chants (dharani) to Jizo Bodhisattva. The priest may pick a *kaimyo*, a posthumous Buddhist name, for the infant, writing it in black calligraphy on a thin wooden plaque called an *ihai*. The ihai has a rounded shape at the top representing a pagoda or stupa, the traditional memorials constructed for the dead in India or China. The ihai can be left in the temple in a memorial room full of plaques, or in a cemetery, or taken home to the family altar. The priest gives an invocation asking Jizo and the other Buddhas and bodhisattvas to watch over the mizuko, says a prayer for the mizuko, and also reads the names of the people who sponsored the ceremony. Typically those who attend are asked to offer incense individually during or after the service. At a temple specializing in mizuko kuyo for abortions, a family may purchase a small statue of Jizo to place in an area especially designated for Jizo statues, often containing rows of hundreds of Jizos. In the case of an infant who dies, the parents may place the baby's ashes and a Jizo statue at their family grave site.

Some priests also offer counseling to those who request it. Here is what one priest has written about the type of advice he provides:

Neglecting a mizuko without having a (mizuko-kuyo) service for it is like trying to run or swim with a heavy weight attached. . . . If a couple has a mizuko they must, while one of them is still alive, have a suitable and proper memorial service for the mizuko. One should not have to live a gloomy life and not having a memorial service by the law of delayed cause and effect is tantamount to leaving sin unatoned for future generations. Mizuko prayer should be carried out by parents as the fundamental and natural thing to

Family plot (outlined by the cement curb) in a cemetery in Kyoto. A small mizuko Jizo is at right with offerings of flowers. The wooden slats (ihai) are for deceased family members.

do. Let us say that a child is born, and then dies one minute later. The parents [would not] say to the doctor, "Take the child away and bury it." No, of course they would not. They would call a priest, have him say at least one sutra, and hold a funeral for the child with all due ceremony. But [since] the child is in the womb and they [have not] actually seen it, they do not do these things. Just a slight gap in time makes the difference between abandoning it on the one hand and holding a funeral service for it on the other. I feel that prayer for the mizuko ought to be carried out as the parents' role—or rather duty. Is that not true parental love?

The book this priest has written contains testimonials about the benefits of the mizuko ceremony. These letters are typical:

Thank you very much for your letter acknowledging my contribution for the mizuko prayers. I had just gone to bed with [your letter] under my pillow when I dreamed my child came to me and smiled all over his face. I felt so glad!

Thanks to you the soul of my mizuko baby is living perpetually free from sadness and suffering at the feet of the Buddha.

At the end of last year my girlfriend became pregnant. As we were not married and too young, we had an abortion. After that there was a rift between us and I felt her heart had gone far away from me.[By trying] the mizuko prayer, my girlfriend and I recovered our love for each other which had cooled off after the abortion and now we plan to get married and to have children as the happy result of our love.

I am embarrassed to say it, but until this year although I did have the mizuko on my mind, I did not know what to do about it, so I tried not to think about it. Thank you very much for praying for my mizuko. The burden I had been carrying for such a long time was lifted from my shoulders and I started to get up each morning feeling that life was really worth living.

Some historians note that the peak in mizuko ceremonies was reached in the 1980s and assert that the practice is dying out. A stone mason in Kyoto told me that demand for Jizo statues had fallen dramatically in the last ten years. Others feel that even when the rate of abortion drops in Japan, which seems inevitable—oral contraceptives became legal in the year 2000—the ceremony will always be needed. Babies will always die and parents will always grieve.

THE BUDDHIST VIEW OF LIFE AND DEATH

People might think that the acceptance by Japanese society of infanticide (until the last few centuries) and of abortion (through modern times) would lead to weak family values. In fact the opposite is true. The Japanese value the family highly. Children are noticeably cherished in Japan today, as they have been for centuries. The high regard of the Japanese people for their children was observable even to a European who worked for the Dutch East-India Company in Japan in the 1600s. He wrote:

> Children are carefully and tenderly brought up; their parents strike them seldom or never, and though they cry whole nights together, endeavor to still them with patience; judging that Infants have no understanding, but that it grows with them as they grow in years, and therefore to be encouraged with indulgences and examples. It is remarkable to see how orderly and how modestly little Children of seven or eight years old behave themselves; their discourse and answers savoring of riper age, and far surpassing any I have yet seen of their times in our Country.

In times before effective birth control was available, abortion and mabiki were means to try to attain what we all wish, a society in which all children are wanted and have a high quality of life. The Japanese have been remarkably successful. Their infant mortality rate (after birth) is much lower than that in the United States and among the lowest in the world. The literacy rate is 99 percent and few children drop out of school or live in poverty. These attainments have not come without a price. The popularity of mizuko ceremonies indicates that many people feel sorrow and shame over abortion. It is a great consolation to those who suffer over abortion to believe that Jizo Bodhisattva protects and guides all children, those who die early and those who live.

Japanese attitudes about abortion or early death have as their partial foundation the Buddhist belief that life continually arises and disappears like waves on the surface of the ocean. In the largest view then, a life is not a discrete event with a certain beginning and end, but a constant appearing and disappearing due to the working of cause and effect. When causes and conditions are appropriate, life appears in this realm where we are aware of it and call it "newly born." When causes and conditions no longer support the temporary aggregation of the five elements they deteriorate, die, and decay. They separate back into the constituent elements, physical and psychical energy, which is recycled into new life.

If we can predict that a newly conceived life will be born in a situation of suffering, for example, to parents who could not care for an infant because of poverty or illness, then it would be seen as an act of mercy to return that life to a realm of no suffering, back into the ocean of life, the great mystery from which it emerged, and then for the parents to pray that those life elements would reemerge in a time and place where they could be loved and cared for properly. This view of life and death is extremely helpful in relieving the emotional pain that can accompany abortion, miscarriage, or early death.

The healing aspect of the mizuko kuyo was experienced by one woman who came to our ceremony grieving over an abortion that had occurred ten years before. She said that at the time she had been unmarried, very young, and unable to support even herself. Her family was angry with her and insisted that she terminate the pregnancy. She felt that to bring a new life into such an environment would cause only misery, and reluctantly underwent an abortion. Now she was mature, financially secure, and in a loving relationship; she wanted a child but had been unable to conceive. Her life was undermined by sorrow, her pain deepened by each baby she happened to see.

As she was listening to a description of life as a continuous process, appearing and disappearing, her sorrow for herself dropped away. It was transformed into an energy that moved outward, a sincere wish that the child whose life had touched her very briefly go on to find happiness. In releasing the child at last, she also released herself.

The Buddha helped a grief-stricken mother to this realization. The woman must have been young, perhaps thirteen or fourteen years old, and had never seen a dead person before.

At the time of the Buddha there lived a young woman from a poor family. She was so thin that she was called Kisagotami, which meant Haggard Gotami. A rich merchant fell in love with her and married her over his family's objections. When she gave birth to a son her in-laws accepted her at last and she was completely happy. One day the little boy became acutely ill and suddenly died. Kisagotami became distraught, and never having seen death before, refused to believe that her son could be dead. Carrying the baby in her arms she went from house to house asking for medicine to re-

vive him. At last a kind man advised her to go to the greatest physi-
cian, the Buddha, for a remedy.

The Buddha told her to go into the village and bring him a few
mustard seeds from a house where no one had died. The young
woman went from house to house with her dead child, asking for
the seeds. Everyone was glad to give her a few seeds but at each
house she heard of someone beloved who had died there, a child,
a wife or husband, a mother, or a father. She was told, "The dead
are more numerous than the living."

By evening she understood for herself how brief and fragile life
was and that death and sorrow came to all who were born. She
took her child's body to the cemetery and buried it. Then she re-
turned to the Buddha and entered the order of nuns. The Buddha
told her, "When a person's mind is deeply attached, infatuated
with sons and cattle, death grabs him and carries him away, as a
flood does a sleeping village." Later Kisagotami became enlight-
ened as she was watching the flickering flame of an oil lamp. The
Buddha appeared before her and said, "Though one should live a
hundred years without seeing the deathless state, yet it is better in-
deed to live a single day seeing the Deathless."

In the West we view life as a discrete, personal event. We are
born at a certain hour on a specific date. We live a certain number
of years, months, days, and minutes, and at a certain time on a specific date we die. Our life has a start and a stop point.

The Buddhist concept of life is different. Our life is only a small
part of the eternal life. It is interconnected with that huge body-
mind always. Birth is not a complete separation but rather the appearance of a new bud, branch, or leaf. Death is not the end of life
but one step in a dynamic of change that has no beginning or end.
A leaf emerges from a small bud when conditions are right in the
spring. It is visible on the tree until autumn when it changes color,
falls, and disappears from our view. We do not say the tree dies, only
the leaf. To say a leaf—or any individual—has died is not incorrect
but is only a very small part of what we see if we enlarge the frame-
work of time and place.

When a leaf falls, it decays, turning into oxygen, nitrogen, and
carbon in the soil. It is taken up into roots of trees, usually the very

same tree it fell from, and is literally turned into new leaves. If we fast forwarded a video of its life it would appear as bud, leaf, dry husk, $C+N+O_2$, sap, bud, leaf. Increase the speed and it would appear as a flickering, leaf, leaf, leaf. Only its location on the tree would change. If we, like Kisagotami, could perceive clearly and continuously the constant birth and death that comprise the Deathless, our suffering would not increase but would end.

No one believes that abortion is good. Some sincerely believe it to be killing and therefore wrong. They believe that each human life is a spark of the divine that must be allowed to be born and to grow. They believe that the creator had the largest view and has made each life to be "right." Others believe that abortion is in some circumstances the more appropriate of two very difficult choices. They believe that humans, in open and humble communication with the divine, can hold a larger view and realize circumstances into which a life would be born only to endure terrible hardship and abuse.

Neither view is right. They are only views, part of what the Buddha called a "wilderness of views." Either view can be taken to an unhealthy extreme. The "right to life" for every human conception can be taken to the extreme of human overpopulation and destruction not only of other human life but of many other living creatures, and finally to the extreme of killing people who do not agree with you. While fighting for the survival of each fetus, this view evades the subsequent and huge responsibility of ensuring the support and care of each life after it is born, for instance, to a poor single mother or into an abusive family.

The "right to choose" can be taken to the extreme of selection of the fittest or the preferred sex or race and disposal of all those currently unwanted or potentially of a type currently undesired—the extreme of the Holocaust. Both of these points of view, right to life and right to choose, have merit, and both are needed to balance each other and prevent deterioration into the harmful extreme on either end. Both have the potential to degrade the human condition and move further from enlightenment or heaven on earth—the right-to-life movement through anger, self-righteousness, and justification of killing, the right to choose through hubris, greed, self-righteousness, and justification of killing.

The Enduring Value of
the Mizuko Ceremony

As in America, in Japan there are people who approve of and perform abortions and people who do not. But Japanese people do not
go to battle or kill each other over this difference of opinion. It may
be that the mizuko ceremony has helped to maintain a balance by
embracing the universal human sorrow over abortion and early
death in a sacramental and ceremonial way. The religious aspects
of the mizuko ceremony speak to the heart of all religion, the pain
of being a human and (apparently) separate from the One and
therefore the pain of always acting with imperfect wisdom and partial compassion.

Abortion is a fact. It occurs thousands of times a day throughout
the world. It can cause physical pain to the mother and fetus, and
emotional suffering to many. This includes those who believe abortion to be an appropriate action in some circumstances and those
who perform abortions. For these, the mizuko ceremony offers consolation and witnessing, a place to say good-bye, a touching in sadness and in the human confusion of love.

The sadness we all share about abortion arises from the fact that
this is not a world where all children have a place that fits their individual needs, supports them in developing their talents, and
brings them happiness and fulfillment. No one wants a world where
babies are killed. No one wants to condemn unwanted children
to a life of abuse and contagious misery that spreads relentlessly
through society generation after generation.

Jizo Bodhisattva provides consolation for those who have lost an
infant or young child. No matter how the infant or child died,
through miscarriage, abortion, sudden infant death, accident, or illness, no matter how old the child was, there are those who grieve.
Their grief is honored and gently held in the ceremony of Mizuko
Jizo. In America we have expanded the ceremony to include children lost in other ways, such as children who have been abducted
or are alienated through a painful divorce or separation and also
children given up for adoption.

The term *water baby* recognizes the essential purity of the infant mind as it emerges into this world of sound and light from the great unborn. This is the mind of the unborn we all once lived within. When we grieve for a lost child, we grieve also for our own lost innocence, the pure mind and heart we once had before conditioning and circumstances of the environment closed in with the walls of reactivity. Fortunately there is a path to recover what we have lost. It is the path of practice.

chapter four

Jizo Bodhisattva Protector of Children

First days of spring—blue sky, bright sun.
Everything is gradually becoming fresh and green.
Carrying my bowl, I walk slowly to the village.
The children, surprised to see me,
Joyfully crowd about, bringing
My begging trip to an end at the temple gate.
I place my bowl on top of a white rock and
Hang my sack from the branch of a tree.
Here we play with the wild grasses and throw a ball.
For a time, I play catch while the children sing;
Then it is my turn.
Playing like this, here and there, I have forgotten the time.
'Passers by point and laugh at me, asking,
"What is the reason for such foolishness?"
No answer I give, only a deep bow;
Even if I replied, they would not understand.
Look around! There is nothing but this.

RYŌKAN

HISTORY OF JIZO AS SPECIAL GUARDIAN OF CHILDREN

Jizo Bodhisattva became the special protector of children during medieval times in Japan. He never assumed that role in China, Korea, or Tibet. The Japanese aristocracy was the first to take on worship of Jizo. They favored an artistic style that depicted Jizo with a handsome, youthful face. As Jizo became associated with children he was depicted with an even more childlike face and body. He was shown as a monk carrying a child or later, in a combination of these aspects, as a child monk. In modern Japan this trend has continued and Jizo is sometimes portrayed as a *kawai* (cute) baby monk, almost a cartoon figure.

How did Jizo become associated with children? One possible origin lies in the *Earth Store Bodhisattva Sutra* that was written in China in the seventh century and later introduced into Japan. In this sutra there are a few short passages related to children, specifically at the time of their birth. In one section the Lord of Longevity speaks to the Buddha about childbirth. The Lord of Longevity, who will become a Buddha in the future, is in charge of the life span of each human, determining the time of their birth and death. He advises:

> *When a birth is expected or has just occurred, people should practice good deeds. Then the local spirits will not only protect the mother and the newborn child, but will bestow peace and happiness upon the entire family. After the birth, all killing or injuring for the purpose of offering fresh foods to the mother should be avoided carefully, as should assembling and entertaining the family with wine, meat, music, and singing. This is because at the difficult time of birth there are uncountable evil ghosts who wish to drink blood. The local earth spirits should be honored instead and they will protect the mother and child.*

The implication is that evil spirits could be attracted by killing, by offerings of meat, and by the immoral behavior of celebrants who are drunk. These spirits might harm the infant and its mother. In another passage Shakyamuni Buddha speaks to a bodhisattva called Universally Expansive of the benefits to an infant if the parents honor Kshitigarbha.

> *The parents of new born children should chant the name of Kshitigarbha and this sutra ten thousand times within the seven days before the birth. Then, if the new born child was to have had a disastrous life, he will be liberated from this fate and be peaceful,*

happy, easily raised, and long-lived. If he was to have received a
life of blessings, his life will be even longer and happier.

The implication is that our life span is not fixed, and that good
deeds can both prolong it and make us happier, while bad deeds
will make our life brief and more miserable.

These short passages in the *Earth Store Bodhisattva Sutra* did not
seem to result in any strong association of Kshitigarbha / Ti-tsang
with children in China. Ti-tsang did have some connection with
women's concerns in China but did not assume a clear role as
guardian of women until after Buddhism entered Japan in the sixth
and seventh centuries. Women of the Japanese nobility soon took
up the worship of Jizo, some honoring him as their tutelary deity. By
the eleventh to twelfth centuries, devotion to Jizo had arisen among
the common people accompanied by a rich folklore from which
many of the legends in this book are taken. Associations of people
devoted to Jizo, called *Jizo-ko*, arose, usually attended by more
women than men. At the monthly meetings of these "Jizo clubs,"
older women prayed for deliverance after death and younger
women for easy deliveries and healthy children.

Jizo may have become the guardian deity of children precisely
because many of his devotees were women petitioning for help with
their particular anxieties. These worries often centered around their
children. They included successful conception, easy childbirth,
conditions like diseases of the nipple that might interfere with nursing, and the many contagions that imperiled young lives and made
passage through childhood quite uncertain. There are Jizo images
in the Kyoto and Nara area that have reputations for curing typhoid,
smallpox, and even measles. Why measles? Although it is an illness
we regard now as relatively trivial, in years past it killed many children or left them blind, deaf, and retarded.

There are other theories to explain how Jizo became associated
with children after Buddhism entered Japan. One is that infants
who died before birth and children who died before their life span
was complete would need divine help because they would find it
difficult to settle down and adjust to life in the next realm of existence. Another theory postulates that parents grieving for the many
children who died in the epidemics that swept frequently through

Japan found natural solace in the figure of Jizo Bodhisattva who, with his hairless head, smooth round smiling face, bare toes and simple garments, reminded them of their lost children. In support of this idea, there are modern Jizo figures fashioned like a cherubic toddler, with a robe dragging around its feet like a nightgown that is too big.

THE LEGEND OF THE RIVERBANK OF SAI

According to Japanese Buddhist beliefs, young children are innocent souls who are unable to understand the teachings of the Buddha or to separate right from wrong. This also means that through no fault of their own, they cannot become enlightened and pass on to the realm of the Buddhas after death. They are stuck in a kind of limbo. Mythology locates this intermediate world on the banks of a river that must be crossed after death.

Jizo Bodhisattva protecting newly deceased children by confronting a demon on the banks of the River Sai. From a religious comic book, O Jizo Sama.

An old Japanese legend tells of the fate of children who die young. They gather on the banks of a river called *Sai*, where they pile up beach pebbles to make small stupas in remembrance of their parents and siblings. They say, "This one is for my mother who protected me, this is for my father who held my hand, this is for my sister. . . ." In sunnier versions of this legend, the children are playing and Jizo helps them. The children make these stone cairns in order to build enough merit to cross to the other shore of the river where they will be able to be judged and to pass on to the next rebirth.

There is a more distressing version of the Sai no Kawara (river-bank of Sai) legend, which is described in one religious picture book for children as "so frightening that if you heard it in summer you would start to shiver and wouldn't be able to stop." The beach is lonely and desolate and the children are grieving for the families they have left behind. An ugly hag with burning eyes called *Dat-suba* (or *Shozuka no baba*) strips the children naked and hangs their clothing on a tree. Because they have died young, the children can-not fulfill their filial duty to care for their parents in old age. To make up for this they must spend each day building stone stupas. Every day at dusk the wicked *oni*, fierce demons with horns and fangs, emerge from the gathering gloom and descend upon the chil-dren, yelling insults. "You weren't even around long enough to learn how to pray! You mis-erable brats who died before your parents!" With their iron staffs they demolish the piles of stone the children have labored to build.

Then Jizo Bodhisattva appears and the frightened children run to him, taking sanctuary under his flowing monk's robes. The littlest among them cling to his staff or are taken up in his arms. He soothes them, say-ing, "There's nothing to be

Datsuba, the old woman who strips people of their cloth-ing on the banks of the River Sai.

frightened of. From now on I will be your mother and your father."
The wicked oni demand that Jizo return the children, but he stands
firm, radiating brilliant light, and the demons retreat. This is the suffering even innocent children undergo in the netherworld. Only
Jizo can rescue these little ones.

The origin of the legend Sai no Kawara is not known. It may
come from the *Sutra of the Ten Kings*, which was written in China
in the eighth century and includes a detailed and vivid description
of the journey that each person must undertake after death. In the
second week the spirit must cross the River Sai. A medieval Japanese version of the sutra adds Datsuba (Old Woman Who Pulls Off
Clothes) and *Ken-eo* (Old Man Who Hangs Up Clothing). This
couple strips sinners naked and hangs their clothing on a tree whose
branches tilt, acting as a scale that weighs their sins. There are three
ways to traverse the River Sai. Virtuous people are able to cross easily by means of a bridge. People with less merit can cross at a shallow ford. People whose sins weigh heavily must struggle across
where the water is deep and swift and many drown. All who cross
the river then pass before ten kings who interrogate and sentence
them. In the last court, outside the iron gates of the city of hell,
stands the shining figure of Jizo Bodhisattva, who argues for leniency. The kings are subordinate to Jizo. He can release those im-
prisoned in wooden neck shackles, give the thirsty broth to drink,
and successfully argue for leniency if he can find even one deed of
kindness in each soul.

Japanese belief in the River Sai also may have originated in medieval times with a desolate stony area outside Kyoto called *Saiin no
Kawahara*. This field, bounded by a stream, was used as a potter's
field where the bodies of unwanted children, suicides, and the
homeless were discarded or buried. It is said that the tenth-century
priest Kuya performed funeral and burial services there for these
discarded souls. Additionally there also are records from the tenth
century of a village and nearby river, both called Sai. Peasants were
buried in Nether or Upper Sai and funeral processions stopped before crossing the bridge over the River Sai. Thus the Jizo images
that were placed in those graveyards may have been called "Jizo of
the beach of Sai."

There are a number of places in Japan designated as Sai no
Kawara. Often the name is applied to a deserted and rocky stretch of

beach by a river or the sea. One such is Sai no Kawara of Numa no Uchi, used since the Edo period as a Jizo shrine. There grieving parents pile stones in memory of their dead children before Jizos in a cave. Hundreds of small Jizo images and toys line the rocks and fill a sea cave at another Sai no Kawara on the northernmost tip of Sado island. Yet another Sai no Kawara is the mountain Osorezan. In the thirteenth century Abbot Ennin of the Tendai sect collected hundreds of human remains there, built a temple, and performed proper funerals for these forgotten spirits. Over the centuries Jizo statues have accumulated on many riverbanks and stretches of rocky beach, places where families still go to make stone stupas and pray for their dead children. These piles grow as pebbles are added by kind believers who are moved to help the souls of unknown children travel on to an earlier and more fortunate rebirth. This practice may derive from an ancient Japanese custom of placing simple stone phallic images at entrances to villages and at crossroads. Travelers petitioning for protection placed small pebbles in a pile before these pillars. As Jizo worship grew and spread, these stones began to be called Jizos.

There is a children's game in Japan called *kotoro-kotoro* (taking a child) based upon the legend of Sai no Kawara. One child who is "it" represents the demon and tries to catch the other children. Another child, who represents Jizo, tries to prevent their capture or rescue them. In talking of this game, Morinaga Roshi pointed out that the demons of Sai no Kawara are partners of Jizo Bodhisattva and "contribute their half to Jizo's virtuous action." Jizo does not do the work for the children, nor banish the demons. This is because children cannot develop courage and grow into their full potential without facing hardship and exerting themselves fully. Jizo simply shelters the children under his robe when they are afraid and encourages them to continue their efforts. This, Morinaga Roshi says, is "the essence of religion."

JIZO AS PROTECTOR OF CHILDREN IN JAPANESE LEGEND

Jizo Bodhisattva's role both as a special guardian of children and as a bodhisattva who could appear as a child was developed through the many miracle tales that arose during the Heian period. This was a time when the misery of war, social upheaval, and coincident natural disasters caused large numbers of suffering people to believe that a degenerate age had arrived and that people could be saved only by divine intervention. Here are a few Jizo tales from that time:

During the reign of Emperor Go-Ichido there was an epidemic of smallpox. No one, noble or commoner, escaped, and the sound of pitiful human lamentation filled every household. Priest Ninko was deeply moved by people's suffering and prayed to Jizo Bodhisattva for help. That night Ninko had a dream of a handsome boy who said, "You are observing the impermanence of life." Ninko said, "Those I meet and talk to in the morning are dead by nightfall. Even if we have happiness today later sorrow will come. Nothing is permanent."

The boy smiled, saying, "Do not lament over life's sufferings. Was there ever a time without sorrow? If a person wishes to be free from sufferings he should listen to the teachings of Jizo. Then he and others will be delivered into the peace of the serene light of the Buddha."

When Ninko awoke he went to master sculptor Kojo and asked him to make a gilded statue of Jizo. When the statue was done Ninko held a dedication ceremony and delivered teachings on Jizo. Priests and lay people together were moved to worship Jizo. Everyone in the temple and those who came to hear the Jizo sermons escaped infection. Those who were too proud to attend met with disaster. The epidemic soon ceased but people still continue to venerate Jizo.

The next tale is from the thirteenth century:

Once there was an old nun who was devoted to Jizo Bodhisattva and had always wished to see him, not just as a statue, but in person. Hearing that Jizo went out at daybreak to help people, she set out walking early one morning, wearing the best of her two robes, hoping to meet him. She soon met a man who, when she told him her errand, promised to lead her to Jizo if she would give him her robe. The nun was innocent in the ways of the world and did not recognize that the man was a thief. She readily gave him her robe. Laughing at her foolishness, he led her to a small house where a man and his small son lived. The boy's name was Jizo.

The pious woman did not realize that she had been tricked. She knelt reverently before the boy and worshiped him. The neighbors all laughed to see the old nun bowing down in her under-kimono. Just then the little boy scratched idly at his forehead with a stick he had been playing with. Suddenly his face split from top to bottom and inside was the shining face of a beautiful golden Jizo! Thus the nun was granted her wish and when she died was rewarded for her devotion by being taken straight to heaven.

Another tale concerns the plight of a stepchild. If life was difficult for children in medieval times, it was even harder for stepchildren. Recognizing this, there is a specific retribution for cruel parents or stepparents in the *Earth Store Bodhisattva Sutra*: they are to be flogged in future lives.

A thousand years ago in Anwa there was a woman who believed in Jizo and prayed that she might have an image of the Bodhisattva in her house to make offerings to. One day she found an old wooden Jizo in the river in front of her house. She rejoiced and prayed to this Jizo every morning and evening to be granted a child. She became pregnant and delivered a boy, but when he was four years old, she suddenly died. Her husband took a second wife who was very cruel to the little boy. The child had learned from his mother to pray to Jizo. One day when his father was away he took a little rice and, weeping for his dead mother, offered it to Jizo and to his mother's memorial tablet at the family shrine. When the stepmother came into the house she found the child kneeling before the shrine and flew into a rage. She seized the boy and threw him into a kettle that was boiling over the fire.

At that moment the father, who was traveling on a road, became very confused and was unable to go on. He felt compelled to return home. As he turned back he saw a Buddhist priest standing by the road with a child on his back who cried out with a voice that he recognized. It was the voice of his own son! The man asked who this child was. The priest answered, "I have substituted my own body for this child when his stepmother was about to kill him. You must entrust him to other people who will raise and educate him well." He put the child in the arms of his frightened father. The man asked the priest where he lived. The monk replied,

"Near the Temple of the Repository King," and disappeared into thin air. After giving his son over to the care of kind friends the father returned home. There he found his wife stoking the fire under a kettle. When she saw her husband she quickly put out the fire and became quite distressed. He asked her, "Where is my son?" Pretending grief she told him that the boy had been playing by the river and had drowned. The man strode to the kettle and took off the lid. There he found the old wooden Jizo floating in the boiling water. He realized the terrible thing his wife had done and saw that indeed Jizo had changed places with his son to save the boy's life. Weeping bitterly he left the life of a householder and became a monk. From that time forth he was utterly devoted to Jizo Bodhisattva.

THE JIZO FESTIVAL FOR CHILDREN IN JAPAN

Jizo's *ennichi*, special or saint's day in Japan, is the twenty-fourth day of the seventh month of the traditional lunar calendar. Temples especially dedicated to Jizo may hold services every month on that day. A festival to honor Jizo still is celebrated in August in the Kyoto and Osaka region, at the end of the Obon or festival for the dead.

During the weeks of Obon the "gates" between the human world and other realms are believed to open. The spirits of the dead are welcomed and honored as they return to visit family and friends. Priests are very busy making rounds to parishioners' homes to chant sutras in memory of relatives who have died. Traditionally bountiful offerings of food, especially cookies, candy, canned fruit, and also sake, are placed on the altar for the hungry ghosts. The best offerings, however, are the sutras, for only the Dharma will slake the unending thirst of all beings and relieve their gnawing hunger.

The Obon festival often ends with bonfires and a ceremony in which hundreds of little boats made of leaves, each bearing a lighted candle, are floated on rivers or lakes. The fires light the path for the dead to return to their homes in the other realms. At Nembutsu-ji Temple in the hills above Kyoto myriads of candles flicker in the darkness, illuminating hundreds of ancient gravestones that have been gathered there from out of the forests to honor the nameless dead. The *Jizo-bon* (festival) occurs at the end of Obon because the gates that allowed spirits to return and visit will soon close and lock behind them for another year. It is an appropriate time to ask Jizo to assist these loved ones as they journey back, possibly to difficult realms.

The Jizo-bon has become a festival for children, a time to express gratitude to Jizo and to invoke his special protection for little ones making their way through the perils of childhood in the coming year. Here is a lovely description of the Jizo-bon in Kyoto from an article in a Japanese newspaper for foreigners:

The surface of this religious observance looks like a gay neighborhood party to end the summer. Children under thirteen and the adults of the neighborhood take part in the festival. On the morning of the 24th a canopy is set up in front of Jizo's shrine or statue. If the image is in a crowded area, a neighbor living close to the statue will open up his front rooms for the festivities. The point is that Jizo should be able to enjoy the fun too.

[Jizo and his shrine have been thoroughly cleaned.] From early morning, offerings of food and drink, and of incense, candles and flowers are made. The statue and/or its shrine will have been draped with red and white bunting and red lanterns with Jizo-bon and each family's name written on them will have been hung before each door. These will be lighted in the evening to give a soft rosy glow to the streets and alleys of the neighborhood.

Excited children gather early in the day for games (organized and spontaneous), the drawing of prizes, snacks and general fun. Some neighborhoods serve a communal supper of curry, noodles or sushi prepared by children under adult supervision.

Nightfall brings the magic of sparklers and fireworks, cold drinks and watermelon, and perhaps bon-odori [dances]. The children and their parents, bathed and dressed in colorful cotton summer kimono, enjoy the cool of the evening and its festivities with their neighbors. At bedtime a final thank you to Jizo for past health and safety, and supplications for future protection are made.

Jizo-bon is over and so is summer. Children must return to school, farmers must start preparations for the autumn crops and harvests and businessmen their autumn "sales offensive."

PROTECTION OF CHILDREN AS OUR PRACTICE

Fresh morning snow in front of the shrine,
The trees! Are they white with peach blossoms
Or white with snow?
The children and I joyfully throw snowballs.

RYŌKAN

The aspect of Jizo Bodhisattva that moves us to protect children is an aspect we all share. We see children at play and smile, thinking, "Oh, they're so cute and happy! If only they didn't have to grow up!" We know this is unrealistic, but it points to qualities of child-nature we would like to preserve. What are they?

When we asked this question in a practice group, we came up with these qualities:

innocence, openness, acceptance, curiosity, energy, unself-consciousness, a natural loving quality, spontaneity, freedom and flexibility, lack of anxiety and worry.

We also asked what qualities of childhood we would like *not* to retain. These were:

vulnerability, ignorance, helplessness, and self-centeredness.

The childlike figure of Jizo appeals to us because it portrays what we all wish to regain, our original nature, innocent, happy, open and curious. Infants have the quality of not judging right or wrong. They accept milk from a breast or a bottle, and love a sober or drunk parent. They are relaxed taking breaths of fresh or polluted air and are happy clothed in rags or satin. They embody the line from the sutra which says, "the Great Way is not difficult for those who do not pick or choose." Through their wondering eyes and fresh minds we glimpse what we have lost. We have all emerged, newly born, again born, from that Great Unborn. We appear in this world of bright light and sharp sound, blinking and startling at the sensational extremes we were buffered against in the womb.

No one emerges as a tabula rasa. The karma of genetics and environment are already active. Some infants emerge placid and unconcerned, some are puzzled and curious. Some are shy and overreactive, and some worried and protesting. The environment interacts with these innate patterns to shape action and reaction as we learn about dangers and pleasures, at first overt and then more subtle. We shape an armor of strategies to avoid these threats, real or imagined, and eventually do not know how to escape. We are locked away from others and out of God. We grow unhappy in our self-made prison and long to return to a time of freedom and innocence. But we do not know how to do this.

The word *infant* literally means "not speaking." Before words arise, what is our experience? This is the state of the second *jyana* (meditative absorption). It is characterized by joy and vitality, the happiness of being aware of all that is speaking, moving, and vividly alive, before we cover it up with words.

When the mind becomes quiet during a retreat you can look down and see ten marvelous fingers taking care of you, all by themselves. Picking up spoons, wrapping around mugs, bringing food to the mouth, what wisdom they have! Just like our tongue, our liver, our pores. Working to take care of us all the time. This itself is the unselfconscious operation of the innate goodness of existence. A poet named Ozaki Hosai wrote, "Cutting my fingernails I have ten fingers!" That's the mind of every infant who has just discovered his own toes and can play with them for hours! "Oh look! These marvelous pink playthings that keep appearing in front of my face and moving!"

These childlike qualities can reemerge through sincere religious practice. They are qualities that draw others to practice. They are qualities that enable bodhisattvas and saints to forget themselves in joy and thus to serve others fully. Are these qualities prerequisites *for* a bodhisattva life? Or do they emerge *from* a bodhisattva's life, a life deliberately given over relieving the suffering of others? Cause, result—or both?

The Bible relates the story of a group of mothers who brought children to Jesus, asking him to touch and bless them. Like all mothers, they worried about the safety and future of their children, and they were asking for his protection and guidance. The disciples of

Jesus were annoyed and told the mothers to go away, feeling that Jesus was too important and busy to bother with a group of noisy, dirty children. But Jesus called the children over to him and rebuked the disciples, saying "Let the little children come to me. Never send them away! For to such, people with hearts as trusting as children, belongs the kingdom of Heaven. I say to you, whoever does not receive the heavenly kingdom like a child shall never enter."

What is being said here in Buddhist language? That we cannot enter nirvana, the gateless gate to our true and enduring life, unless we have the hearts and faith of children.

CHILDLIKE, NOT CHILDISH

This does not mean to become childish, to run around, giggle, and act silly, or to take on any of the self-centered, stubborn qualities children acquire as protection from the perceived threats of the world. Childish is different from childlike, and childlike is different from being a child. Infants newly born and unconditioned live in a state of open-ended interest and awareness, experiencing everything as it is. They live in Buddha-nature but are unaware of it, having nothing to compare it to. They are unaware of suffering. They feel simple pain and hunger, and react to it. They don't worry, does this pain in my stomach mean I have cancer? They just feel it and cry out! The *Tao Te Ching* says:

> *He who is in harmony with the Way*
>   *is like a newborn child.*
> *Its bones are soft, its muscles are weak,*
>   *but its grip is powerful.*
> *It doesn't know about the union*
>   *of male and female,*
>   *yet its penis can stand erect,*
>   *so intense is its vital power.*
> *It can scream its head off all day,*
>   *yet it never becomes hoarse,*
>   *so complete is its harmony.*
>
> *The Master's power is like this.*
> *He lets all things come and go*

effortlessly, without desire.
He never expects results;
  thus he is never disappointed.
He is never disappointed;
  thus his spirit never grows old.

Babies are not aware of their vulnerability or their separation. But inevitably the sense of a separate self emerges, and every child feels lonely, ashamed, and afraid, evicted from the Garden of Eden.

Children are not enlightened. The Buddha spoke about this quite clearly. He was asked about the teaching of another religious wanderer who said that if a person did no evil actions, uttered no evil speech, had no evil intentions and did not make his living by any evil livelihood, then he had done all the spiritual work that needed to be done, was perfected, invincible and enlightened. The Buddha refuted this, saying:

> A young tender infant lying prone does not even have the notion "body," so how should he do an evil action beyond mere wriggling? A young tender infant lying prone does not even have the notion "speech," so how should he utter evil speech beyond mere whining? . . . [He] does not even have the notion "intention," so how should he have evil intentions beyond mere skulking? . . . [He] does not even have the notion "livelihood," so how should he make his living by evil livelihood beyond being suckled at his mother's breast? If [what the wanderer said] were so, then a young tender infant lying prone is perfected, invincible, and [enlightened].

The Buddha said that it is not enough to cease doing and saying things that cause harm. Under the external words and actions are the internal thoughts and feelings that drive them, primarily the thoughts and feelings that construct and reinforce the notions "I am" and "I must survive." Under the thoughts are what the Buddha called "latent tendencies." Unless these are completely cut off down to the finest root hair they will, like weeds given the right nutrition, always grow again. We know this ourselves. We emerge from a long retreat feeling clear, clean, and loving. But as soon as we pull out onto the highway and someone cuts in front of "our" car, or as soon as we arrive home and see the pile of "our" bills or dirty laundry waiting, or find that "that" dog has destroyed the window screens or our grubby, demanding children pile on us—the latent tendencies explode full blown into speech and action.

A young tender infant may feel with open heart and and observe with open mind, but it is not enlightened. The events of life always will cause those latent tendencies to emerge. All it takes is "No, that's bad!" or "You idiot!" or "You adorable thing! I love you." and the cycle of conditioning begins again. The only way to stop the merry-go-round is to get off. The only way to get off is to let go of the self we are riding on and the support posts we are gripping. This is only possible through the power of practice.

Another aspect of childishness can be heard in the mind when we encounter obstacles on the path of practice. Impatience arises. "Let's get on with this!" says the mind. "Nothing's happening." If we weren't so entangled in this voice it would remind us of someone we know, or knew—a three-year-old on a long car trip. "When are we going to get there? I'm bored! Aren't we there *yet*?" When we hear this voice or, more often, when we feel the restless three-year-old energy arise, first we have to turn around and face it. Then we can handle it in two ways. We can take it lightly, ask ourselves, "Will you be the first person in the history to die from boredom? I could write you up in a medical journal and we'd be famous." Or we can take it seriously. "What is it you want, Mr. Impatience?" How would it answer? "I'm impatient for clarity. For enlightenment. For an end to suffering—even in its mild form, boredom." Then we can respond, "You're absolutely right. Me too."

Then the impatience, instead of being an obstacle on the pilgrim's road, instead of putting the brakes on, can become a push from behind. It can be transformed into an energy of determination, an appropriate sense of urgency. Life is very short, we've suffered enough, we've caused enough suffering. Let's get on with it! That very impatience becomes the medicine to cure the disease of indifference, laziness, and boredom.

If we honor the voice of our own impatience, hear it with compassion and a touch of humor, find its real purpose, yield to it gently instead of fighting it, it's like a tai chi movement. The yielding turns the opponent's energy over to us, to use to our advantage.

Other energies that arise during a retreat are the "I'll do it my-self!" voice. How old does that sound? You discover after a while that many internal voices are those of a two- to five-year-old, thinly disguised. They resist the sesshin schedule or what the teacher or those in charge say to do. They get irritated at other meditators ("If he clears his throat one more time!"), at the ceremonies ("I hate that chant!") or at guided meditations ("I won't do it. It's distracting me from my lovely tranquil mind state.").

They say things like, "I want to do it myself. I'll tell them to change the schedule. I sit best at night. The mornings are terrible for me. I'm lonely when we all sit in silence. I want someone to talk to me. We should get up later and sit late at night. Next time I'll just stay home and do my own retreat, my way."

Right. Sure you will.

You'll convince yourself to sit a whole week, eight hours a day. No cheating, no skimping. Push yourself beyond your limits. No way. This is why we need sangha, good companions, on this pilgrimage. To make vows to. To hear our vows. To help us uphold vows.

How do we transform the stubborn "I do it myself!" aspect of mind? Take away what is extra, the childish, self-aggrandizing part, and it becomes the voice of the Buddha who told us not to believe anything simply because "the monk said it is so." This is the man-date of our practice. Not to accept at face value the words of any-one, the Buddha, the Dalai Lama, Christ, our mother or father. The voice that insists, "I want to do it myself!" is right. It is the only way it can be done. The voice is crying out desperately, "I won't be satisfied until I know it, experience it *myself*, in every corner of my existence. I want to be able to say, "The depths and shallows of the world are all in *my* grasp, are all myself."

There is a difference between childish and childlike. Our prac-tice enables us not just to unfold the qualities of a child, but to man-ifest them in a truly adult body, a body of stability and wisdom, with a mind that is not just aware of our own suffering and the suffering of all beings, but has experience, and thus confidence, in the way to end that suffering. This, the rediscovery of our beginner's heart and our ageless mind, brings us happiness. Their merging makes us inwardly comfortable, truly at home in the full possession of all of our faculties.

CHILDREN AS SPIRITUAL PILGRIMS

In a practice group we asked the question, "When did my spiritual life begin?" Everyone remembered the beginnings in childhood. One college student said, "When I was about six or seven I found a dead bird on our front lawn. I suddenly realized that everyone, my parents, my favorite uncle, my cousins and I, all were going to die. What then was life about, if everyone was just born, lived a little while, and then died? It was all a trap. I began crying without stopping and my parents couldn't help me." This question never left him and now has propelled him into full-time Zen training. I asked my mother, still a spiritual seeker at age eighty, this question, and instantly she said, "Of course I remember. I was two or three years old. My mother would let me ride on her Hoover upright while she was vacuuming the house. As we passed a bookcase I saw my reflection in the glass doors and suddenly realized that I was unique, different from everyone else in the world. I began to wonder how this could be."

It is fortunate to be born to parents who know they are seekers. If we were born to parents who were "lost on the dark paths," at some point we realized they were not going to be much help. If I'm going to figure it out, I'll have to do it myself. The advantage of that particular karmic situation is we can embark on home-leaving early. We know the truth earlier than most people, that each one journeys alone. We set out like small but erect pilgrims. The great Zen teacher Dōgen Zenji began the journey early. His father died when he was two and his mother when he was seven. He began studying sutras at age eight and became ordained at age eleven. Unsupported but determined children find other ways to keep the spiritual doors open despite their inhospitable surroundings, through music, art, or nature.

Looking back at how we started out, child pilgrims all, squaring our shoulders as we faced the travails of life, taking up any kind of staff that offered support, it's very touching. We are like Christopher Robin determinedly setting out to find the North Pole that Pooh and Piglet have decided is lost and must be found. This is a true representation of something lost or missing that *must* be found and a quest that does begin in childhood.

I once evaluated a ten-year-old boy whom police brought to the child-abuse program after he had called 911 because his schizophrenic mother was climbing on top of him nude and touching his private parts. His father was retarded. The boy was quite bright, but no one had ever spoken to him about his parents' conditions. The boy was very worried about being taken away from home and denied to me that his mother had done any touching. I soon dropped any questions about abuse and moved on to what seemed more important. I asked if his mother or father ever did or said things that didn't make sense. It poured out of him, his frustration at being born to and loving, but being unsupported by, these two peculiar adults. I explained briefly what mental illness was. He seemed relieved to know it could be treated and that we would try to help.

After finishing his exam I left the room to let him get dressed in private. When I returned I asked my standard question for wrapping things up, "Do you have any questions you want to ask me?" Most children have no questions, and jump down from the exam table in relief, scooting out the door before we think of something else to do with them. But this boy didn't move. He had a question.

"Do you know the meaning of life?" he asked me very seriously. Halfway out the door myself, I stopped. Whoah. I sat down and asked him, "What do you think the meaning of life is?" He said, "I wonder if God is hiding." What a wonderful koan, I thought. We had a long discussion, touching on his worries that he would go to hell because he hadn't kept a small promise, and many other questions. We both left the room smiling. Age and circumstance do not matter. A pilgrim recognizes a pilgrim.

The following passage is from the diary of a seven-year-old girl named Opal who lived in a logging town in Oregon in the late 1800s. She was a bright child who was not only in love with the world but who was able, because of her intelligence and sensitivity, to write about her natural joy and innate spirituality in a unique way, a way that opens the door of time and invokes our own child-heart of pure love and flowing gratitude for all existence.

Today the grandpa dug potatoes in the filed. Too, the chore boy did dig potatoes in the field. I did follow along after. My work was to pick up the potatoes they got out of the ground. I picked them up and piled them in piles. Some of them were very plump. Some of them were not big. All of them wore brown dresses.

When they were in piles I did stop to take looks at them. I walked up close; I looked them all over. I walked off and took long looks at them. Potatoes are very interesting folks. I think they must see a lot of what is going on in the earth—they have so many eyes. And after I did look those looks as I did go along, I did count the eyes that every potato did have, and their numbers were in blessings.

And all the time I was picking up potatoes, I did have conversations with them. Too, I did have thinks of all their growing days there in the ground, and all the things they did hear. Earth-voices are glad voices, and earth songs come up from the ground through the plants; and in their flowering . . . they do tell the earth songs to the wind. And the wind in her goings does whisper them to folks to print for other folks, so other folks do have knowing of the earth's songs. When I grow up, I am going to write for children—and the grownups that haven't grown up too much—all the earth songs I now do hear.

I have thinks these potatoes growing here did have knowings of star-songs. I have kept watch in the field at night , and I have seen the stars look kindness upon them. And I have walked between the rows of potatoes and I have watched the star-gleams on their leaves. . . . And as the wind did go walking in the field talking to the earth-voices there, I did follow her down the rows. I did have feels of her presence near. And her goings-by made ripples on my nightgown.

On the afternoon of today, when I did have a goodly number of potatoes in piles, I did have thinks of how this was the going-away day of Saint Francois of Assisi, and the borning day of Jean Francois Millet—so I did take as many potatoes as they years did dwell upon the earth. Forty four potatoes I so took for Saint Francois of Assisi, for his years were near unto forty-four. Sixty potatoes I so took for Jean Francois Millet, for his years were sixty. All these potatoes I did lay in two rows.

And as I had seeing of them all there, I did have thinks to have a choir. First I did sing, "Sanctus, sanctus, sanctus, Dominus Deus." . . . And the choir, there was a goodly number of folks

in it, all potato folks wearing brown robes. Then I did sing one
"Ave Maria."

After we had prayers, I did sing one more "Ave Maria." I was
just going to sing the all of it. I did not so. I so did not, because the
chore boy did have steps behind me. He gave me three shoulder
shakes, and he did tell me to get a hurry on me and get those po-
tatoes picked up. I so did in a most quick way.

Just as the chore boy stopped Opal's song so she could finish her
work, a necessary aspect of our growth is to assume responsibility
and, with it, the anxieties of heart and mind that cover our original
nature. As young children we all naturally possessed many of qualities that are manifested by the enlightened. These have not been
lost, only obscured. Through practice we are able to open this kind
of awareness again. Then impermanence and not-knowing no
longer make us afraid. They become a source of continual wonder
and delight. It is said that Jizo Bodhisattva likes to stand at crossroads because he is curious and wants to be able to learn about new
things. Out of this childlike curiosity flows an ever-fresh intelligence, the experience of a warm and ever-spreading web of connection to all that exists.

When these qualities of Jizo become our own, then, like Opal,
we do not know boredom and loneliness. We are always accompanied. I accompany myself. I as the myriad living beings, grass
blades, scurrying mice, swooping bats, dropping lichen, flittering
tree spirits. I as multitude accompany I as temporary warm spot,
padding and crunching along the path. Never alone, never ignored,
never useless, never disconnected, never unsupported, never outside the vast web of loving-kindness extended by all beings.

There are ancient legends from many countries—including
India, Greece, China, and Tibet—of a river like the Styx that must
be crossed by those who have died. The story of the Jizo and the
children on the banks of the Sai undoubtedly arose from a combination of imported and indigenous sources. It is the universal story
of human existence. Each of us is born helpless and naked, stripped
of whatever had been accomplished in past lifetimes (whether we
believe them to be our own past lives or that of our ancestors). We
set out to achieve and make a mark upon the world, but all our

creations are built upon the shifting sands of impermanence. The demons of karma inevitably emerge to help us understand that actions based upon worldly ambition and selfish desires cannot bring us happiness. Jizo appears as a symbol of our only true refuge, the shining, eternal, mysterious beauty of the selfless Dharma. If we are able to surrender our fear to this truth, to live with a simple, child-like faith in the mystery that is beyond our childish understanding, we will find ourselves at ease, sheltered within the very Source of everlasting peace and comfort.

Resting in that Unborn Mind, we look out and can clearly see the child, frightened, barely daring to hope, hidden in the heart of every angry and disordered person. The parental mind embodied by Jizo Bodhisattva naturally opens within us and embraces every being as our child. We accept our duty to protect and nourish all children so that they are able realize their full spiritual potential. We are moved to join the task of Jizo, extending our support and protection to every being born in ignorance and struggling toward freedom.

chapter five

THE *Stone* *Woman* *Dances*

Long ago, a pretty girl lived next door:
She used to pick mulberries in a distant grove,
Returning with her white arms full of gold and silver branches.
She sang with a heart rending voice
And sparkled with life.
Young farmers put aside their hoes when they saw her,
And many forgot to return home when she was around.
Now she is just a white-haired granny,
Burdened with the aches and pains of old age.

RYŌKAN

THE FEMININE ORIGINS OF JIZO BODHISATTVA: HISTORICAL ASPECTS

Jizo Bodhisattva and Kannon (Kuan-yin) are the two most revered bodhisattvas in China, Korea, and Japan. Both Jizo and Kannon have feminine as well as masculine aspects. Some authors postulate that Jizo's ancestor in India, Kshitigarbha, was a Buddhist transformation/assimilation of Prithivi, a Vedic earth goddess. This is congruent with the Sanskrit name of Jizo, Kshitigarbha, which can be translated as "Womb of the Earth" or "Earth Womb Receptacle." There are four stories of the genesis of Kshitigarbha in the *Sutra of the Original Vow of Earth Store Bodhisattva*. The longest and most detailed stories are of two women whose sincere vows and devoted practice led them to become Kshitigarbha (see chapter eleven).

There also is a Japanese legend ascribing a mixed feminine and masculine origin to Jizo. A devout priest named Myogwan prayed for several nights to see a living Jizo. A woman appeared in a dream and pointed the way to Mount Iwafune. There he met an old priest who transformed into a golden Jizo and then appeared again as an ordinary monk. He gave Myogwan miraculous rice that radiated light. If a few grains were cooked they filled an entire pot, enabling Myogwan to feed many starving people during a famine. Both the woman and old priest were declared to be manifestations of Jizo.

After Jizo was introduced into Japan he gradually became known as a protector of women and children. As Jizo worship was taken up by the aristocracy, a number of shoguns and their consorts adopted Jizo as a tutelary deity. Masako, daughter of Hojo Tokimasa and consort of Yoritomo, had a picture of Jizo dedicated in her private chapel in 1223 on the twenty-fourth day of the month, the day dedicated to the bodhisattva. After the death of her lord, Masako became a nun, and, while reigning in the place of her sons, was called Ama-Shogun or "Nun Shogun."

NUDE JIZOS

Hojo Tokiyori (1226–1263) and his consort were devout worshipers of Jizo. One day as this couple played at a dice game similar to backgammon they decided that the loser would have to disrobe. The consort lost the match, but she was ashamed to undress and prayed to an image of Jizo to rescue her. Suddenly the little Jizo statue disappeared, reappearing as a naked woman standing on the game board. This image was enshrined in Kamakura at Emmyō-ji, Temple of Long Life. It was dressed in robes sewn of cloth and stood on a backgammon board instead of a lotus pedestal. When pilgrims came the image was sometimes taken out and its robes parted to reveal that this Jizo had female pudenda. Because it substituted its own body to protect the modesty of the consort, it is called a Migawari (Substitute or Surrogate) Jizo. It is also called a Hadaka or "Naked Jizo" because, unlike most statues that had robes carved of wood as part of the statue and decorated with paint, this Jizo was carved as a nude image and was later dressed in clothing made as miniatures of actual priests' robes.

There are other "nude" Jizos in Japan. Two are in the city of Nara, one now found at Shinyakushi-ji Temple and another at

Denkō-ji Temple. Both of these Jizos have genitalia that are neither clearly feminine nor masculine. The Shinyakushi Jizo has a simple lump in the groin and the Denkō-ji Jizo has only a line carved in a corkscrew shape. There is speculation that these are representations of the "sheathed" or "retractable" penis, one of the distinguishing marks of a Buddha. The ambiguous genitalia of these Jizos also may reflect the dual male and female origin and attributes of Jizo Bodhisattva.

"Nude" Jizos are not displayed naked. They wear priests' robes and *o-kesa*, a pieced rectangle made like the Buddha's original patchwork robe, that are sewn by women as a devotional practice. The priest's wife at Denkō-ji told me that she and other women of the temple make by hand an entirely new set of clothing for the Jizo

The "nude" Jizo at Denkō-ji Temple in Nara. Once a year, the women in the congregation dress it in new robes, which they sew themselves.

each year, including underwear, kimono, robe, and o-kesa. During the August Jizo-bon festival the statue is dressed in its new clothes.

Accounts from the tenth and twelfth centuries tell of women of the Japanese nobility sewing clothing and ceremonially dressing religious statues. This custom has ancient origins. From the time of the Buddha, lay people have offered robes or robe-making material to monks and nuns along with food, soap, and other necessities. The *Earth Store Bodhisattva Sutra* tells of the merits of offering "scented flowers, clothing, food and drink" to Kshitigarbha. The recommendation in the sutra (along with the fun of dressing small beings like children, pets, and dolls) may have given rise to the devotional practice of making priest's clothing for Jizo images. This practice, in turn, may have been the origin of the modern custom of making capes, hats, and bibs for Jizo. You can see small items of clothing on most Jizo statues or any upright rock that is even vaguely human shaped all over Japan. Some old Jizos even have fresh "makeup" on their stone faces, bright red lips, white cheeks, and blue eyeshadow.

When the nude Jizo at Denkō-ji Jizo was taken apart for restoration in 1950, the curators were surprised to find it was hollow. In a cavity in the thigh they found a Kannon Bodhisattva holding a monks's staff in the left hand and a lotus in the right. Inside the head of the Jizo was a small blue glass vessel of fifth-century Chinese origin that contained a diminutive sandalwood statue of Yakushi nyorai (the healing or medicine Buddha) and three tiny fragments believed to be relics of the historical Buddha. The Denkō-ji Jizo likely was fashioned in 1228 under a joint commission by three women. The torso of the Jizo was filled with scrolls of Buddhist sutras. Two women, one a nun of 83 years, had written dedications in classical Chinese, offering the merit of the statue for the salvation of their parents. A third woman, also a nun, included prayers to Jizo Bodhisattva asking to be reborn as a man.

JIZO AND PREGNANCY

A temple to Jizo was built in 851 by Fujiwara no Akiko, the consort of Emperor Montoku, after prayers to Jizo ended her long and difficult pregnancy. After giving birth to a son who became the first boy emperor of Japan, she erected a Jizo temple in Nara called *Obitoki-dera* or "Temple for Loosening the Girdle" (granting easy birth). The press of pilgrims visiting this temple was described as like the crowds on a busy market day. Thousands of easy births have been ascribed to this Jizo.

There are many Jizos in Japan dedicated to the particular concerns of women. There are Jizos that assist women with birth, the Belly Band Jizo (Hara-obi no Jizo) and the Easy Birth Jizo (Koyasu Jizo). An eighteenth-century Jizo specialized in curing women with nipple problems. There are also Prosperous Birth Jizos (Tai-san Jizo), Child Granting Jizos (Ko-sazuke Jizo), and Child Rearing Jizos (Ko-sodate Jizo) usually shown with a child on their laps. Pregnant women still apply sand to their bodies from a Jizo temple in Mibu to be assured of an easy birth. After the birth they return the sand to the temple.

There is a custom in Izumo province in which young people carry a stone Jizo to the gate of the house of newly married couple on the bridal night. In Iwami province several stones are carried to the bridegroom's home. According to modern explanations the images help remind the woman to be firm like stone in her fidelity and to have the love and compassion of Jizo. Also it is hoped that the union will be as hard to turn over as the stone Jizos, and divorce will not occur. These customs are probably remnants of ancient rites involving stone phallic images. It is likely that they were begun to ensure fertility and easy births.

The association between Jizo and pregnancy is implied in the Japanese Jizo statues that are fashioned with small Jizo images hidden within them, much like a baby in the womb. These are called *haragomori* (hidden in the belly) images. The term for fetus is *haragomori no ko*. A story from the 1600s tells of a small Jizo made of aloe wood that was kept by a courtesan on her body. One night a Buddhist priest heard the mysterious crying of a child. He found it was the little Jizo weeping for the immoral company it was forced to keep. The priest retrieved the image and placed it inside a bigger Jizo statue in Nembutsudo in Nara. It is known as the "Jizo who wept at night."

I wonder. Are there unborn children whose tears add salt to the amniotic sea they float in, weeping in the dark for the suffering humans who will soon become their guardians or tormenters? Who will rescue them? Who will help them return to their place of ease within the large and sacred body?

Another standing Jizo attributed to the twelfth-century sculptor Unkei had a small copper Jizo enclosed in its belly. The small Jizo was said to have emerged from a pool. There are many stories in Japan of Jizo images found floating in rivers, drifting ashore on beaches, or being dug out of the earth where they were hidden for centuries. Often the image was found because it was radiating light. In these stories Jizo miraculously materializes in the water like a fetus (called a "water baby" in Japan) or emerges like a baby from the womb of the earth.

THE BUDDHA AS PROTECTOR OF WOMEN

Why would women need extra protection from Jizo Bodhisattva or anyone? In the time of the Buddha, the special needs of women were so obvious that the Buddha was reluctant to allow women to be ordained until his disciple Ananda intervened on their behalf. This is the story from the Pali canon, a historical record of the Buddha's life and teaching:

> *Mahapajapati was the Buddha's aunt and a second wife to the Buddha's father Suddodhana, who was a ruler of the warrior clan called the Sakyans. The future Buddha's mother had died after giving birth to him and Mahapajapati, another of his father's wives, nursed and raised him. After the Buddha became enlightened he returned to his birthplace to teach and both his father and stepmother became his followers. Several years later when Suddhodhana died, his widow Mahapajapati became determined to become ordained although the Buddha had ordained only men. She went to her foster son, the Buddha, paid homage, and requested that women be allowed to be ordained. The Buddha told her, "Enough, do not ask for the going forth from the house life into homelessness for women." Twice more Mahapajapati asked him and twice more he refused her. She departed in tears.*
>
> *Mahapajapati continued to follow the Buddha's teaching and became a lay teacher for many women who had been cast into*

uncertainty and personal suffering. These included women who had belonged to the future Buddha's harem before he left the palace on his spiritual pilgrimage and women whose husbands died in local wars.

Seeing first hand the benefit of the Buddha's teaching Maha-pajapati renewed her determination to become ordained. She cut off her hair and put on a saffron robe. She and a number of her women followers walked 150 miles barefoot to speak with the Buddha again. She stood outside the hall where he taught, her feet swollen, her body covered with dust, her face wet with tears. The Venerable Ananda saw her in this pitiful condition, and inquiring, learned of her sincere desire to enter the homeless life. He went to the Buddha and asked on behalf of the women that they might become ordained. The Buddha again refused. After asking and being refused three times Ananda realized he would have to use the truth that he had learned from the Buddha himself.

He asked, "Lord, are women capable, after going forth from the house life into homelessness in the Dharma and Discipline you have taught, of realizing the fruit of practice, and becoming fully awakened?" The Buddha replied, "They are." Ananda then asked the Buddha not to deny the wonderful fruits of practice to the woman who had nursed the Buddha with her own breasts when his mother had died. The Buddha was won over by his own truth and agreed that women could join the sangha of the ordained.

Ananda is venerated by Buddhist women because of his advocacy for the spiritual potential and integrity of women.

Why would the Buddha be reluctant to ordain women? Why would women need extra protection? At the time of the Buddha, health and safety problems existed that were particular to women. Rape was common and women were not safe walking alone or even in small groups. When there was no birth control, women could be continually pregnant and caring for numbers of children from the age of fifteen on. Each pregnancy meant not only pain but a high risk of dying in childbirth, as the Buddha's mother did, despite the extra care and nutrition afforded a queen. Women lost blood with menses and childbirth and without adequate iron in the diet could be chronically anemic, weak, and prey to infection. Average life expectancy was about thirty-five years. The care and feeding of many children meant a life of unending labor and also terror if her husband and in-laws were cruel. Women who did not bring a good bride price or bear a son could be cast out or killed.

These problems are not two millennia distant. When I lived in Korea in the early 1960s after the Korean War, the orphanages were filled with infant girls collected each morning from the trash heaps. Girls were a liability; they would cost their families a dowry. When even well- and Western-educated Asians found that my father had three daughters, they would shake their heads in pity, saying, "Well, maybe next time." In the 1970s I taught in Africa. Half of infants died there before age five. In some cultures babies were not named before age one because the chance of survival was so low. To know that half their children would die must have caused women constant anxiety and suffering. Even as we entered the new millennium, we heard news reports about women who had been raped during the war in Serbo-Croatia. Their families told reporters it would have been better if the women had not survived the rape, because of the shame they brought upon the families. Some of these girls, as young as twelve or thirteen, have been cast out of their homes and reporters say they will not survive.

Buddhism as a Refuge for Women

A prevailing belief at the time of the Buddha was that a woman's spiritual role was to bear sons, preferable ten in number. She could not become enlightened until she was reborn as a man. Her access to the divine was through men: her father, her husband, her sons. The Buddha gave spiritual protection to women by allowing no distinction based upon sex or caste. He accepted women as full members of the sangha whether they remained in lay life or underwent ordination, whether they had been queens, prostitutes, or victims of rape. The poems of the early Buddhist nuns in India tell of the hardships endured by women and the freedom, consolation, and safe refuge they found as followers of the Enlightened One.

Some of these were women who had gone mad with grief over losing a child or after being put out of their homes for failure to bear a son. One was Vasatthi, who went crazy and roamed, homeless, mourning for her dead son until she met the Buddha. Then she entered the enlightened state, an entirely different kind of homelessness. This is her poem:

Grief-stricken for my son,
mad-minded, out of my senses,
I was naked with wild hair
and I wandered anywhere.

I lived on trash heaps,
in a graveyard,
and by the highways.
Three years' wandering,
starved and thirsty.

Then in the city of Mithila
I saw the one who tames
what is untamed
and goes his way in happiness,
enlightened, unafraid.

I came to my senses,
paid homage
and sat down.

Out of compassion
Gautama taught me the way.
When I heard his words
I set out into homelessness.
By putting his teachings into practice,
I realized great joy.

My grief is cut out,
finished, ended,
for I have understood the ground
from which all grief comes.

Chinese women also took refuge in ordination when it was introduced into China. Buddhist convents became places of asylum for women escaping cruelty in marriage and the dangers of war or homelessness. This occurred despite the rule that a Chinese woman who wished to be ordained was supposed to have the permission of the man who had authority over her—her father, her husband, or her son. In the fifth century, a thirteen-year old girl named Radiance of the Dharma, determined to enter a convent, vowed to immolate herself if her parents forced her to marry. Her teacher raised money by begging to pay off her betrothal fee. She became a skilled Dharma teacher who could not be defeated by the questions of famous masters, and built a temple and three convents before dying at age eighty-three.

Three girls played a pivotal role in the introduction of Buddhism into Japan by becoming the first ordained Buddhists in the country. An envoy to Korea had returned in 577 C.E. with Buddhist sutras, a sculptor of Buddhist images, a temple architect, a nun, and masters of the precepts, meditation techniques, and mantras. In 584 a Korean master ordained the eleven-year-old daughter of a Japanese government official and gave her the name Zenshin. Two of her companions also became nuns and a temple was built so offering could be made to them.

Several months later a severe smallpox epidemic broke out and many died. Advisors to Emperor Bidatsu convinced him that the cause was his support of the foreign religion. As a result the nuns' temple was destroyed and the charred remains of a new Buddha statue thrown in the canal. Government officials arrested the young nuns, stripped them of their robes, and had them publicly whipped. When smallpox erupted again, people said it was in retribution for the burning of the Buddha image, and the temple was rebuilt. A few years later the nuns went to Korea to study and receive the full precepts. Upon their return many others entered the Buddhist order. Within thirty years there were a total of 816 monks and 569 nuns. Even if these three girls were ordained for political reasons, the new religion must have affected them deeply, giving them courage to face public humiliation and remain steadfast in the face of turning tides of public superstition.

BUDDHISM AND HARASSMENT

The Buddha protected the spiritual potential of women, and of men, by forbidding sexual harassment. These are examples from the Pali canon:

> Once a monk saw a woman who was wearing a rough blanket and said, "Sister, is that thick, short hair yours?" Being naive she did not understand and said, "Yes, master, it is a rough blanket."
>
> At one time a monk was infatuated with a woman and said, "You are a faithful follower but you do not give the highest gift." "What is the highest gift, sir?" she asked. "Sexual intercourse," he answered.

In each case the monk was remorseful and went to the Buddha to report what he had done. The Buddha ruled that such offenses were "wrongdoing" and prescribed ways to atone.

Jizo Bodhisattva embodies the protection offered to women by the Buddha's teachings. One legend tells of a thirteenth-century female pilgrim who spent the night in a Jizo temple in Kyoto. During the night the lecherous priest pretended to speak to her as she slept, as if it were Jizo Bodhisattva himself. He directed her to have intercourse with the first man she met the next morning as she left the temple. The next day as the priest prepared to intercept her and be the first man she met, he could not find his sandals. Jizo had hidden them. The woman met another man instead, a widower who married her (and presumably cared well for her).

PROTECTING THE FEMININE

If Jizo is a protector of women, does it mean that we, as Jizo, do not protect men? Of course not. But we have to ask, why should we, as manifestations of Jizo Bodhisattva, be particularly concerned with the protection of women? What is it in the feminine that we wish to protect?

The metta sutra instructs us,

> Even as a mother protects with her life her child, her only child, so with a boundless heart should one cherish all living beings.

This word "love" is much richer in the Buddhist context than in the West. It has four aspects to be cultivated. They are *metta*—loving-kindness, *karuna*—compassion, *mudita*—rejoicing in another's happiness, and *upekka*—equanimity. The Buddhist teacher Gunaratna distinguishes these aspects using the example of a mother's love for her child. When she first learns that she is pregnant she is filled with loving-kindness. Even though she has never seen this being she wants to protect and care for it. When the infant is born and cries in hunger or pain, the mother feels compassion. Intuitively she feels the baby's suffering and develops the skill to help relieve it. As the child grows and takes joy in learning to walk, play, talk, and explore the world, the mother feels sympathetic joy in the child's happiness. She is free of jealousy. When the child grows up, moves away, and encounters problems in life, she must develop equanimity, not clinging, not becoming too anxious about the child's individual path through life. These are all qualities manifested, transmitted, and protected by the existence of bodhisattvas. To see these qualities of love in the face of a Jizo image or manifesting in a living Jizo inspires us to recognize them as characteristics of a rare, endangered, and vital species, to cultivate them in our lives and doing so, to protect them.

Jizo Bodhisattva protects those who are helpless. A mark of civilization is the recognition that those who have less power, those who are born into less fortunate circumstances and are vulnerable, have rights that should be safeguarded. It is a mark of empathy, the recognition that any of us could, in the turning of a moment of cause and effect, be stripped of our intelligence, talent, power, money, or sexual functioning. We know, but do not want to think, that this could happen to us. Thus we are morbidly fascinated when these sudden overturnings happen to others. The Titanic sinks and hundreds of the wealthy and powerful are plunged into an icy sea. Millions have watched this occur over and over in the glow of a TV screen in their dry and comfortable living rooms. The handsome athletic movie star who epitomized invulnerability to us when he portrayed Superman becomes the helpless captive not of super villains but of a motorized wheelchair and a respirator after his horse stumbles. We must have reminders like these and the presence of Jizo Bodhisattva to be compassionate toward those who suffer or we risk reverting to the mind of the ruthless conqueror who tramples and gloats.

Shodo Harada Roshi has said, "No one should be teaching Zen unless they do not see male and female in their students." The enlightened eye of Jizo Bodhisattva and all other Awakened Ones penetrates superficial differences and sees at the core of all beings the innate potential to awaken to the truth and manifest it fully. Jizo manifests loving-kindness toward all beings who are unseen and live in darkness just as a mother loves the unborn infant she can sense but has not yet seen. Jizo manifests compassion and brings aid to those who suffer, rejoicing in the faltering steps we make along the path. Jizo shows equanimity and optimism when we fall back into old habits that cause us difficulty.

We perceive the fragile nature of our human life and it makes us afraid. As protection against the inevitable assaults of a human life—separations, failures, abuse, illness, and death—we construct a set of strategies and defenses called a self. Each time we perceive danger we fortify the defenses until we find ourselves trapped and isolated inside its walls. Like a stone or wooden Jizo, we are frozen and lifeless. We long for—and fear—someone who can see through the thick shell to the nascent Buddha inside.

The feminine aspect recognizes and operates from the truth that we are all weak and powerless in relationship to that great power that animates our life. The feminine aspect is aware of the immensity of the field in which we are but tiny figures. It yields, surrenders. Unless we allow that feminine aspect to emerge, unless we surrender completely to That Which Is, we keep at bay that which we most desire. We must yield to our deepest yearning, and allow ourselves to be completely interpenetrated by that overwhelming mystery, to nurture it in awe within our own life. Then the wooden man will walk and the stone woman will dance. Then the Jizo Bodhisattva within us will come to life.

chapter six

The *Pilgrimage* of *Jizo* *Bodhisattva*

> *My bowl is fragrant from the rice of a thousand homes;*
> *My heart has renounced the sovereignty of riches*
>   *and worldly fame.*
> *Quietly cherishing the memory of the ancient 'Buddhas,*
> *I walk to the village for another day of begging.*

RYŌKAN

FROM INDIA

The history of Jizo Bodhisattva before his arrival in Japan, the history of his birth, travels, and transformations, is a story that can be pieced together out of fragments found along a path of pilgrimage that stretches over four thousand miles, from the jungles of India through the desert oases of central Asia to a sacred mountain in China. The fragments include faded frescoes on the walls of forgotten caves, fragile hangings of painted silk, statues fashioned of stone, clay and metal, and sections of sutras sung to celebrate the virtue of this beloved bodhisattva. The travels of Jizo parallel the history and spread of Buddhism in Asia.

He was born in India in the first or second century, about six hundred years after the Buddha died. His name, in Sanskrit, was Kshitigarbha. He came to life within a family of bodhisattvas as the Mahayana school emerged from the original teaching of the Buddha and the elder monks. In the Mahayana school the ideal practitioner was a bodhisattva, who sought not only personal enlightenment but the welfare and spiritual liberation of all beings. There is no evidence that Kshitigarbha was ever very popular in India. Only a little historical evidence remains in India to hint at how he was portrayed and venerated. His image is found in mandalas of Shakyamuni Buddha and the eight great bodhisattvas carved in the walls of the cave temples of Ellora (fifth to sixth century) near modern Bombay. Groups of eight bodhisattvas surrounding a Buddha have been found in other ancient sites in India, but no early image of a single bodhisattva clearly identifiable as Kshitigarbha has been found yet in India. The diaries of seventh-century Chinese pilgrims to India do not mention Kshitigarbha although he and his sutras certainly were known and studied at the great Buddhist university and monastic complex of Nalanda in Magadha.

As the new religion of Buddhism spread to Central Asia, Jizo Bodhisattva followed its path. Upon entering a new country Jizo, as any good immigrant, became assimilated into the culture. In this process he took on new names, new forms, and new dress. Through intermarriage with indigenous religious practices and folk beliefs he also assumed new powers and functions.

To China

Buddhism arrived in Turkestan, the part of China that borders on India and Pakistan, about 140 C.E. Buddhism was spread by missionary monks traveling the Silk Road. The journey between India and China was long, arduous, and often dangerous. Travelers encountered difficult terrain and hostile peoples. A biography of a Chinese monk of the times tells of his courage in leading twelve fellow pilgrims west to India in order to study the Dharma. As they struggled through the deserts of northwest China they used the skeletal remains of dead men as landmarks to keep them on the path. Veneration of Kshitigarbha as the protector of pilgrims may have begun at this time in order to meet a very real need. In painted silk banners from Turkestan he wears the "shawl of the Traveler." This garment is described either as a monk's cloak thrown over the head or as a head scarf or turban with loose ends covering and protecting the traveler's neck and shoulders. A cult of Kshitigarbha as guardian deity of travelers was flourishing in Turkestan by the ninth and tenth centuries.

Kshitigarbha Bodhisattva entered central China around 400 C.E., taking on the name Ti-tsang Pusa. It does not appear he was venerated widely until the middle to late 500s when the sect of the Three Stages promoted veneration of Ti-tsang as the most appropriate form of Buddhism for that era, which was felt to be degenerate. "Degenerate era" refers to a prediction that the original teachings of the Buddha would become so corrupted over time that eventually people could not hope to become enlightened through their own study and practice. They would have to depend upon the intercession of someone who had become enlightened in an earlier time, a Buddha or bodhisattva.

This prediction, which is attributed to the Buddha himself, makes Buddhism subject to the law it teaches, namely the impermanence of all things. Buddhism is the only religion to forecast its own demise. According to the scriptures, the first five hundred years following the death of the Buddha would be the time of practice of the True Dharma. During the next period, the era of the Counterfeit Dharma, the practice would be outward only, a false show of religiosity. In the third period, called the time of the Collapsed Dharma, the teaching and practice would degenerate completely and enlightenment would not be possible. This period was known in China as *mo fa* and in Japan as *mappo*. The Japanese calculated that this period would begin at the end of the eleventh century. In Japan economic and social conditions did deteriorate at this time and people who felt that salvation was no longer possible under one's own power turned to religious teachings that focused on calling upon the beneficent "other power" of Amida Buddha or bodhisattvas such as Jizo.

There are many images of Ti-tsang in the caves at Lung-Men, where he was worshiped from 650 to 700 C.E. The construction of this extensive complex of twenty-one thousand sacred caves and one hundred thousand Buddhist images was supported by the imperial family, indicating that Ti-tsang was revered by those of power and wealth. There also are many images of Ti-tsang / Kshitigarbha in the grotto of the Ten Thousand Buddhas in the Tun-huang caves, located in Turkestan, now the province of Kansu in north-western China. In frescoes and banners there from the ninth and tenth century he is portrayed with a shaven head, wearing monk's robes and carrying a staff and jewel, a savior of those in the six realms. Worship services in the Tun-huan caves included hymns to Ti-tsang, chanting, bowing, prayers, rites of repentance and divination, and the traditional offerings of incense, flowers, and money.

The art of the Sung dynasty testifies to the popularity of Ti-tsang in the tenth through twelfth centuries. He was depicted in stone statues used for veneration and offerings in temples, in hand scrolls used for sermons, in portraits painted on silk banners, and on frescoes painted on the walls of temples and grottoes. The sermons that unfolded as the illustrated scrolls were unrolled probably were aimed at impressing believers with the pain suffered by unrepentant sinners and the benefits of confession, repentance, and a life guided by the precepts.

Three Chinese Sutras about Ti-tsang

Sutras that refer to Ti-tsang provide clues about how the Chinese viewed this bodhisattva and came to revere him. Three texts were instrumental in shaping Chinese views of Ti-tsang and his powers, because of their popularity among the laity and their wide dissemination. These were the *Sutra of the Ten Kings*, the *Transformation Text on Mu-lein Saving His Mother*, and the *Sutra of the Past Vows of Earth Store Bodhisattva*. The first two texts give bare mention to Ti-tsang. The *Sutra on the Past Vows of Earth Store Bodhisattva* provides more information about Ti-tsang / Kshitigarbha and is excerpted and discussed separately in chapter eleven.

The sutra on the Ten Kings was written in China in the ninth century. The sutra represents a synthesis of Indian and Chinese beliefs. Indian Buddhism focused upon practice as a means to escape from the endless round of birth and death driven by karma, that is, the effects of unenlightened thought, speech and action. The Buddha had described five realms of existence (see chapter ten on the Six Realms). The Chinese were particularly focused on the hell realm to which they added a new concept, that of purgatory. In the *Ten Kings Sutra* these ideas were combined with several Chinese ideals. The first was the ideal of filial piety, particularly as expressed through veneration of ancestors and concern for their fate after death. The second was the ideal of harmony and order that was possible under a strong, well-organized system of government. The third was the attainment of immortality after death.

Chinese sutras document the way in which Buddhist teachings flowed into China and blended with existing beliefs. The *Sutra of the Ten Kings* is a synthesis of Taoist, Confucian, and Buddhist views. It describes a cosmology in which the Taoist hierarchy is intercalated with a Buddhist one, as might occur if the rulers of two merging countries worked out the delicate task of deciding who is in charge of what without demeaning or insulting anyone. In the *Sutra of the Ten Kings* a Taoist deity is Emperor of Heaven and under him is the Buddhist Ti-tsang, called Lord of Hell. Ti-tsang Pusa is in turn overlord of the Chinese Ten Kings of Hell including Yama, the ruler of hell. Yama has three messengers, Old Age, Sickness, and Death, who go forth into the world to warn humans that life is fleeting and they should mend their ways while there is still time left.

The *Ten Kings Sutra* combined all of these beliefs and personages in purgatory, which was both a physical location and a process that each person must undergo after death. The first forty-nine days after death became a time of particular concern, when the fate of the deceased was uncertain. Before death a person's own actions and mind-state were important in influencing their destination. After death it was the actions of friends and relatives that could tip the scales and determine a pleasant or horrible future existence.

The Chinese moved the Buddhist hell from India to China, to a location in Szechuan province, 280,000 miles under the surface of the earth. The entrance to these Infernal Regions was thought to be in a desolate area on the side of a specific mountain where, during the night, terrifying shrieks and wailing could be heard. Hell was vast, containing great seas and mountains of iron, encircled by an iron wall with a huge gate studded with countless nails. Purgatory was located outside the gates to hell.

The *Ten Kings Sutra* taught that after death a person entered purgatory, where they became the defendant in a series of trials. They passed from one court to another, once a week in the first forty-nine days after death, then again on the one hundredth day, the first year, and the third year, for a total of ten trials and ten judges or kings. It must have been frightening for a Chinese peasant in medieval times to be called before a powerful and educated judge or king. The tests imposed by the ten kings included such things as being burned with scalding water and searing fire, and having one's beating heart cut out and examined. Death itself is fearsome, but to believe in ten terrifying interrogations, judgments, and punishments after death might frighten anyone into more moral behavior.

In the ten courts many clerks maintained written records of each person's actions during his or her lifetime on earth. Each king reviewed these files, administered certain tests, and then passed sentence. When a good person died he was led by a good demon before the judge of the first court. The judge took measure of the person's life. If he determined that the good deeds outweighed the sins, he sent the deceased directly to the tenth court and thence on to another existence in the human realm. The circumstances of his next existence would depend upon how his life account was balanced. A man could be reborn as a woman, a woman as a man, a rich person could be born to experience poverty, or a sick person who was virtuous, into a long and healthy life.

The sutra created a stage setting with characters taken from the ubiquitous imperial bureaucracy of the times. Virtuous people appeared serene, wearing fine garments and jewelry. They carried scrolls of sutras that they commissioned while alive, visible proof of the meritorious acts that resulted in their happy destination. Unhappy sinners, in sharp contrast, entered the stage as prisoners. They wore only their underclothing and were shackled at wrists and ankles, with iron yokes around their necks. Demon guards pulled their hair and beat them with whips.

If in the first court a person's evil deeds were found to outweigh the good he had done, the demon guards forced him to kneel before the great Mirror of Guilt that reflected the evil acts of his recent life. The mirror showed times when a person had been cruel or killed another living being, providing visible proof of the past actions that had resulted in their current miserable state. Once the deceased had witnessed all of the suffering he had caused for others, he was sent on through the next nine courts, for a succession of trials and judgments. The punishments were appropriate to the crimes. Even Buddhist monks could not escape the inexorable workings of the law of cause and effect, as this example of just retribution shows.

> [In] this First Court of Hades, a group of Buddhist monks may be seen squatting in a narrow corner, and atoning for all the short-weights they have given in the exercise of their professional duties when living on earth. The dungeon assigned to them is one from which the light of day is wholly excluded. A lamp with a wick composed of a single thread is allowed them, and by this weak, flickering light, they have to repeat all the prayers and chants they skipped while in life, to the material detriment of those who had paid for their services.

The second king was stationed on the banks of the River Sai (River of No Recourse). People of virtue could cross the river on a bridge but sinners struggled across in deep water, prodded by ghosts and ox-headed demons wielding clubs and pitchforks. The tenth and final court was very large, furnished with many tables, chairs, and benches where numerous officials worked to carry out the process of transmigration. They determined in which of the six realms a person would be reborn. The determination was made purely in accord with the person's past actions, under the laws of cause and effect. To Christian missionaries this process was "fatalistic in the extreme." To Buddhists it was objective and fair.

Before leaving purgatory to go on to the next realm, souls were led to the Hall of Oblivion. There an old woman named Granny Meng made them drink a special broth that wiped out all memory of their previous existence. King Yama appointed her to this task so that no one could divulge what happened in the underground realms. If a person refused to take the broth, two demons forced a bamboo pipe in his throat and poured the liquid down. At last the souls could leave purgatory. In some versions of hell, the dead again crossed the bridge over the River Sai. Engraved upon a stone pillar on the opposite shore were these words, hopefully to be imprinted deeply upon their newly cleansed minds, "To become a human for the first time is easy, but to act truly human is difficult. If you did not behave well, it is almost impossible to be born again as a human. If you wish a happy transmigration, do good during your coming life so that you can reap its rewards." As the deceased approached the opposite shore two demons hurled them into the dark red foaming waters beneath the bridge and they were carried away by the torrent to their next existence.

Ti-tsang is mentioned only once in the *Ten Kings Sutra*, but he is a prominent figure in the many illustrations added to the picture scrolls of the sutra that monks apparently used in their instruction of lay people. He appears upon the tragic stage of purgatory and hell as a figure offering mercy and hope. Ti-tsang had been a relatively minor bodhisattva until he was assigned, through the widespread propagation of this sutra, the power to deliver souls from the many ghastly forms of torture in the Chinese hells. Ti-tsang was portrayed as a powerful overlord who could intercede with the Ten Kings, argue for leniency and soften their judgments. He was also a compassionate priest. If he knocked on the doors of hell with his ring staff, they had to open. As he descended into hell, the cintamani jewel brought light into realms of utter darkness and despair. If he could discern even one good deed in a person's life he could plead for leniency. If he were able to find more virtuous actions, he might win acquittal. He could release prisoners from their shackles and, in some illustrations of the sutra, it is he who gives those who have undergone torment in hell the broth of oblivion to drink.

A second work that spread faith in the savior Ti-tsang was the *Transformation Text on Mu-lein Saving His Mother*, written in the eighth century. It is the story of a disciple of the Buddha named Mu-lein (Mahamogallana, or Mogallana) who searches for his deceased parents, trying to discover their fate. He finds his father in heaven. His mother, however, had acquired an unhealthy appetite for meat, roasting a live goat and even eating the family dog. For this she was reborn in hell, where Mu-lein finds her nailed down by forty-nine huge iron spikes. The Buddha releases her and she is reborn in a slightly higher realm, as a hungry ghost with a huge belly, a needle-thin neck and skin hanging off her bones. Mu-lein tries to send his mother food through offering it on the altar, but it becomes flaming coals as it enters her mouth. Mu-lein appeals to the Buddha for help. The Buddha tells the sorrowing son to provide a feast for the monks on the fifteenth day of the seventh month, at the time they emerge from the summer retreat, three months of intensive and aesthetic practice. He does so, and through this offering his mother is freed. As the story ends she ascends into heaven.

This tale became the basis for the Festival of the Hungry Ghosts (in Sanskrit *ullambana*, in Chinese *yu-lan-p'en*, in Japanese *obon*), now celebrated throughout Asia. This holiday occurs on the full moon in the late summer when people make offerings from their harvests to the sangha of monks. Lay people hope to transfer the merit of these offerings to their ancestors to ensure them an easier time in hell or a better rebirth. Temples are cleaned and decorated, and families go to cemeteries to sweep and tidy ancestral graves, and sometimes to picnic. It is a time that the dead may be allowed a brief visit with their relatives on earth. In medieval China professional storytellers and troupes of actors entertained crowds at Hungry Ghosts Festivals with renditions of the story of Mu-lein rescuing his mother.

Ti-tsang plays a minor role in the *Transformation Text*. Mu-lein meets him as he journeys through the underworld and the bodhisattva advises the monk to look for his mother in hell, as she had committed a number of sins. As the *Transformation Text* and *Sutra of the Ten Kings* barely mention Ti-tsang, devotees who wanted to know more about him had to rely on the *Sutra of the Past Vows of Earth Store Bodhisattva*. It helped "flesh out" this deity, explaining more about his origins, his vows, and his functions.

A Mountain Sacred to Ti-tsang

The most famous site dedicated to Ti-tsang Pusa in China is Chiu-hua Mountain, which lies in a high range on the south bank of the Yangtze River in Anwei Province. The name of the mountain means "Nine Flowers." It is said to come from the famous poet Li Po who saw the peaks from his boat on the Yangtze River and compared them to the petals of a lotus flower. Li Po was reputed to be a friend of the hermit monk Mu-lein, who lived on the mountain for over fifty years.

According to the annals of the Tang dynasty, a Korean monk landed on the coast of China in 742. His surname was Chin (in Korean, Kim). He was a prince in a royal family of the Silla Kingdom in Korea. He had renounced earthly riches, been ordained, and was given the Dharma name Lofty Enlightenment. He settled on the mountain, living in austerity in a stone hut. In 756 C.E., visitors found the only food in his cook pot was a meager amount of white clay mixed with boiled millet. They worshiped him as a holy man, building a monastery and providing food for the disciples who gathered around him. The hermit monk was protected by many spirit beings. Once when he was bitten by a poisonous creature he was saved by a *deva* who caused a spring of healing water to issue forth from a rock.

Lofty Enlightenment died at age ninety-nine while seated in meditation. The noise of crashing rocks and moaning came from the hills around, sounds of the spirits of earth and water mourning his passing. When his disciples opened his coffin three years later to move his remains to a newly built tomb, his body was not decayed and his complexion was fresh and glowing as if he were alive. As the body was lifted out of the coffin his bones gave forth a sound like the rattling of golden chains, the sign of a saint. His disciples reflected on his qualities of compassion and mercy and realized that he must have been an incarnation of the bodhisattva Ti-tsang. When his body was placed in the new tomb a tongue of fire erupted from the ground and remained burning over the grave for a long time. Various miracles occurred around his tomb and crowds began to flock there. He soon became known as Chin Ti-tsang.

The pilgrimage to Mount Chiu-hua became one of the most famous in China. Chiu-hua was one of four mountains, each sacred to a different bodhisattva, that every devout Chinese monk hoped to visit within a lifetime. Writers from the early 1900s give a picture of what occurred there. The pilgrimage season was September to November, a time when the air was cooler and the maples became brilliant among the groves of bamboo and pine. Over one hundred thousand people visited the mountain annually. Every family tried to send one or two members to pray for their relatives. The pilgrims arrived in thousands of boats decorated with religious banners and painted lanterns. A Buddhist monk was assigned to each boat to pray and offer incense to Ti-tsang on behalf of the pilgrims. The path to the sacred mountain led through azaleas and rhododendrons that grew in the lowlands around the mountain. On the slopes the monks cultivated a special tea to sell to pilgrims, a tea reportedly brought from Korea by Chin Ti-tsang. Once the pilgrims ascended the mountain there were many sights to see.

Young men arrived at the temple dressed in women's clothing, asking the monks to print the seal of Ti-tsang on the dresses. Then they removed the clothing and folded it carefully to take it home as a sacred treasure for their aging mothers. Rich people paid thousands of dollars to sponsor religious plays, generally on the theme of the deliverance of Mu-lein's mother from hell. Famous actors were commissioned for the plays, which were believed to have the power to free one's ancestors from hell. Firecrackers were set off and piles of mock money were burned, to be used to bribe the officials in hell.

The paths leading to the temples on the mountain were lined with shops and booths selling goods to the pilgrims, sweets, children's toys, Buddhist books, and images. Fortune-tellers and palm readers plied their trade in the crowds. Poorer pilgrims treasured paper amulets that sold for a few cents. They bore the image of Ti-tsang and were thought to protect against demons, disease, and other misfortune, as well as conferring health, happiness, and long life. Pilgrims could ask the monks to pray for their relatives and to stamp the amulets with the seal of Ti-tsang.

Chin Ti-tsang's tomb, guarded by two Taoist deities, was preserved in a temple reputed to be the original one built for him. The flame that hovered at his enshrinement was said to be visible occasionally after nightfall. There was a shrine containing the guilded mummy of a former abbot and a large library and printing house where the *Sutra of the Past Vows of Earth Store Bodhisattva* was never allowed to go out of print. The walls of the main temple on Mount Chiu-hua bore a painting of Ti-tsang surrounded by the Ten Kings. Ti-tsang also was depicted with the "Inspired Drunkard Poet" Li Po, who was shown offering the enthroned bodhisattva a cup of wine. A legend says that Li Po rescued Chin Ti-tsang when the saint fell into the Yangtze, and they became as close as brothers.

A modern miracle tale indicates that Ti-tsang remains alive in China. In the preface to a twentieth-century translation of the *Earth Store Bodhisattva Sutra* there is a description of curious circumstances that occurred at the temple where work on the translation was being carried out. One evening two monks and two laymen

completed their day's labor at ten o'clock and immediately retired to their beds. After they had extinguished all lights they were amazed to catch sight of a dazzling light of electric blue in the locked shrine room. . . . The light was of human shape and size . . .

transparent [and] very similar to the marble figure of Kshitigarbha Bodhisattva on the shrine. A staff was in its right hand. The luminous figure . . . lasted for perhaps half an hour at full brilliance and gradually diminished.

Six days later when the two monks locked up for the night at eleven o'clock they saw

six luminous figures seated before the main altar. These lights were not in human form—but merely uniform areas of light, vertical and of about the height of men seated in the lotus posture. This phenomenon persisted for perhaps half an hour before fading . . . strange lights of bluish radiance. Be it remembered that Kshitigarbha Bodhisattva's color is a jewel blue—of the shade referred to in modern times as "electric blue."

OTHER ASIAN COUNTRIES

Because Kshitigarbha Bodhisattva arose from Mahayana Buddhism, he is not found in Southeast Asian countries such as Thailand and Cambodia where Theravadin practice persisted. He is known in all the countries to which the Mahayana doctrine spread from China including Tibet, Manchuria, Japan, and Korea. He is also known in Vietnam where Tien (Zen) Buddhism is practiced. There is a stone image that may be Kshitigarbha, who is called Ji-jang Bosal in Korea, in the Sokkuram caves dating from the late 700s. Beautiful paintings of Ji-jang Bosal from the Koryu dynasty show him wearing a head scarf and holding a mani jewel that is completely transparent. In Tibet Kshitigarbha is called Sati-snin-po. Sati-snin-po was not as popular in Tibet as Ti-tsang was in China or Jizo in Japan. Statues of Sati-snin-po are uncommon in Tibet, but he frequently appears in Tantric mandalas of the Eight Great Bodhisattvas.

TO JAPAN

Buddhism was brought to Japan from Korea and China during the fourth or fifth centuries. The first official record of worship of Jizo Bodhisattva is a repentance rite held for the ailing emperor in

850 C.E. Jizo was seen as an absolver to whom harmful or wrong actions were confessed in an annual ceremony. Jizo rapidly became popular, first among the nobility and later common people. There are Jizo statues preserved in Nara and Kyoto that date from the 800s. Pilgrimages to Jizo images and temples were practiced from the late Heian period on, becoming very popular in the Tokugawa period. In Japanese temple paintings he often appears as master of the six realms because he can move unhindered through them all. He is surrounded by six figures, one for each world, a bodhisattva from the heavenly realms, a man from the human sphere, a horse and ox representing the animal realm, a demon from the hells, an *asura* and a hungry ghost. Many sutras related to Jizo were copied from Chinese originals during the Nara period. In the Kamakura period a Japanese sutra appeared, the *Enmei Jizo-kyo*, its text promising longevity to believers in Jizo.

Several traditions surrounding Ti-tsang in China also were adopted in Japan. The first series of miracle tales about Ti-tsang were assembled toward the end of the Sung dynasty in China. In these stories, Ti-tsang was able to free many people from hell, at times by substituting his body for theirs. He rescued deceased parents if their children made offerings to him, commissioned statues, or made copies of his sutras. These stories influenced the miracle tales that arose later in Japan, and seem to be the basis for belief in the *migawari* (surrogate) Jizo. In China the local gods were adopted as protectors of Buddhist temples, and were depicted as ferocious guards standing at the temple gates. In Japan a similar process occurred when Shinto kami were adopted as the original manifestations in Japan (*honji*) of the Indian Buddhas and bodhisattvas. In this way the deities of indigenous religions and of Buddhism—and more important, their believers and priests—developed a peaceful coexistence.

Chinese Buddhists believed that punishment for sins was not permanent, but temporary. Once restitution had been made the person would move to a new place of existence. If they were unable to do so under their own power, Ti-tsang would help deliver them. The Japanese adopted these beliefs. When Christian missionaries arrived eight centuries later, the long-held faith of the Japanese in the infinite mercy of bodhisattvas such as Jizo who would descend into hell to redeem the lowliest sinner became a problem. Compared to Jizo, who embodied the spirit of pity, or compared even to the impartial bureaucratic justice of the hall of the Ten Kings, the Christian God seemed hardhearted. As the Jesuit missionary Francis Xavier recorded:

> *The Christians of Japan are afflicted with sadness, and the reason for this is that they feel keenly what we have told them, that there is no remedy for those who go to hell. They feel this because of their love for their fathers and mothers, wives, children and others who have died in the past and they feel pity for them. Many weep for their dead, and they ask me if there is any remedy for them through alms and prayers. I tell them there is no remedy for them. [T]hese people . . . had great doubts about the supreme goodness of God, saying that he could not be merciful since he had not revealed himself to them before our coming; if all was true (as we said) that those who do not adore God all go to hell, God had no mercy on their ancestors, since he had let them go to hell without having given them a knowledge of himself . . . They do not cease to weep when they see that their ancestors cannot be helped. I also experience some sadness when I see my friends, so loved and cherished, weeping over things for which there is no remedy.*

The Jesuits also reproached the Buddhist monks for allowing lay people and women to make offerings during the Obon festival for the dead. While some Japanese believed in the cosmology of the underground realms of hell ruled by the Ten Kings, and were troubled by the Christian idea of a hell without possibility of salvation, some clearly were not. When sixteenth-century Jesuits asked Zen monks about hell, the monks replied that hell and punishment were in this world. They said,

> *. . . that there is no hell after a man's death and that hell is in this world. And when through death we are liberated from these physical miseries by leaving this hell, we shall be at peace. There is a principle from which all things arise: men, animals, plants: every created thing has in itself this principle, and when a man or animal dies, they return to the four elements, into that which they were, and this principle returns to that which it is.*

Asked how one could become a saint, the Zen monks replied that there were no saints or Buddhas to look for outside of ourselves.

MUDRAS AND ATTRIBUTES

How to Recognize Jizo Bodhisattva

The historical Buddha asked that no statues be made of him since he was, as a human being, an example to be followed, not a god to be worshiped. After his death such symbols as the Buddha's footprints or the eight-spoked wheel connoting the eightfold path were used to represent the World Honored One and his teachings. By the second century C.E., statues and artwork began to portray the Buddha in human form. Buddhas and bodhisattvas were shown with mudras—hand gestures indicating aspects of a Buddha or bodhisattva's manifestation in the world—and with attributes—objects held by bodhisattvas, symbolic of their powers. The Buddha is seldom shown holding objects other than his begging bowl. Most bodhisattvas were shown with certain mudras and attributes that later became characteristic and could be used to identify them. The number of mudras and attributes is small and no gesture or object is unique to a particular bodhisattva.

The clothing, mudras, and attributes of Jizo Bodhisattva vary according to country and era. Jizo appears in two forms, either as a simple monk or as a royal bodhisattva. In China and later in Tibet Kshitigarbha appears in the bodhisattva form, wearing silken garments, jeweled necklace and crown, and seated on a throne. He may be accompanied by a winged lion or a tiger. In the art of the Tun Huang cave she is shown standing on a single lotus and also with a white lotus under one foot and a yellow lotus under the other. The lotus is a symbol of purity arising from defilement or the sacred blooming in the ordinary. In Korea Ji-jang Bosal is shown wearing a pilgrim's head scarf that touches his shoulders.

In Tibet Kshitigarbha usually holds the mudra of fearlessness and charity as in Japan, but he is also shown in the mudra symbolic of speaking and teaching. In mandalas he is seated at the right of Shakyamuni and opposite Akasagarba, the Womb of Space (or Sky) Bodhisattva. His color is white or flesh, because, as white is the source of all colors, he is the source of all virtues, and because he appears on earth in flesh, as a human being. In mandalas of the eight bodhisattvas he is often shown with an alms bowl in the left hand. In Tibetan art he holds various implements, a fly whisk (symbol of repelling obstacles to enlightenment and of not harming any creature), a book (the sacred texts and teachings), a vase (symbol of being most useful by virtue of emptiness), or an alms bowl (symbolic of being a receptacle of the Dharma).

In Japanese art Jizo Bodhisattva rarely appears as a regal bodhisattva. He usually has the shaven head of a monk and wears a Theravadin monk's robes. Sometimes a more ornate over-robe (o-kesa) is added. Either his feet are bare or he wears a monk's sandals. Jizo is usually shown standing quietly with eyes lowered or subtly poised with the toes of one foot lifted slightly or a foot turned as if he is about to walk. Less often he sits, either in meditation posture on a large lotus, or as if resting during a long journey. Seated Jizos are sometimes shown in the earth-touching gesture appropriate to the Earth Store Bodhisattva.

Early Jizos in Japan had mature faces. Immature and somewhat effeminate faces began to be shown in art from the twelfth century, becoming overtly childlike in the Mizuko Jizos of the twentieth century. The first Jizos in Japan had empty hands, making the mudras of fearlessness with the raised and extended right hand and the mudra of charity or giving the gift of the Dharma with the left hand open, facing out and pointing downward toward the earth. By the ninth century Jizo began to be shown holding the radiant cintamani jewel of the Dharma in the left hand, and by the twelfth century the ringed staff appeared in the right hand. Japanese statues of the Mizu-ko Jizo, protector of children, have children in various poses around them, clinging to their robes, holding on to the staff for support or held securely in Jizo's arms. Not all Jizos carry the traditional attributes. A group of Roku (six) Jizo may each hold a different object and make a different mudra appropriate to each of the six realms. In one representation, the Jizo who visits hell holds a staff topped by a skull or a human head, the Jizo who visits the realm of the hungry ghosts carries a begging bowl to feed the hungry, the Jizo of the human realm carries a rosary, the Jizo in the world of animals holds a banner, Jizo of the asura realm carries the triple cintamani, and the Jizo of the heavenly realm holds a solar disk and vajra. The Shogun Jizo rides a horse and carries a sword (symbol of the power of wisdom to cut the fetters of delusion) and a banner. One Jizo statue at Kongorin-ji holds a huge arrow (symbolic of the Dharma as the weapon against evil) instead of a staff.

Jizo may have two young monks as attendants, Sho-zen and Sho-aku. Sho-zen controls good and harmonizes the underlying nature of all things. He is dressed in white and holds a white lotus. Sho-aku controls evil and subjugates ignorance. He is dressed in red and carries a vajra or thunderbolt. The custom of dressing statues of Jizo in red or white garments in Japan may have its origin, now forgotten, in the red and white attendants.

The Greatest Gift: No Fear

Jizo Bodhisattva is usually shown with the right hand making the mudra of fearlessness or holding the six-ringed staff. Like other Buddhas and bodhisattvas, she is fearless because she has seen through the illusion of self. One Dharma teacher has defined *self* as the process of defining and defending personal territory. When we think our puny little self is all that we are, then we are afraid when there is any threat to it. That fear is the source of all anger. When the self is seen as empty, that is, simply an ever-changing process with no thing at its heart, then there is nothing to defend and nothing to fear.

Fearlessness also arises when someone we love is at risk and must be saved. The mudra of fearlessness is said to come from a gesture the Buddha used in subduing an attacking elephant.

Devadatta was a monk who became jealous of the Buddha and tried to kill him by many and various means. Once he went to the elephant stables where a savage, man-killing elephant called Nalagiri was kept. He bribed the mahouts to let Nalagiri loose in the road where the Buddha was walking. When the elephant saw the Buddha he raised his trunk and charged. The Buddha's disciples tried to convince the Buddha to turn back but the Buddha told them not to be afraid. "It is impossible, cannot happen, that anyone can take a Perfect One's life by violence," he told them.

As the maddened elephant thundered toward him the Buddha raised his right hand and encompassed it with thoughts of loving-kindness. The elephant lowered his trunk, stopped and stood quietly before the Buddha. The Buddha stroked the elephant's forehead and spoke to him quietly. Nalagiri took the dust of the Blessed One's feet with his trunk and sprinkled it on his forehead. Then, keeping the Buddha in his sight as long as possible, he re-treated backwards to the elephant stables, peacefully entered his stall and was thenceforth tame.

It is her great love for all living beings that renders Jizo fearless. It is said that Jizo can use her staff to strike the iron doors of hell and they must open and release those who have done even one good deed. Love has this, the greatest power—the power to over-come all fear.

Jizo is often shown with the mudra of charity or the cintamani jewel in his left hand. These indicate the best gift that can be given to those in need, the clear light of Dharma truth. Those who live by that truth lose personal fear and are able to walk straight along the twisted paths of human suffering. When energy is not wasted on fearing for and protecting the individual self, it finds another outlet. It turns around and flows outward. A kind of miracle occurs. As the energy flows out, the innate heart of compassion is opened and there is the experience of a pure love for everyone and everything. People's faces change when this transformation occurs, becoming bright and radiant like the glow of an inner jewel. The outward-di-rected light illuminates the source of people's suffering. Its warmth brings them hope and ease. The mudra of charity is also called the mudra of consolation because the teachings of the Buddha provide us with an inner refuge in times of external or internal turmoil. The combined mudras of fearlessness and charity show the serene con-fidence that arises from taking complete refuge in the Dharma.

For over fifteen hundred years Jizo Bodhisattva has been a spiri-tual pilgrim, traveling from India to Northern Asia and now to America and Europe, fulfilling her original vow not to rest until all beings are saved from hell. As she travels, her body and dress trans-form according to need. As she enters new countries new forms of practice develop that make her more accessible and are most suited to the suffering particular to each time and place. Whatever her external appearance, male or female, monk or royalty, Oriental or Western, she always can be recognized by the benefit that appears in her wake.

In the next chapter we will look at how we ourselves are spiritual pilgrims and can be inspired by the example of Jizo Bodhisattva to continue on the spiritual path.

chapter seven

Jizo Bodhisattva
AND THE
Path of Pilgrimage

Early on the first of August
I take my bowl and head for town.
Silver clouds accompany my steps,
A golden breeze caresses the bell on my staff.
Ten thousand doors, a thousand gates open for me.
I feast my eyes on cool groves of bamboo and banana trees.
I beg here and there, east and west,
Stopping at sake shops and fishmongers, too.
An honest gaze can disarm a mountain of swords,
A steady stride can glide over the fires of hell.
This was the message the Prince of Beggars
Taught his disciples over twenty-seven hundred years ago.

RYŌKAN

PILGRIMS

Jizo Bodhisattva has been a pilgrim for two thousand years. What can we learn from Jizo's pilgrimage about our own spiritual journey? A pilgrim is defined as a person who travels a long distance to a sacred place as an act of devotion. In the West we do not generally encounter people on the roads and sidewalks who are identifiable as pilgrims. They are more common in Asia, particularly in

India, where wandering holy men with matted hair and convoys of trucks packed with religious pilgrims on their way to a temple celebration are an everyday sight. In Japan, too, there are group pilgrimages by bus to temples in a series, each with a different image of a particular bodhisattva such as Jizo. In recent years, as the population of Japan has aged, a new image has been created, the anti-senility bodhisattva. A ten-foot bronze statue portrays an old man and woman kneeling in prayer at the feet of a benevolent standing Kannon or Jizo. Busloads of elderly Japanese tour the chains of temples that have installed these new images, offering prayers at each one for longevity and freedom from dementia.

Although modern pilgrims travel by plane or bus, the tradition of the walking pilgrimage does persist. In Japan pilgrims climb the sacred mountain Fuji carrying wooden staffs purchased for the occasion. On the path up the mountain they stop for tea and have the staff stamped at each way station. Other pilgrims undertake a walking tour of several weeks to thirty-three temples on the island of Shikoku. The tradition of a pilgrimage to six Jizo temples in Kyoto began in medieval times and continues to this day.

Jizo Bodhisattva is often portrayed carrying a pilgrim's staff and wearing pilgrim garb. In the ancient Chinese caves of Tun Huang and also in Korea he was shown with his robe worn as a traveler would, draped over his head and shoulders for protection from the weather. Statues of Jizo are found at thousands of crossroads in Japan, from intersections of major highways to the divergence of dirt paths among rice paddies. His presence helps travelers choose the right direction. Jizo is the guardian not only of those who travel on the earthly plane but also of those at crucial crossroads in the spiritual journey.

As we consider these aspects of Jizo we should assess our life honestly. Am I a pilgrim, or more of a wanderer?

There is a difference between a pilgrim and a wanderer. Buddhist teachings use "wanderer" to refer to someone who is lost in the rounds of suffering existence, transmigrating through the six worlds. As we move day by day, hour by hour, among states of ignorance and stupidity, irritation and anger, greediness, coveting and jealousy, pain and mental discomfort, we are like people wandering in a dense primal forest, unable to find a way out or even to climb above the trees to see if there is an edge to this tangling wilderness. We will do this until we realize, hear, or are shown that there is a way out.

PATH CONSCIOUSNESS

What is the difference between a wanderer and a pilgrim? First we must know there is a path. If we are lost and can't find a way out, our only choices are despair, a grim determination just to survive, or for some who suffer terribly, suicide. What transforms despair and resignation to hope and joy is to know there is a path.

The Story of Sara

We have a number of nurses, doctors, and therapists in our sangha. There often is a reticence among helping professionals to even admit, let alone attend to, their own physical and mental problems. They are the ones in charge, fighting and conquering disease. They have to be strong for the sake of helping others, with no time for vulnerability, rest, or self-care. Eventually they "burn out" or become victims of what is called "compassion fatigue." When we first offered meditation retreats for health-care professionals, we asked those who came whether their primary interest was in learning meditation for themselves or for their patients. "For ourselves!" everyone responded. "If we are healthy, our patients will benefit."

I heard Sara's story at one of these retreats. Sara was a social work student at the University Hospital. She was assigned a preceptor who had trained with Dr. Jon Kabat Zinn and who had begun a mindfulness meditation clinic for patients with chronic pain and disease. In her previous work in the university pain clinics, the preceptor had not been impressed with the results, which were mostly unhappy patients on a rotation of medications. The mindfulness meditation techniques seemed much more effective.

Sara had been suffering from headaches, by her own estimate, twenty-seven days a month, with no relief after complete medical evaluations. She was taking painkillers almost daily. Her preceptor suggested that the student join the mindfulness meditation group for patients with chronic disease and pain. Sara was skeptical, but it would look bad to refuse her mentor. She committed to the course, eight weeks of meditating forty-five minutes a day, and to learning and trying several new techniques of meditation. To her surprise the meditation worked. Within five weeks her headaches had been reduced from twenty-seven days to three days a month.

Sara had discovered that if she could be mindful of a small spot between her eyebrows, checking it many times a day and keeping it relaxed, she could prevent the headaches. She was quite delighted with the technique and with herself. When the doctors had failed, she had been able to find the source of her suffering and to treat it successfully.

First Sara needed to be told there was a path. To know there is a way to freedom is called "path consciousness." Next she needed practical instruction to begin practice, to step onto the path and begin to walk. Listening to her story, feeling her happiness, I realized that if I know of such a path, the way taught by the Buddha, it is my obligation to use it to relieve suffering. If I do not, I condemn others to pain and despair. It would be like having a cure for cancer and keeping it to myself. In Christian terms, not sharing the path is a "sin of omission." This is the birthplace of the bodhisattva vow. Jizo Bodhisattva is sure that sentient beings do not have to suffer. Her certainty that the path brings ease and happiness manifests as Jizo's great optimism and is the source of Jizo's unflagging determination and energy.

The difference between a pilgrim and a wanderer is to know there is a path and to set out on it. We also need guides, both printed maps and also human guides. The Buddha provided the first map in the teachings he expounded so thoroughly, adjusting them to the individual and the circumstances. Surprisingly, many people who follow Buddhist principles have never read the original teachings. This is akin to Christians not reading the Bible. It is important to return to the source. Books on the direct teachings of the Buddha appear in the notes for this chapter.

Books and audio-tape teachings by current Buddhist teachers also provide maps for us, describing parts of the path and giving hints for the traveler. We should realize that all of these, including this very book, are interpretations of his teachings and insights by individuals less enlightened than the Buddha. Be discriminating.

Students often ask if they should read books about Zen. I say to read books that inspire you to sit down on the cushion and practice, not books that entice you to hide out in information acquisition or in more intellectual speculation. If you find a book that inspires you to meditate, read a little upon first awakening, and a little just before going to bed. Begin each day with practice; and end each day with practice taken into sleep time.

PREPARING FOR THE TRIP

Setting Aside Resources

Before setting out on the journey we must set aside the resources. These include time and money. How much time should be set aside for spiritual practice? In other religious traditions, there is the practice of tithing. People give one-tenth of their gross income to the church. This is a good principle to apply to the energy resource we call money or income.

What if we applied this same principle to the resource of time? If we gave one-tenth of our day, that would be 2.4 hours. If we gave even one-tenth of the sixteen hours we are vertical and have our eyes open (I hesitate to say "awake") that would be 1.6 hours of practice a day. Few people do this. It is ironic that in this age when we have so many gadgets to "save time" that the pace of our life is more frantic than ever. We have less time than previous generations for spiritual practice. Time has to be deliberately and repetitively set aside.

Gathering the Needed Equipment

A pilgrim carries only the essentials. Jizo has a robe and bowl, a staff, and the Dharma jewel. Nothing extra. What do we need to step out on the path of practice? Just the equipment we were born with. A body and a mind. Actually, a body that is breathing.

Body, breath, and mind. That's all that's needed. The beauty of this is that it means you can practice anywhere, anytime. In line for the bank, in a traffic jam, rocking your child to sleep. Just align body, breath, and mind, and there you are. There is no longer such thing as "waiting." Only a gift of additional time to practice.

Students ask, "How do you find time for practice?" There are two answers. First, my life makes me practice. I could not do what I do without practice. Second, I turn my awareness around. Instead of looking for time to practice and trying to expand it, I look for time I am not practicing and try to shrink it. One way to begin to make a seamless practice is to pick points of awareness. These points depend upon your particular life. They could be upon opening the eyes, upon sitting on the toilet, upon putting your hand on a door handle and before opening it, upon entering an elevator, upon looking in a mirror, upon stepping into a shower. These many small moments of mindfulness, a pause to take one or two breaths in awareness, eventually fill in the background of "not practicing" like many small dots of paint eventually fill in a canvas.

I recently discovered a new one. I became aware of restlessness arising when the hourglass icon (meaning "wait a bit") came up on my computer screen. My mind and often my body would run off to another place, unable to endure even ten seconds of waiting. I decided to use the hourglass icon like a mindfulness bell to move mentally back from the computer and take a few slow breaths. This "paint by dots" method for weaving a tapestry of increasing awareness works well and prepares the way for the great reversal of figure and ground we call enlightenment.

What Vehicle to Take?

Buddhist practice traditions are divided into three schools—sometimes called "vehicles"—the Theravada, the Mahayana, and the Vajrayana. Theravada means the "way of the elders" and is closest to the original form of Buddhism. Mahayana means "great vehicle" and includes Chinese Ch'an and Japanese Zen schools. Vajrayana means "diamond vehicle" and includes many forms of Tibetan Buddhism. These paths are only different ways to approach the same Truth. Any statements about a particular school being better or best arise from insecurity. The only thing we can really say is, "This practice is the best for me at this time." There is only one Truth. If there were more than one, it would not be the Truth.

In America, the great melting pot, the differences between different schools of Buddhism seem relatively unimportant. We are all working against the same enemies: delusion and suffering. There is plenty of suffering to go around, an unending supply. We needn't compete for customers. As my husband says, "The more Dharma, the more Dharma." What is most important is to find a good teacher. The trappings of the tradition are only a kind of lure to get you practicing until the practice begins to practice you.

Setting out on Pilgrimage

Our pilgrimage began very early in our lives, so early we can't really remember. It began before we had mind-words to hold memory. It began as soon as we were born into separateness, as soon as we experienced separateness and therefore discomfort.

Once in a practice group we asked the question, when did our spiritual journey begin? Some students had a clear memory of the pilgrimage starting as early as ages two to five. One student recalled at age four seeing a tomato plant in the sun, glowingly alive. She knelt down and offered her life to God. Another student recalled walking down a road at age three wearing a red-and-white gingham dress. She saw a rainbow on the road ahead and wondered if she walked into the rainbow would she continue to exist. Thus began the asking of the great spiritual questions: Who am I? Is there a meaning to my life?

Even though the pilgrimage begins very early, perhaps before we are born, our experience is that of setting out over and over. Each period of meditation, each retreat is a venture into unknown territory. It's not so easy to keep setting out. We're reluctant to undertake a small journey into our minds, one that lasts only for the three or seven days of a retreat. The most difficult parts of retreat are actually deciding to go and then physically getting there, stepping around all the detours the ego lays out. There are so many cogent and tempting alternatives. And they don't even have to be that attractive. Faced with the prospect of sitting still for seven days and looking straight at what the mind is up to *now* or *again*, faced with having to acknowledge what we are clinging to, faced with giving up our neurotic habits—habits that make us suffer but that give us a lovely sense of security and familiarity, a specialness, an identity—faced with stepping out into what we think is unknown territory, staying home even to scrub the kitchen floor or do the taxes looks pretty good.

But a very wise and intelligent and compassionate part of us knows that the work we really have to do is home-leaving. The work that is most essential if we are not just to cling to survival in our dirty nest of self is the scrubbing of the mind, the meticulous accounting of the taxes we pay to the action of karma, the cleaning out of the old trash of conditioning. This work we do best on the cushion.

The most wise and warmly compassionate and intelligent part of us is our True Mind. It calls to us in our little not-so-cozy nest, "Remember me? Remember me from when you were a child? From when you fell in love? From when your life hung by a thread? From when you looked through the stars that dark night and opened to your existence as a speck on a tiny globe whirling through vast space? Remember me from when you first looked through a microscope into a world of billions of exquisite, dancing living beings all interconnected by strands of light? Remember me from when sound became color and color became taste and taste became shape and shape became sound?

"I'm still here. Just waiting for you to give up all the confusion, desperation, cleverness, climbing, dullness, restlessness, pursuit, and the running away. Just waiting for you to sit quietly and discover you're home."

The most wise and compassionate part of us is what signs us up for retreats, makes us pack up and leave home, gets us there and sits us down. A small step in a long pilgrimage.

The Discontent of Being a Bystander

Once as Dipankara Buddha walked by, a bystander stepped forward and laid down his hair upon the mud in the path for the Buddha to walk on.

This is part of a story about the Dipankara Buddha, who was a Buddha many eons before the Buddha Shakyamuni of our historical time. This phrase "a bystander stepped forward" is important. Are we content to stand by, eon after eon, as Buddha after Buddha arises, passes by us and disappears? Are we happy sitting in the pews, listening to sermons preached from the front of the assembly and then returning home, lives unchanged? If so, we step back from our palpably real potential. We cannot be bystanders, for to take no action is to be tossed about by the action of cause and effect, by the evil of other's actions, and to condemn ourselves and others to lives of pain and unhappiness.

Why did the bystander lay his hair on the path? Hair is very personal. It is a statement of who we think we are. Hair has human warmth, human scent. To lay our hair down for someone to walk on is an act of extreme humility. There is the story in the Bible of the woman who anointed the feet of Jesus with costly perfume that she had been saving for his burial. She used her long hair to dry his feet. To use our hair as a foot towel, to lay down our hair for someone to walk on—what acts of deep humility and love!

The Buddha lay down his long hair, cutting it off when he stepped out of palace life, surrendered his future as a king, and began the spiritual search. This is what our practice is fundamentally about, home-leaving. It means to leave the safe, secure "home" we have constructed for ourselves, woven together out of the myths about our family of origin and mistaken ideas about what we need to survive and be safe. It doesn't mean to break off ties to our biological family, our spouse and children. It means to take off the blinders and the binders.

No one is truly content being a bystander. We want to walk the path ourselves, feel the lovely ache of stretched muscles in our own body-mind. We want to be able hear the truth of Dharma spoken by all creations, everywhere, not just in temples on Sunday. We want to live and speak the truth ourselves, the truth of the Dharma that we have realized as our very life. Only then will our restlessness cease and will we find true contentment. Every day, every minute we must summon the energy, let go of that which is static. Step out!

A GUIDE FOR THE JOURNEY

The example of bodhisattvas like Jizo or Kannon can inspire us, but to make significant progress a living human guide is needed. Shodo Harada Roshi said that a Zen teacher is like someone who teaches you to rock climb. To a beginner, the mountain looks like a sheer rock face, impossible to climb. The experienced climber can show you where there are hand- and toe holds and chimneys to use to find your way up. The teacher can show you how to use the tools of practice. A teacher helps you climb safely, knows when you need an assist or belay, when you should climb hard, and when you need to rest. The teacher encourages you when you are backing uncertainly over the edge of a precipice, scared/exhilarated about stepping out into thin air and rappelling down. In Zen practice this is called the step "off the top of a hundred-foot pole."

The teacher says, "Start right there, that place in front of you that you're gripping so hard. Let go of it." "Who, me?" we say. "Holding on? I'm not holding on to anything!" "That ledge you're standing on, that's the one you have to step off," says the teacher.

The ledge could be almost anything. It's any position we are stuck to, any judgment. It is technique we've developed to get our way and feel safe, by bullying, by whining, by being cute, by making people laugh, by being a smart aleck, by hiding.

A journey of a thousand miles actually begins with one step into empty space. This is not a metaphor. A young couple came to me to plan their wedding ceremony. As often happens, plans for the wedding had flushed a few problems out of their hiding place in the herbaceous border. In a recent argument over the invitations, Jane had declared that maybe she didn't want to get married after all. She had sent for college catalogs for schools back East. Maybe she'd go to graduate school instead. Noah was completely baffled but supportive. If she wanted out, he'd help her face her parents with the news and share in paying back the four thousand dollars already spent on the event.

We began to tease out what was going on. Jane had just graduated from college a few weeks before. She had no clear direction in her life at this time, no plans for a job or graduate school. Her mother had taken firm control over the wedding, controverting every one of the young bride's wishes. Jane had wanted the men in the wedding party to wear pale green linen pants. Her mother had promptly bought dark green wool pants. And so on. Jane said she didn't really want to go to graduate school on the East Coast but suddenly and somewhat inexplicably found herself sending for the catalogs.

What was going on? The common theme was stepping forward into uncertainty. No structure of school or job. Moving into adult married life, she wanted to be out from under her mother's control but panicked at the thought of becoming subservient to her husband's life. She had grabbed at graduate school as structure. I asked, "Can you just wait in uncertainty for awhile? Can you move deliberately into the spaciousness of the unknown without clutching at anything? Jane moaned. "I've heard you give Dharma talks about stepping out into emptiness before, but I didn't know it would be like this!"

Correct. One of the ways I know I am on the path is that what occurs, what teaches, what cracks, what opens up, is *never* what I expected it to be. The ego cannot foresee its own demise.

When we do let go of some chunk of who we think we are and step out into the unknown, we feel naked. We are afraid—of the emptiness. The teacher's words (and hopefully his or her life) encourages us to take this step, which we already know we must take, to taste freedom. The teacher says, "It's beautiful up here. You can see forever. It's worth the climb. You can do it!"

Jizo Bodhisattva is often portrayed with one foot raised slightly, as if to take a step. This is the awareness of mind and body we seek, not dragging or holding on to anything, poised for what life calls us to do in this moment.

The next point is very important. *The teacher must be alive.* As Jiyu Kennett Roshi said, "It's easy to practice with a dead teacher." I add, "Or a teacher three thousand miles away." In the Zen tradition we insist upon "face to face." Even that is often not enough. People can hide things from teachers for years when their only encounters are in *dokusan* (private interviews). We do not want to reveal our hidden ugly, pitiful, selfish parts. A teacher must be living with you for a goodly piece of continuous time to feel your energetic blocks, to watch how you react to uncomfortable situations and difficult people. Our ego's project is to shape the world so we are not uncomfortable or revealed. The teacher's job is the opposite, to make us sit through our discomfort and be revealed completely. The teacher has radar to detect each layer of "invisible" (or so we like to think) protective shield we have erected over the years. Next the teacher helps us to see it and deconstruct it, reassuring us as it comes down.

Much of the ego's working is unconscious and therefore inaccessible to us. As Jung said, "The unconscious is unconscious." A person who is observing from the outside and who has done at least part of the dirty and thrilling job of dismantling themselves is the only person who can help you do the job fully. Teachers know the rat holes where the ego hides out squeaking. They have compassion because they know how frightening nakedness is. They have strength when you need it because they know the difference between whining and deep sobs.

Although the teacher entices us from the front and pushes us from behind, each person has to do the climb alone. We would never be satisfied with a slide show of lovely views from the mountaintop, or with someone else's description of their rock climb. In fact it would be very boring.

Have you ever tried to recount to a friend who does not meditate, the highlights of your recent meditation retreat? "For the first day I sat still for eight hours and followed my breath. My breaths were pretty short. I couldn't hold my attention on the breath for more than two breaths. By the second day my breaths got a little longer. Some were short and some were long. I was able to follow them better, once in a while for five breaths in a row. Then I . . ."

"Really?" your non meditating friend replies, looking at you a bit askance. "And you paid money for this?"

The climb, the following of the breaths, is only interesting and satisfying to the person who is actually doing it. The true joy is in the doing of it, facing our fears, our boredom, our deep and petty emotions, and continuing to go on. Our happiness is in feeling the body and mind become still, in the taste of simple food well earned by a day's work, and in the touch of a breeze on the face and sounds of the forest and earth during nighttime meditation.

It is in each step that we find our pleasure. Each step, marked by the sound of Jizo's pilgrim staff. Tap. Tap. Tap. Here. Here. Here.

FELLOW PILGRIMS

My companions
Trekking
The six realms—
I recognize my father!
There is my mother!

DŌGEN ZENJI

After being born into separateness, at some point we realize this isn't all. Something's missing. The grown-ups don't have it all figured out. They're fooling themselves into thinking they're happy, and now they're trying to fool me. At that point we actively step out on the pilgrimage road. It's up to us to start out alone. Then help begins to flow toward us, including the necessary guides and supplies for the journey.

If our parents are spiritual seekers, they may assist us. One of the clearest childhood memories is calling down the stairs after I had gone to bed, asking my mother, who had gone down to the living room after tucking me in, questions about the nature of God. Was God a man or a woman? How old? Present always or not? The questions were asked in a casual afterthought way, but I remember holding my breath until I heard by the directness and care and weight of her response that these were very important questions to her too.

The answers didn't matter so much; I don't even remember if she gave me any answers. Knowing my mother, probably not. What mattered was the understanding that flowed between us, up and down those dark stairs, that this was *the* most important thing. Here is where two human beings could truly meet, in that great questioning. A pilgrim recognizes a pilgrim.

Pilgrims are found everywhere. Among Jews, Christians, Hindus, agnostics, Muslims; among the poor, the homeless, the dying, the white or blue collar, children or the elderly — it does not matter. A pilgrim recognizes a pilgrim.

On a recent plane trip I was seated next to an older man who had a warm feeling to him. He wore clean Western clothes and a cowboy hat, but he looked like these were his real clothes, not ordered from the Coldwater Canyon catalog. We talked about a house he was building, which led to a church he had built in Latin America, which led to my favorite topic, spiritual life. It was an easy, gentle ramble through spiritual experiences and findings. We agreed that the spiritual search is the underpinning of all other activity, and that spiritual truth is revealed to us to the degree we are willing to use it in our life for others. Only as we finished the conversation and turned to our books did we clarify our traditions. He was Mormon and I was a Zen Buddhist. At that point it made not a ripple of difference. A pilgrim recognizes a pilgrim.

This is always true, once we have been seized by the great question and set out on the quest. Our antennae are up. We recognize someone who also knows they have been seized by the scruff of the neck. There is a look, a humor, a determination. They have been pierced through by the sharp pointed staff of that great question, and being pierced, no way to pull it out.

We can let ourselves be tortured by its point, a point that can never be covered over by soft wrappings, fur coats, leather seat covers or down comforters, a point whose needling pain can never be dulled completely by alcohol or drugs. We can be made miserable by the heart-piercing wound that can never be healed by human embraces or insertion of body parts into body orifices. We can try to hide the staff or run away from the staff that has penetrated us through and through, but we are like a knight with a lance protruding fore and aft. It will keep tripping us and others up.

Or we can acknowledge that great question, and use it as a staff—to support us as we set out on the pilgrimage, to help us cross rivers when the current is so swift it pushes and pulls at our legs, knocking us off balance. We can plant the staff down here and now, regain our balance, and move on.

When we have plumbed ourselves to the bottom of our minds, and have seen through its most silly, superficial and pitiful aspects, down to that which is fundamental and unadorned, then no one else is a mystery. Everyone else is known, and thus a friend. Angry only because they are afraid. Afraid only because they are ignorant and confused. Everyone else is also—a pilgrim.

THE PURPOSES OF PILGRIMAGE

There are many reasons to undertake a pilgrimage: to seek new teachers and new truths, to find freedom of religious expression, and to seek a cure.

Visiting Spiritual Teachers

There is a koan about a monk on pilgrimage, carrying his six-ringed staff, sharpening his understanding against a teacher's whetstone.

BLUE CLIFF RECORD CASE 31:
MAYOKU COMES TO SHŌKEI

Mayoku came to Master Shōkei's monastery, carrying his six ringed pilgrim's staff with him. He walked up to the teacher's high seat where Shōkei was sitting, walked around Shōkei's seat three times, shook his staff, ringing the bells, stuck it in the ground, and stood up straight. Shōkei said, "Good."

Mayoku then went on to the monastery where Master Nansen was in charge. Again he walked around the Master's set, shook his staff, ringing the bells, stuck it in the ground and stood up straight. Nansen said, "Wrong."

Mayoku objected. "Shōkei said, 'Good,' why do you say 'Wrong'?" Nansen replied, "Shōkei is 'good' but you are wrong. You are blown about by the wind. That will lead to destruction."

The young monk's actions might sound quite brazen to us, like a young priest walking into a church where an old minister or priest is giving a sermon before the congregation, striding up to the pulpit, circling it three times, and standing in open challenge. But this was part of good Zen etiquette, a custom dating back to the time of the Buddha. The disciple circled the master's seat three times keeping him to the right, bowed before him, and moved back to an inconspicuous seat to await instructions.

Mayoku has had fresh insight, perhaps a glimpse that his own body is the Buddha body. A genuine opening is very compelling and can cause people to behave in peculiar ways. Mayoku stands boldly before Shōkei, who acknowledges this frisky puppy politely.

Then Mayoku picks up his staff, departs, and travels on to Nansen's temple. By the time he arrives, the insight he is carrying is stale and Nansen is aware of it. No dragging bags of rotting garbage around my temple!

Harada Rohsi was asked if Zen training was different in these times. He said that the training is the same, but it takes much longer. This is, he said, because people have too many choices. They won't settle down for the length of time it takes to do the work of radical transformation. There is a danger in visiting teacher after teacher. It can become a form of spiritual materialism, collecting Buddhist merit badges. "I've been to retreat with the great X and been blessed by the holy Y and had three empowerments from the great Z." It is a defense of the ego against settling down to do the sometimes uncomfortable and dirty, sometimes pleasurable and pure, work that must be done. Zen is not a perfume to cover up the stink of our ego temporarily. Zen is the work of digging out and eradicating the source of the stink.

New Places, New Truth

Buddhist pilgrims often visit places of significance in the life of the Buddha: Limbini, where the Buddha was born: Bodgaya, where he was enlightened; Benares, where he gave his first teaching; and Kusinagara, where he died. It can be inspiring to visit old Buddhist sites and to feel the energy of many lives dedicated to practice in one place. Some places have an energy of great power and determination. Some are tranquil, soaked in silence.

That tranquillity can be palpable, even in the middle of a city. When I lived at the Zen Center of Los Angeles, we had periodic open houses, inviting the families of those in residential training to come visit, ask questions, and to poke around that place. This was to help dispel concerns that their child (who might be forty years old) was involved in a cult.

During one of these events I was giving a tour to someone's relatives who were somewhat cool and skeptical. The Zen Center wasn't a very impressive place physically. It consisted of several houses and apartment buildings clustered on a noisy block in the L.A. ghetto near Watts, with drug deals going down in the adjacent park, boom boxes blasting all night, and gunfire around the block most weekends. The *zendo* was a small remodeled house in need of paint. Inside most of the downstairs walls had been removed, and sitting cushions put down on the wood floor. As we entered, I expected the guests to take a quick peek and leave. But they stopped and looked around. Then one said in a hushed voice, "It's so quiet in here." The others nodded. "It's like the silence is soaked in the walls." We all stood there for a few minutes, relaxing in the oasis of quiet in the midst of chaos.

I was surprised that strangers could feel that silence. I realized then that our practice of zazen has a physical effect upon our surroundings. And that effect can radiate back to inspire and affect (infect?) others. Even when our motive in practice is to benefit ourselves, if undertaken properly, it will benefit others.

My husband and I experienced the benefits of pilgrimage when we first traveled to Japan. More than a decade before, we had each separately taken forks in the road that led away from conventional success. At age nineteen, my husband had dropped out of college to help build the fledgling Rochester Zen Center. At age thirty-three I had left a tenure-track job at the University of California School of Medicine to live and train at the young Zen Center of Los Angeles (ZCLA). After devoting our lives to Dharma training, we had decided to leave ZCLA to move to Oregon, to take up jobs in "the outside world," and live as a single family, alone, not associated with a Zen community.

We left Los Angeles in great doubt about Buddhist practice in the West. Several Buddhist centers had been disrupted by the discovery of abuses of power by teachers. We were in a crisis of faith. If these were examples of the behavior of the most "enlightened" of the Buddhist teachers, what benefit did the practice have? Our relatives had wondered about this foreign religion for a long time. Maybe they were right.

We took the trip to Japan because my teacher Maezumi Roshi was insistent. We were unprepared for how the trip transformed itself from obligation into privilege, and how we also were transformed in the process. Because of this, it became a sacred pilgrimage. We were moved deeply to be standing small in the presence of huge Buddha images in Zen temples filled with the energy of thousands of people practicing over hundreds of years. On our last day, trying to squeeze in one more sight, we dashed to a long dark wood building over seven hundred years old called Sanjusangen Do (Hall of Thirty Three). Stepping into the dim barnlike structure, we stopped in awe, moved to tears at the sudden sight of one thousand life-sized images of Kannon, the bodhisattva of compassion, like a golden army with forty thousand arms holding every needed tool. They stood still and serene for our inspection during the day, but gave the sense of being poised, ready at the slightest signal to pour out the doors of the wooden building housing them, and disperse under cover of night to relieve the suffering of the world.

In Japan we were no longer members of a strange minority religion. We entered the huge stream of faith and dedicated practice that had been flowing for two and half millennia, and we felt the power of that practice to inspire humans to give their lives to build temples, make gardens, and create works of spiritual art. We saw that this great river had been flowing on, despite the centuries of human frailty, greed, and political machinations, to bring relief to those who suffer. Our wavering faith was renewed.

At one temple we joined in a celebration of the Buddha's birthday. In this rite a line of people chant and walk slowly in a serpentine form in front of a statue of the baby Buddha, which stands in a small open-sided building covered with cascades of fragrant fresh flowers. As they pass the bower, they pause to offer incense and to pour sweet tea over the baby Buddha.

For several days before the Buddha's birthday we had been working nonstop from 4 A.M. to 10 P.M. taking care of *kenshukai*. These are young people newly hired by Japanese companies and brought to the temple for a few days of Zen boot camp. If they couldn't make it through this, they wouldn't get the jobs. During this time we were feeding and training between fifty and a hundred extra people. "We" were a motley group of staff in full-time training at the temple, about twenty Americans and Europeans. We communicated in English, Japanese, Spanish, and French, with bits of Greek. Our own zazen was crammed into the early morning and late night hours. Many people were nodding off, exhausted during evening zazen. Tempers were on edge, occasionally spilling over when, for example, the cook was told an hour before lunch that there would be twenty-four extra people arriving.

All of this activity and tension dissolved the morning we began the Buddha's birthday chant. We were suddenly all united in a beginning-less, endless ribbon of humans walking the path like Jizo Bodhisattva, inspired by the birth and life of that one most human being to realize our own continual awakening to each new breath. In an instant all our difficulties and failings were put into perspective. For over twenty-five hundred years, millions of practitioners of the Buddhist Way, none of them perfect, have upheld this Way, have been rods and staffs and bridges and roofs and pillars that have enabled this wonderful practice to be handed down to this place and time where you sit as you read this book.

The most important foreign territory we have to explore is the land that lies within our own body/mind/heart. Ultimately we must sit down on the seat of zazen and undertake for ourselves this long, exciting, difficult, and most rewarding of journeys. This is the journey undertaken by the Buddha, by Jizo, and all other awakened beings. It is our duty. It is our privilege.

Seeking Religious Freedom

> *Master Hima on Mt. Godai had a forked stick. When he saw a monk coming he would hold it up and say, "What kind of demons made you take up this pilgrimage?"*

The American pilgrims came to the New Country fleeing religious persecution. Are we also subject to persecution? Who persecutes us most severely? Who has the greatest potential to destroy our spiritual life? It is not others. The harm others do to us is very small compared to the harm we do to ourselves. We are the biggest threat to our own spiritual health and freedom.

There is a demon, a deadly part in us that says, "You're not doing this practice right. Everyone else is sitting better than you are. You got started too late. If you can't do it right you might as well forget it." Or more vicious versions. "You're an idiot. You don't deserve peace and contentment in life. You shouldn't even have been born. This is sham. Your whole life is a sham."

These inner voices persecute us and destroy our religious potential, the potential to open to our innate wisdom and compassion. How do we deal with them? As the American pilgrims did, as Jizo Bodhisattva and all spiritual pilgrims do, by leaving home. First, leave the place and circumstances where these energies have set up housekeeping, have dug themselves in. Strike out for a place of freedom. This is one reason we go on retreat.

Second, take away their fuel, their lifeblood, which is the internal process of comparing, judging, and criticizing. We quiet the mind. If we ignore the welter of internal voices, they lose energy and interest. If we can get some space between "them" and "us," if we step back even a bit, we decrease their power to harm.

Jizo Bodhisattva is able to move through hellish and heavenly realms without becoming entangled or entranced. This is because she knows that they are all a fabrication, an imaginary but sometimes frightening landscape woven in the desperate shuttling of the loom of small mind. Jizo and all the saints are "in the world but not of the world," embraced and protected by the One Great

Mind. This aspect of radiant assurance is shown in paintings as a golden halo.

Third, we can turn and face the voices square on. There is a story about Jizo Bodhisattva rescuing children from demons. All Jizo does is to turn and face them. That is all that is needed, to stand still and not run. There is no battle. The demons all just melt away. It is a great triumph to be able to hear the internal voices and not to believe them or identify with them.

Whenever there is a lot of energy around something, I look for the deeper truth underneath. The voice of the internal critic carries loads of energy. What is it pointing to? A simple fact. We are not what we could be. We are not enlightened. If we can hear it without self-loathing or shame, it is telling the truth. We could do better. We can awaken. That is why we practice.

What we seek is true religious freedom, the freedom to be whole and complete, the person we truly are, to live life alive to the presence of that great Body-Mind that is us. To be able not just to know it, but to function with it, as it, to use its eyes to see, ears to hear, voice to speak. To find complete health.

Seeking a Cure

Certain images of Jizo Bodhisattva have developed reputations for curing particular ailments such as eye disease or measles. People undertake pilgrimages to these temples or to sites like Lourdes in hopes of curing terminal illnesses. This is very important to remember: no spiritual path can cure the "terminal" part. We will all die. These bodies are just borrowed. They will grow old, become ill, and die. We can be cured, however, of the misperception that illness, old age, and death are unnatural. They can cease being a cause of our suffering.

There is a Zen koan about this.

Master Ummon spoke to his disciples. 'Medicine and sickness cure each other. The whole earth is medicine. What is your self?"

This is based on a story from the time of the Buddha.

A beautiful courtesan named Salavati became pregnant. She was clever and renowned, "much visited by desirous people, and she went for a night for the fee of a hundred." Salavati decided that if men discovered her pregnancy "all respect for me would dwindle." She hid her condition and after giving birth, had her infant son thrown on a rubbish heap. The king's son Prince Abhaya found the infant and named him Jivaka, which means "He lives!" The prince had Jivaka raised in the women's quarters of the palace.

When Jivaka became an adult he discovered that he was an orphan. Realizing that "it is not easy to depend on these royal families" he decided to learn a craft and undertook studies with a world famous doctor at [the University at] Taxila. At the end of seven years he underwent a final examination. He was given a spade and instructed to do a walking tour all around Taxila, and to bring back anything he found that was not medicinal.

Upon his return he reported, "Teacher, while I was touring . . . all around Taxila I did not see anything that was not medicinal." He passed his exam and was sent out to practice independently. The Vinaya records his skill in curing patients given up as hopeless by other doctors.

The Buddha's teaching is the medicine for our hopelessness. The Buddha is very matter of fact. If you practice, see through your delusion and know for yourself the truth, you will recover. The Buddha's teaching is that everything we need to be cured is present, in our human life, our breath, our heart-mind. Anything we observe with a quiet mind, meticulously and deeply, will open and reveal the truth to us. Our medicine is a blade of grass, a flower, a stone, a feather, a drop of water, a butterfly wing. We have this experience in retreat. After a few days of meditation as we turn around, look and listen, everything is bright and comes to life. Even us. Everything, anything, is a remedy, just waiting for us to be present with / in them.

The cure for our illness is to become aware of the source of our great life and then to step out of the way as it functions through us. It is never any distance away from us. We continually see it and are seen by it. We hear it and are heard by it. It is touching us in our deepest recesses. There is nowhere we cannot touch or hear it. If we put a hand out, it is there. It plays in concert with us, through all instruments. When we are awake, there is nothing that is not medicine, no place that is not a place of holy healing. Jizo Bodhisattva is the protector of this, the whole earth that is our very medicine.

A Sense of Direction

Course Corrections

We cannot be too careless on the path. Small corrections in course are very important. A student named Bob taught me this. Bob came to practice in his forties after a life of addiction to heroin and methamphetamine. He had just been diagnosed with a hereditary kidney disease that can shorten the life span and causes chronic pain. He was on methadone for pain when he first began to sit sesshin. Over a few years he gradually weaned himself from pain-killers, went through a painful divorce from an alcoholic spouse, returned to college to get a graduate degree, and began a successful career in addictions counseling. He worked effectively and patiently with the emotional pain addicts face in being in the present moment. Here is the principle of small course corrections that has been helpful to him and his clients.

If you make a small change today, it may seem an insignificant alteration, not worth bothering about. In geometric terms let's say the change is five degrees. Now move forward in time. In one year, or ten years, the result in terms of where you actually end up, is very significant indeed. This means that a small difference in how strongly we express anger, a remembering not to gossip about someone, a little more care about how we treat ourselves and others, passed through the chain of cause and effect, can make a very great difference in outcome for everyone over time. We must remember this.

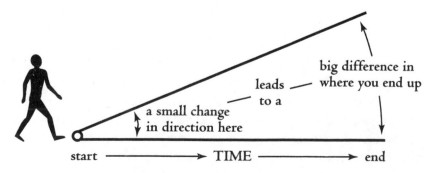

One bit at a time. "Dan, dan, dan (step, step, step)," my teacher told me. That's all that's needed. Our best effort in taking the next step on the path. Step, step, step. Don't count or measure them. We can't worry about how much there is to accomplish, because we don't really know. We can't worry about how small each step seems, because when we let go of the frames of the squashed sense of the time and space in which we operate, small and large are not to be distinguished.

Jizo Bodhisattva has vowed to save each one of uncountable beings in innumerable hells. Does she stop to count and worry how many are left? No time to worry, just keep going. Worrying is a big waste of energy.

Wandering off the Path

We are never off the path of pilgrimage. We are only confused, temporarily made deaf and blind by the clamor of our minds. Although we are never off the path, there are detours and blind alleys. We may perceive these as "being off the path." How do we know when this is occurring?

We can wander off the path bit by bit or quite abruptly. It is my experience that once I stepped firmly on the Buddhist path, *karma speeded up.* By this I mean that when I stray off the path, the consequences of my straying come back to "hit" me very quickly. If I become overconfident, within minutes or hours, something occurs to take me down a peg. If I lack empathy, watch out! I'll have to suffer the same pain.

At ZCLA I worked at the center's medical clinic as a Western doctor and also did acupuncture. Several residents came to me over a few weeks' time to be treated for hemorrhoids, apparently brought on by hours on the sitting cushion. As I treated them I thought, "Hemorrhoids, schmemorrhoids, what's the big deal? I sit as much as they do and I don't get hemorrhoids. They must be doing something wrong when they sit, and obviously, I'm sitting right." Within a week I had bad hemorrhoids. They hurt! A lot! I had not had enough sympathy for my patients. The hemorrhoids were stubborn too. I had to try every remedy I recommended and find some new ones before I got rid of them. I quickly became a much better hemorrhoid doctor. Too bad, it seems we humans learn most rapidly when we are in pain. This is how Jizo Bodhisattva became so wise. All Buddhas and bodhisattvas have bodies and minds that feel pain and once also suffered.

How do you know whether you are on or off the correct path for your life? The Buddha said that we can tell whether we are on the path by the fruits of our activity, the results of our thinking, our speech, and our bodily action. If the effects are wholesome or good, then we should continue in that way. If the effects are unwholesome for us or others, then we should not continue.

SOMETIMES WE WANDER OFF the path so gradually that we are not aware that it has happened. One day something happens to make us realize how far off we are, and we are shocked or saddened.

I was asked to visit a forty-year-old woman in the last days before she died of liver cancer. In outward appearance she was a skeleton covered by yellow skin, lying in a big white bed. She asked me to teach her to meditate. I taught her the meditation on listening to sounds, since the sense of hearing is said to be the last to fade during the transition of death. She enjoyed the meditation and said at one point during it she thought death had come, and found it very pleasant and tranquil possibility. She was a little disappointed to come back.

As I prepared to leave her room, I began removing my robes. She told me she appreciated my wearing the Zen robes, which are Chinese T'ang dynasty in style. She had been a brilliant scholar specializing a certain period in Chinese history, able to read ancient Chinese characters. She looked at me wistfully and said, "I was always too busy learning and studying. I planned to practice Zen 'later.' Now there is no later. I wish I had practiced." I heed her words.

The image of Jizo Bodhisattva in his monk's robes reminds us daily of the path of practice. It is always open, always awaiting our "later."

Wandering that Is Not

It is important to distinguish wandering off the path from a needed sabbatical. When we are deeply immersed in the practice, we can lose perspective. Sometimes we need a break, to stop meditating for a few days or even months. When we start again, we can see afresh what regular meditation does for the body and mind. Our desire and dedication for practice became newly informed and much stronger. We can see the effects of even a brief one- or two-day sabbatical. Not to meditate for a day feels like not sleeping enough or like not brushing your teeth. My mind-heart feels sticky and dirty. Meditation becomes a health-care essential.

There is another distinction to make, a variation in practice that might be mistaken for a wandering. I call this a *plateau*. This occurs after a period of intense practice, usually a long sesshin, when important shifts in the sense of self have occurred. It feels like surgery has been done, hunks have fallen away, and a rest is needed. We cannot work full out for too long. We need a time to rebalance the system, to incorporate what has occurred and see how it informs our life. During this time a more relaxed but very regular daily practice seems best. The temptation is to say, "I worked very hard, I need a complete break." But not to practice during this time means important doors close again. What has been gained slips quietly away and eventually the work has to be done again. Daily practice is vital at these times.

It is like training for a marathon run, putting all you have into the race, breaking through some barrier, and then reverting to couch potato. After the event, good nutrition, regular stretching, exercise, and maintenance runs are important to keep the benefits to mind and body fluid and functioning.

There are statues and paintings of a seated Jizo Bodhisattva. These remind us of the importance of resting in practice. There are two kinds of resting: refreshment and refuge. Refreshment means to rest body and mind. Even the Buddha needed to lie down to rest his back when it was painful. The body wears out and must be attended to. Meditation is the best rest and refuge for the mind. Refuge means to rest in the lap of the Buddha, to find sanctuary in the One Mind.

Returning to the Path of Practice

Wandering off can be a deep crisis of faith. Or it can be the wandering off that occurs daily, hourly, even minutely. Our practice consists of noticing and returning. We tend to become exasperated when our minds wander off the practice. "Not again! You idiot! How many years have you been practicing and your mind still wanders?"

We know that in physical exercise it's the actual exercise that is the practice, the lifting and putting down of the weights, the climbing and descending of the steps, the stretching and relaxing at the bar. It's not the miles or the pounds of barbells. Those are only tools. In spiritual practice it's not the number of retreats or initiations or a count of the years of practice that give us joy or fruit. They are only tools. The practice is the actual exercise, over and over again, of noticing and returning. The lifting up and putting down of thought. The holding steady, the expanding, the contracting of mind.

Our practice is to return over and over to this day, this very moment of pilgrimage. Where am I now? That very awareness is a function of a bigger mind. We don't have to wait for a teacher to ask us or check us. We can develop the ability to look clearly at our mind state and to adjust it. "Now I'm awake, focused—oops, asleep! Try again. Take a deep breath." Returning is the practice of Jizo Bodhisattva, a patient returning to each realm of suffering, to each being that has slipped back in to hopelessness. Practice *is* returning.

When Paths Diverge

A couple in our sangha are divorcing after more than two decades together. The woman has decided to train at a monastery overseas and hopes to become ordained. In his shock and grief, her husband has worked extremely hard at directing the ferocious anger that arose at his feeling of abandonment into useful channels. As he spoke to me about this, his eyes filled with tears of sadness, then with tears of joy at how much he has learned from this terrible time. He has assumed responsibility for his daughters, and has become much closer to them. His work has mysteriously benefited as energy tied up in the difficulties of relationship has begun to flow again. He has a new and welcome sense of the usefulness of the energy of anger. It rises and falls, minute by minute as we talk. It is becoming a companion, an inducement to stay on the path. He is using the energy of anger and transforming it into determination.

A cause of his sadness is the loss of his best friend, now ex-wife. They were practicing together, now apart. A small source of comfort is to know that both are on the path of practice, though in different places in space. Can the heart that hurts stay open? Open enough to close the apparent gap of space and divorce papers?

A monk friend says he sees everyone, even the man on the couch drinking beer and watching football, as on the path, trying in his own way to find freedom from suffering. Shunryu Suzuki Roshi asks if we can see this in a spouse who snores while we meditate. "True zazen is beyond being in bed or sitting in the zendo. If your husband or wife is in bed, that is zazen. If you think, 'I am sitting here and my spouse is in bed,' then even though you are sitting here in the cross-legged position, that is not true zazen."

A Catholic monk told me that in the contemplative monastery only one in ten monks is doing the work of deep contemplation. The rest are chanting, cooking, helping to keep the schedule. Support Bodhisattvas.

Can we see everyone who seems to us not to be practicing as Support Bodhisattvas that make our practice possible? Growing the food necessary to nourish the body of practice, generating the electricity to light our meditation hall, paving roads that lead to our teacher, cutting down trees for our sutra books? How can we say that any paths diverge?

DESTINATION:
ENLIGHTENMENT IS NOT IN THE FUTURE

Do not ask me where I am going
As I travel this limitless world
Every step I take is my home.

DŌGEN ZENJI

Most Zen students begin spiritual practice with the goal of enlightenment. We used to advise new students to read the book *Three Pillars of Zen* but *not* to read the section at the back relating various people's enlightenment experiences. No one could resist. Any old copy of *Three Pillars* will automatically fall open to those, the most well-thumbed pages. Most of us secretly picked the one that read, "All at once the Roshi, the room, every single thing disappeared in a dazzling stream of illumination and I felt myself bathed in a delicious, unspeakable delight." Who could resist?

We want to know ahead of time: Where am I headed? What will it be like? Can I have just a hint? Unfortunately reading or discussing such experiences often puts a roadblock in the way, as the mind grasps at a phantom, in this case a memory of something once read or heard about what enlightenment will be like. This very grasping shuts out the present moment, which is the substance of enlightenment.

One student came to me from another Zen center, full of enthusiasm to race through koans. She became very upset when I told her to stop working on koans for awhile and develop a stronger basic meditation practice. She was obsessed with "finishing all the koans." "Why?" I asked. "To get enlightened," she replied. I pointed out that the Buddha did not work on koans and he certainly became enlightened. Nor did most people who have awakened. It did not satisfy her.

I tried a new tack. "Let's assume you finish all four hundred koans, then what?" "Then I'll be enlightened." "When you're enlightened, what will you do?" "I'll save all sentient beings," she said. "Then what?" I asked. She was stuck. "I don't know."

To have your course in practice all planned out means you are never fully present in the moment. You are always sliding forward into an imagined future, comparing what is occurring now with what you plan to have happen. And you are always disappointed, because the future is seldom as we plan it. At least 90 percent of our dreams for the future never come true and are wasted mental effort. The only place we are truly alive is in the present moment. This experience of being fully awake in the present moment happens so seldom that when it does we call it a "peak experience" and remember it all our lives. What if fifty percent of our life were as vividly lived as those rare peak experiences? One hundred percent?

The best way to handle the mind's anxiety about endings is to live as if there is no end to practice. This can be a source of joy, not disappointment. The Buddha taught us that everything is impermanent. This means no real endings. This is good. Although we think an ending will satisfy us, if we reflect on our experience, it never does. Let's say I decide to buy a new car. For weeks I read *Consumer Reports*, canvass new car owners, and test-drive cars. I daydream and night dream of cars. Finally I decide what car to buy, negotiate a deal, and drive it home. For a few weeks I am so pleased, so aware of this, my glistening car, its nice smell, how well it drives.

I am surprised and happy to see it in my driveway each morning. Then I begin to notice small defects. A lock sticks. A scratch or two mysteriously appear, marring the bright surface. I no longer notice what I am driving. Back to the old dreams and thoughts. It was the search and the capture of the living thing that was exciting, not the carcass once I got it home.

The greatest benefit of our practice is that it does not seem to end. It continually opens before us. As soon as we have opened to a new aspect of that Great Life, as soon as our small mind claims it, names it, and begins to suck the life out of it, before we have even burped, along the path comes the next challenge. It often seems to me the next thing is more than I can bear or handle, but this has never been so. The path seems to have a wisdom about exactly what is needed and how much will be almost, but not quite, too much. The path never asks of us what we cannot do. This is something I have grown to trust.

What is the destination of our pilgrimage? It is to return home.

Another meaning of the word pilgrim is "an exile." Hakuin Zenji said, "Is there a soul on earth who belongs on this shore? How sad to stand mistaken on a wave-lashed quay!" We all know that we don't belong on this shore of suffering. We know it is a mistake to be tossed around by waves of thoughts and emotions, living in the midst of a storm. We are uncomfortable inhabiting our own bodies and minds. But we don't know where we do belong. That is why we set out on pilgrimage, hoping to find the place we do fit.

We have an instinct, a vague memory, that there is a place of "original home," a place where we are completely at ease, satisfied, where we can lean back and rest. If there is such a place, we were once there. What we think of as "me" emerged from it at birth into a world of confusion, a mixture of pain and joy. All our longing comes from this. All our sickness is homesickness.

Many people tell me that their experience of Zen practice is the experience of coming home again. With a shock they realize that without knowing it, they have wandered far off. "I once knew this! How could I have forgotten it?" is not a rare realization during retreats.

Like the Buddha we must be clear that samsara will never satisfy us. Like the Buddha we must leave home, the cozy rat's nest of self-satisfaction, self-defense, and self-indulgence that imprisons us.

Like the Buddha we must become pilgrims, seeking that which is truly good and satisfying. At his death the Buddha said, "I was twenty-nine years old when I renounced the world, seeking after good. For fifty-one years I have been a pilgrim through the wide realms of virtue and truth."

Once we find the way home, it is our natural desire to help others who are confused and homesick. Jizo Bodhisattva has been on pilgrimage since the death of the Buddha, carrying on the Buddha's vow to save all beings. We cannot do better than to follow his example.

What can I accomplish?
Although not yet a Buddha,
Let my priest's body
Be the raft to carry
Sentient beings to the other shore.

DŌGEN ZENJI

chapter eight

THE *Ring Staff*

I have an old staff that has well served many.
Its bark has worn away; all that remains is its strong core.
I used it to test the waters and often it got me out of trouble.
Now, though, it leans against the wall, out of service for years.

RYŌKAN

AS HE TRAVELS, JIZO Bodhisattva carries a pilgrim's staff. It is a tall, stout staff cut from a tree branch and topped with a finial of metal. In English it is called a "sistrum," in Sanskrit the *khakkahara,* in Japanese the *shakujo.* The Buddha allowed mendicant monks to carry the khakkhara as they traveled, particularly those who were old or sick and needed its support.

The sistrum has a handle made of wood, round or hexagonal in cross section. The power of the sistrum is said to lie in the finial and rings on the top. The number of rings can be four for the Four Noble Truths, or more often, six rings for the six perfections or the six realms of existence. Some staffs bear twelve rings for the twelve-fold chain of cause and effect. Each number reminds the pilgrim monk of his purpose, to carry and manifest the fundamental teachings of the Buddha in the world. Thus the sistrum can be called the *chi-jo* or wisdom staff of the Dharma.

The metal rings jingle as they strike each other. Thus the name *ushojo,* "the stick with a voice." The rings serve as the voice of a mendicant who has undertaken the practice of silence. As the monk or nun walks, he or she plants the staff on the ground and the rings jingle. This sound warns small animals to move out of harm's way. A Japanese text, the *Shinbunritsu,* says that the bhikshus who had not obtained liberation from fear complained to the Buddha about the snakes, centipedes, and scorpions that were in their path. The Buddha said, "I permit you to take up the shakujo and shake it." Large animals, who might become frightened and attack if a human came upon them without warning, can also move out of the way. The ring staff is a means to practice *ahimsa* or "nonharming." This is to live a life in which there is continual consciousness of the potential we humans have to harm other living beings or to frighten others so they attack us.

The jingling of the rings also prevents the thoughts of the monk from wandering. The sound of the sistrum cuts through even the din of the bustling marketplace, helping the monk ignore the distractions of samsaric existence. The voice of the staff announces the arrival of a monk or nun on alms rounds. A Japanese text, *Ubasoku-gokaiigikyo*, instructs the mendicant, "The shakujo is shaken three times for getting food. If three times produces no results, try five; if five is unavailing, try seven; if seven is useless, go on to another house." Traditionally monks on begging rounds in Japan wear large straw hats to cover their faces. They announce their presence at shops and homes with a sustained hearty cry "Ho!" which means "Dharma!" When alms—generally a small amount of rice or change—are given, the monk recites a sutra but does not thank the donor. To do so would decrease the merit of the offering. Alms are not given to an individual from an individual but are the Dharma supporting the Dharma. This is called the "emptiness of the three wheels, giver, receiver and gift." The three wheels can be thought of as three cogs that turn and mesh to produce a beneficial result. At times we are the giver, at other times the receiver, at other times we are the gift. Our life is made up of all three and is their very turning. The voice of the ring staff and the voice of the monk are the voice of the Dharma.

Bashō's Staff

The pilgrim's staff is a feature in several Zen koans. Here is one from the collection of koans called the *Mumonkan*. The Chinese character *mu* means nothing, without, nothingness, or emptiness. *Mon* means gate or entrance. These koans are stories of Zen teachers and students who, with the mind of deep questioning, challenge each other to awaken more fully. The title, *Mumonkan* or *Gateless Gate* tells us that although we must struggle to open the gate to full awareness of reality, that reality is actually not entered. It has always been there, around us, completely penetrating us, and functioning *as* us. *Our* experience is that the gate must open and be kept open through our continued practice. From the *Gate's* experience, it was never closed.

MUMONKAN CASE #44: BASHŌ'S STAFF KOAN:

Master Bashō said to his disciples, "If you have a staff, I will give you a staff. If you have no staff, I will take it from you."

MASTER MUMON'S COMMENTARY:

It helps me wade across a river when the bridge is out.
It accompanies me to the village on a moonless night.
If you call it a staff, you will enter hell as fast as an arrow.

MASTER MUMON'S VERSE

The depths and shallows of the world
Are all in its grasp.
It supports heaven and sustains the earth.
Everywhere, it enhances the Truth.

When we study a koan we ponder it word by word, phrase by phrase. How does it reveal our own life? Master Bashō's koan taught two things. On the one hand we should realize the staff that we are never without. On the other, if we lean on anything, even that staff, we must realize it will be taken away. If we do not give up our dependence upon it, impermanence will do the job for us.

Master Bashō was a Korean who lived in the eighth century. He went on pilgrimage to China to find a teacher of clarity. When he met Nanto Koyu he stayed to study. Eventually he realized the Truth, succeeded the Dharma of Master Nanto and settled on Mount Bashō, from which his name comes. Many Zen masters were named after a mountain. I used to see this as the teacher taking the name of the mountain where he or she established a temple and taught. Now I see that actually the mountain teaches through the body of the person. The new name is the true name of that activity.

The characters for *Bashō* mean banana or plantain tree. This name is related to the Buddha's teaching about emptiness of the five aggregates (*skandas*). The body, he said, is like sea foam, feeling is like a water bubble, perception is like a mirage in the desert, consciousness is like a magician's trick, and mental formations are like a banana tree. The stalk of a banana or plantain tree is actually made up of overlapping leaves surrounding a hollow core. If we try to look for the "banana tree" by peeling away the leaves one by one, we find there is nothing else there. In the same way, if we look for our "self" by peeling away layer after layer of mental and physical reactivity, we find there is nothing else there that we can touch or feel. Our mind is full of concepts and ideas that overlap so completely that they seem to be something else. The sense of being an isolated person is actually an activity, an ongoing construction project, a changing work in progress.

There is only one other surviving fragment about Master Bashō's life.

> A monk once asked Master Bashō, "What is the water of Bashō?" Bashō replied, "Warm in winter, cool in summer."

When a banana tree is cut, water flows out of the stem. The monk asks, "What is the essence of your Dharma?" or "What flows out of you?" Bashō's answer is, "Whatever is needed."

Water falls from the sky, trickles off leaf tips, joins other drops underground, becomes streams and rivers, and we are able to drink and bathe in it at will. We take this for granted. The earth supports our every step whether we ask it or not. The air supplies 21 percent oxygen and 79 percent nitrogen at every breath, exactly what we need. The essence of all Dharma is that we are completely supported at every moment. Although this is true, we must, however, be willing to practice without counting on any support whatsoever.

Zen Sticks

What was the staff that Bashō held up? Zen masters use several different kinds of sticks in their work, called in Japanese the *kotsu*, the *hossu*, the *kyosaku*, the *shippei*, and the *shujo*. The *kotsu* is a short stick about seven to twelve inches long, carried in ceremonies. It can be a simple smoothed branch or is sometimes carved ornately on one end in the shape of a lotus. If the stick is used every day it seems to take on the personal character of the teacher.

The *hossu* is a fly whisk, a wooden handle with white hair from a horse or deer tail or shredded fiber attached to the top. Originally the brush may have been made from kusa, the grass the Buddha sat upon when he was enlightened. The fly whisk symbolizes observance of the precept of ahimsa or nonharming, because it brushes away rather than killing small insects. It also symbolizes brushing away all obstacles to enlightenment. It is used now in certain ceremonies. Yamada Roshi wrote that each Zen stick is a part of the Buddha's body. The *hossu*, he said, is the Buddha's white, bushy eyebrow. During sesshin in Alaska and Japan, when mosquitoes were out, I could appreciate that the hossu had very practical uses in ancient China. There is no practice quite as exquisite as sitting still while a mosquito leisurely walks about on your face, moves over small hairs one at a time, then chooses a site and drills in. When students are able to do this, to willingly offer a drop of blood and endure a bit of itching to feed a small creature, they have their first inkling of how the Buddha once gave his flesh to feed a starving tiger that was nursing cubs.

Another Zen stick is the *kyosaku* or "awakening stick." It is one to three feet long, shaped with a thin flat blade at one end. During long sesshin the monitors in the meditation hall may strike blows with the kyosaku on the shoulders of those who are meditating. The short stinging pain can be useful to end drowsiness and to help with back, shoulder, or neck pain. Its best use is to bring the wandering mind abruptly back into the body and into the present moment.

The awakening stick is used not just to bring us out of a dull and drowsy mind state, but to bring us out of the pervasive dreaminess that substitutes during most of our lives for being truly alive. When the mind is quiet and aware, empty but taut, a sudden sensation of any kind can bring reality out of hiding. Sound, color, pain can open the door to awakening if the conditions are right. During a certain period in China, Zen masters used sticks like another mouth. A blow could means approval or disapproval. It could encourage or discipline. Although modern people are afraid of or repulsed by the use of a stick, for Zen students of the time, a worse fate than being struck could be not to be hit.

One thousand years ago there lived a monk named Tōzan. He was an ardent spiritual seeker who traveled thousands of miles on foot, from one end of China to the other, an unimaginably difficult journey one thousand years ago, to study with Zen Master Unmon. When Tōzan finally arrived he had dokusan, private interview, with the revered master he hoped could help him become enlightened. But Tōzan's answers to Unmon's questions were so dull that after a few minutes' conversation Unmon dismissed Tōzan, exclaiming, "I spare you sixty blows!" Tōzan's answers were so poor that he did not even deserve a good whack with the master's stick. This so dismayed Tōzan that he sat all night in an agony of questioning. His pride was shattered and with it all his prior realizations, his hope of showing Unmon anything. Whatever was in the way began to move. The next day, Tōzan humbly returned to question Unmon again. Maybe he was very alert, expecting sixty real blows to rain down at any moment. Instead Unmon scolded him, "You rice bag!" This reply opened the mind door completely. Tōzan was enlightened by no stick.

The fourth Zen staff is the *shippei*, a stick about three feet long, with a curve at one end, like half of a Japanese archery bow. Thus it is called the "broken bow." It can be wound with wisteria vine, and is used in ceremonies such as *shuso hossen*, Dharma combat with the head monk at the end of Ango, an intensive training period. That the shippei is a broken weapon tells us that the Dharma is used not to injure another but to pierce through to the truth at the heart of the other. It is a bow that shoots the two arrows that meet in midair. These two arrows are the innate perfection and harmony of the One and the rich diversity and confusion of the many. The arrows meet at the point of space and instant of time called just now, my life, just now, your life. Yamada Roshi calls the shippei the arm of the Buddha.

The last Zen stick is the *shujo* or *shakujo*, the walking staff, six or seven feet long, usually roughly fashioned from a sturdy branch or small tree from the forest around the temple. The shakujo is given now at the time of transmission and is a symbol of the authority of the (new) master to teach the Dharma. Yamada Roshi called the shakujo the Buddha's leg. It is the staff that was carried on pilgrimages and is the staff carried by Jizo Bodhisattva. On the end is a capital made of metal, often pewter, hung with rings. In China the staff was called the "Wind and Water Holding Pewter." Wind and Water was the name for a wandering monk. The staff is the emblem of the lineage, the past Buddha, and the ancestors who walk the path before us. Chinese monks pledged to propagate the Dharma by touching the staff at the time of ordination. For a time in China the staff had a metal spade on the bottom. Monks used this small shovel to bury dead animals they encountered as they traveled. Rings on the top of the staff and above the spade rang as the tool was used, scaring away beetles and worms in the ground so that the monk did not violate the precept of nonkilling.

The staff in the koan about Bashō is the shakujo. A walking staff had very practical uses in ancient times. The daily alms rounds from forest hut to village and back, sometimes in the dark, could be treacherous. It would be easy to wander off the path, fall in a hole, a ditch, a swamp or a stream, or even fall off a cliff. Travel to other countries can make Americans aware of how they are shielded from the reality of how fragile life is. In India night walking can be very hazardous. There are large piles of garbage, dog packs, excrement, sheer drops with no guard rails, and dangerous snakes and animals. Even in Japan, a modern and prosperous country, in most towns the streets are narrow, there are no sidewalks, the road is flanked by open ditches and sewers, and huge trucks barrel along inches from you when you walk along.

In America our roads and sidewalks are so well maintained and lighted that we rarely walk on a path that is dark and dangerous. Only the people are. When an accident does happen, we are taken by surprise. The surprise can pierce through the veil of dreams that muffles the sharp and aching perfection of our life. Once startled awake we have, briefly, a choice—find a way to stay awake or yield to the overwhelming temptation to go back to sleep. One Zen student in his early twenties was rock-climbing on a sunny day with a girlfriend on a rock face near Portland. Suddenly she slipped over an edge and fell eighty feet. In an instant, the illusion of life's security and permanence was shattered. At that moment, he awoke and began his spiritual quest. After a lapse back into the sleep of addiction, he is now firmly on the path of Dharma practice.

The comfort of a staff is described in Psalm 23 in the Old Testament. *"Yea, though I walk through the valley of the shadow of death, I will fear no evil: for . . . thy rod and thy staff they comfort me."* The rod and staff were tools shepherds used to rescue sheep who had strayed and fallen over cliffs or into crevasses. There is a common misunderstanding of the Old Testament admonition *"Spare the rod and spoil the child."* The rod was used to guide and rescue, not to beat.

THE STAFF IN OUR LIVES

The koan Bashō's Staff asks us to find such a staff in our lives, steady, upright, a continual and trustworthy source of support. To find what can be such a source of support and what cannot, it is useful to ponder, "What is it in my life that supports me?"

Answers might include my job, my health and bodily strength, my clever mind, my wonderful family, my loving partner. The next question asks how permanent each of these supports are. Are any of these lifetime guaranteed?

When we look objectively, we find that no external, physical, or material source of support is permanent. I might have a job with benefits now, but I could lose it or my ability to do it. My health and bodily strength are unlikely to improve; they will most certainly ebb away. My clever mind plays tricks on me. It is already becoming forgetful, "losing nouns," as my eighty-one-year-old mother puts it. My wonderful family, if I had one, is dying off one by one. My loving partner is also a frail human being. A virus, a moment's inattention on the freeway, a clot in an artery in the heart, a change in brain chemistry, a sexy young thing could take them away at any time.

This self, a heap of five elements collected in one place, is held together by cause and effect. One small change — in the electrical circuits, in the sodium or potassium ions in the cells — and this temporary warm place here that is called me, or that temporary warm place there that is called you will grow quickly cold and the five elements will become unbound again.

What then is our support in the midst of all this gathering together and falling apart? At the center of all this coming and going, what is its support? What is its essence? Anything? Nothing?

There is a koan *"Hide yourself in a pillar."* It could be, "Hide yourself in Jizo's staff." Usually we are self-conscious, half-naked, shivering little mice. We feel totally exposed. Where to hide? Where to feel safe? We search for security in vain. Using strategies to camouflage the self will never make us feel safe because the problem lies underneath the decoration and insulation. It is a fundamental structural problem. Answering this koan requires taking apart the defective structure we have so carefully built. Only then can we see what its real foundation is: that staff, that pillar, that straight and upright and continually affirming and destroying thing that is the core of all existence. Only as we let go of the idea of that pitiful little self are we able to experience that which is huge, solid, steady, immovable. True security comes not from hiding in the futile strategies of self, but in surrendering, taking full refuge in that which supports all.

When someone meets us in openness, when we are able to experience that nakedness for even a brief time, then we want more. That hunger is good, but how we try to satisfy it usually is not. Most often that moment of openness and complete vulnerability happens with a lover or a spiritual teacher.

Then we make the mistake of thinking that *they* did it for us. They can save us from all of our greediness, ugliness, self-deceit, and pitiful, silly manipulations. We cling tightly to the wrong supports. We are like a drowning person who panics and clutches the person who is trying to save them. Both are dragged down and die.

This is one aspect of Bashō's staff. If you think you have a staff in the form of a young healthy body, a clever mind, a lover, a parent, a master, who will be a permanent support, fine, here, try it! How long does it relieve suffering? How permanent a support is it? If you think you've attained some understanding, passed some koans, had some insights, here, try it! Try it out on the freeway in a traffic jam when you're late for an important appointment. Try it out when your father dies. Try it out when your boss gets angry at you for something you didn't do or don't understand.

There is another koan, "A *wooden Jizo burns, a metal Jizo melts, a clay Jizo shatters.*" Where then do you find *your* indestructible Jizo Bodhisattva? Your permanent place of refuge? Your equanimity and happiness? This is Bashō's challenge. If you think you have a staff, it will be taken away from you. Everything is changing and impermanent. The only thing we can rely upon is the truth of Dharma, which is based upon the very fact of impermanence.

Next Bashō says, *"If you have no staff, I'll take it away from you."* If you think samadhi, emptiness, equanimity, no attachment, no self is your support, fine, try it! Really try it. All supports removed. No teacher, no friends, no lover, no Buddha, Dharma, sangha. Try it in an earthquake, a famine, when attacked by a rapist or robber, in a war, faced with the suffering of millions of beings. Then how does that cold emptiness, that placid unmoving function? How then does the memory of a wonderful experience of quiet mind that you had a week ago, even a second ago, serve you or others? Not at all!

Going beyond artificial, temporary supports, going beyond the emptiness that is at their core and is the field of their activity, how then does it function, that great staff?

Master Mumon's comment says, *"When the bridge is out . . . ."* What does that mean? One of the five bridges in Portland will be out for two years for repairs. People were already upset when it had been closed for only two weeks. Upset at what? The inconvenience. Having to change just a little. Having to be awake just a little and remember to drive a new way to work, not mindlessly as we usually do, arriving at work unable to recall whether any of the stoplights we went through were red or green.

What kind of staff helps us traverse the river of our irritation and anger, anger that the bridge is out, anger at change and impermanence, anger at our anger? What staff helps us cross to the other side?

It is the staff of our practice. Everyone has had even a tiny experience of this. A moment of suffering, irritation, boredom, panic, anger is transformed by the still mind into awareness of a moment in which the touch of a breeze brings exquisite pleasure. A quiet mind turns the tea for washing the eating bowls into fragrant pools. Our practice transforms a bewildering and frightening life journey with irritating and threatening people all around, into an adventure with interesting characters, fellow travelers, who make up a sangha. It opens our eyes so the little dots of color on the rug shine like jewels. It breaks down large boulders that obstruct us into pebbles and paving for a smoother path. It makes the earth and all our lives "wholesome everywhere." Through our zazen, all activity—everything—is enhanced, made fresh, comes to life. This is so.

Master Mumon says, *"The depths and shallows of the world are all in its grasp."* Usually our minds skip along quite shallowly, flitting from memories of the past to fantasies about the future, all mixed in with bits of the present. When we go into a retreat and meditate for a day or so, we realize how shallow our ordinary mind activity is. After three to five days we are able to experience the deep, clear quiet depths of our mind, depths that are usually hidden from us. It is from those depths that our true wisdom, insight into things as they are, comes. The end to our suffering will come as we learn to use not just the small human and conditioned aspects of the mind that we have developed since childhood, but also to enter at will the bottomless clear vast Mind that was ours from before our birth.

Master Suiryuzan once said to his monks, *"Living on the mountain for thirty years, how much vigor I have received from this staff of mine!"* What kind of staff actually gives us energy?

Our deflector shields take energy to maintain. As these drop, more energy is available to us. Not only that, but when the barriers go down, energy from other sources can flow in. When we take a breath, we take it in. When we need to pee, we pee it out. Functioning freely it is our life that *"supports the heavens and sustains the earth."*

"Call it a staff and you enter hell like an arrow." If we call it a staff, if we grab onto it, counting ten retreats to put in our spiritual bank account, ten koans to add to our Zen merit badges, we destroy it completely. We enter hell as fast as an arrow. Grabbing at anything, including the "thusness" of this moment, starts an equal and opposite reaction that will take this very thing away from us. Why is it an equal and opposite reaction? Simple physics. The Dharma is a physical truth. An equal and opposite reaction *occurs because it is only One thing!* It is all happening in One Body, our body.

Where is the staff of Jizo Bodhisattva? It is also our spine, erect in the noble posture of the Buddha. It is body, breath, and mind, aligned in one straight line, all supporting the activity of that Great Body/Mind. We sit here in between. Why do we sit erect in zazen? To make our spine the staff that holds heaven and earth apart, providing a space between for human activity, for enlightenment, to occur.

It is our work to make Jizo's staff thoroughly our own, to awaken completely to that Great Mind beyond naming which functions within us no matter whether we are aware of it or not, no matter whether we are awake or asleep and dreaming. It is our job to make it so much a part of our functioning that it becomes us. No longer is it we who are practicing but it is the practice that practices as us. Crossing the stream, the staff touches down for a moment, then lifts up, moves to the next spot, and down. Useless if it stayed in one spot, it is an aid in its movement, not a hindrance in its stuckness. Functioning dynamically just as needed, the staff is nothing but up, down, up, down, now, now, now.

It is Jizo's staff of Dharma truth that keeps us upright and balanced on the spiritual journey. We can use the staff to cross rivers of impermanence and suffering that almost overwhelm us. We can walk the dark paths one step, one moment at a time. We can use the staff to take the measure of phenomena and to find for ourselves what is shallow, false, and crumbling, and what is deep, solid, stable, and true. If we can wield that staff freely, picking it up to use it, putting it down completely, using it to support others, then all will find their way home.

THE *Cintamani Jewel*

The whole Universe in the ten directions is one bright pearl. How could we not love the bright pearl? Its colors and light, as they are, are endless.

ZEN MASTER DŌGEN

JIZO BODHISATTVA CARRIES the cintamani jewel in his left hand. *Mani* is a Sanskrit word for jewel, precious stone, or specifically a pearl. The cintamani is the jewel that fulfills all wishes. In paintings or statues of Jizo Bodhisattva the jewel can be shown as a single large luminous jewel, as a cluster of three jewels, or as one large gem with three tiers. The cintamani is shown also as a colored jewel, a pearl, or a transparent globe. There may be a halo of flames around the jewel. This indicates the warm and brilliant light that radiates from the jewel and illuminates the deepest reaches of hell. To see this light brings hope and comfort to those who strike out and harm each other in the dark cave of ignorance.

The three jewels or three-tiered gem are symbols of the "Three Treasures": Buddha, Dharma and Sangha. As the Buddha began teaching, people listened to him, heard the truth of what he said, and asked how to become his disciples. He told them to take refuge in the Buddha, the Dharma, and the Sangha. This meant to trust in the Enlightened One as a spiritual guide; to follow the Dharma, his teaching of existential truth and the precepts he laid out for living a virtuous life; and to join or support the Sangha, which was the community of those who followed the Buddha.

The Three Treasures have acquired a wider meaning over the intervening two and a half millennia. The Buddha treasure now embraces the historical Buddha who lived and taught twenty-five hundred years ago, any fully enlightened being, and enlightened nature itself. The Dharma treasure includes all those who teach as well as all the teachings that lead to enlightenment. Because humans have been enlightened by anything—the sound of a stone striking bamboo, the sight of a peach blossom, a drop of water touching the skin—all things can be said to be dharmas. The Sangha treasure includes the original followers of the Buddha in India, all ordained Buddhist monks and nuns, and in the widest sense, the community of practitioners around the world who have taken refuge in the Three Treasures. Sangha also indicates the harmony between the Buddha and the Dharma, or the harmony of unformed original nature with its countless appearances in space and time.

The single gem with three tiers indicates the unity of the Triple Gem(the Three Treasures). No one aspect can function without the others. A Buddha may be enlightened but cannot help others without skillful means to teach. No matter how enlightened, a teacher is useless and his or her teachings are dry pieces of paper or sterile words without people to hear them, to benefit from them, and to bring them to others. The three-tiered gem also shows that the three treasures function within our one body-heart-mind. It is by means of our own body-heart-mind brought into unity by one-pointed practice that awakening can occur, manifest, and benefit others.

When Jizo descends into the realms of confusion and darkness, the pure light of the cintamani jewel attracts beings to him, to hear and see the Dharma. Humans are naturally attracted to jewels. Jewels become coveted and precious to us. Why is this?

They are not precious to dogs or to trees. Jewels are actually rocks, but all rocks are not alike to us. We do not string pieces of slate around our neck. Why are we attracted to some rocks, put them into a separate category called "gems," and pay a lot of money to possess them?

Anything that is especially valued by humans is worth a second glance with the mind of spiritual insight. I have collected glass all my life. Glass is a poor woman's substitute for jewels. It began in childhood. My girlfriend's father had an auto-wrecking yard and we used to play among the rusting car bodies, pretending to drive the cars, scaring each other with the possibility that we would find blood or even body parts in the twisted wrecks. When shatterproof glass began to be used in windshields, we discovered and collected heaps of beautiful "crystals" from shattered car windows.

In the church my family attended, I seldom heard the sermon but simply enjoyed sitting in that peaceful loving place with the stained-glass windows. I would watch the moving light pour through different scenes and figures, staining the congregation with glowing color. My favorite window was a wall of blues and purples with scattered bits of red.

Now as an adult I have in my kitchen window amethyst and quartz crystals, glass marbles, and a hunk of blue glass from a glass-blower's discard heap. Around the house I have glass paperweights, green Depression glass, and a "deck prism" used in sailing boats to let light into the darkness below the decks. I make cobalt-glass windows of Jizo. I don't wear jewelry, I just like to look at glass and jewels.

One day I looked at all the glass and asked, "What is going on here?" (The basic question of spiritual practice.) Why have I collected all of this? Is there a quality I am trying to take on or to constantly remind myself of?

What is it that attracts us to jewels? First, it is their quality of light. Some jewels—like emeralds, tourmaline, topaz, peridot, and diamonds—can be cut so that light reflects off their facets. Some jewels seem to glow with a luminous quality, like moonstones and pearls. Some have light hidden within their depths, like fire opals or star sapphires.

The conventional truth is that we like jewels because they are beautiful and wearing them somehow confers their beauty on us. The deeper truth is that we are attracted to jewels because they show us a truth about our true nature, the inextinguishable light that is hidden in our depths. Gems reflect to us the truth that we are transparent, luminous, sparkling bits, turned on the lathe of time, cut and polished by constant change. There is a Buddhist view of existence called *Indra's net*. It tells of a net formed by the intersecting strands of time and space. Each life is a jewel twinkling off! and on! at the crossing of here! and now! Each jewel life reflects and is reflected by all other life. We are nothing but reflections reflecting reflections, an empty theater full of mirrors, a net of jewels encased in a single great Gem.

Jewels remind us of our true nature, which is brilliant light. We are the precious jewel. Our spiritual practice is to discover and discard what is extraneous and obscures that light, and to become increasingly transparent, until the clear light of truth shines unhindered through us. There is a luminous quality to those who are transparent to that great shining. It can be seen in the sanzen room. During a long retreat, day by day people come in with faces that become clearer, younger, and more luminous.

Gems are made precious by their rarity. Semiprecious stones are those that are more common. Ordinary human life is in one way a semiprecious gem. In the mass of life-forms, human life is not common. Once born human, if we are able to hear the spiritual truth and to practice it, our life becomes more rare and thus a precious gem. If we are able to practice intensively we can burn up obscuring impurities. We become the *sharira*—heart of brilliant jewel, triply rare and beyond price.

The color of jewels also attracts us. If there were no variety of color and quality, if all gems were clear like diamonds, we would find them boring. What is that color in our lives? How are *we* that color?

We are like the pieces of a stained-glass window, bits of colored glass through which the Great Light pours. The more transparent we are to the light, the more it shines through us to illuminate others. If we are able to see our lives from a "higher" and larger perspective, there is a pattern to the moving mosaic of light and glass. If we move in closer, into the perspective of the middle range of vision where we usually function, the different colors and shapes distract us. If we move in very close, into the molecules of glass, the differences and colors again disappear. It is all a-dancing.

The Origin of the Mani Jewel

There are several myths about the origin of the mani jewel that Jizo carries. One involves mystical animals called *nagas* and *gurudas*. Nagas are mystical ferocious but benign beings with the hood of a cobra, the face of a human, and the body of a serpent or a dragon. They live at the bottom of the ocean where they guard Buddhist teachings until the time that humans are ready to receive them. Nagarjuna, the second-century Buddhist who wrote and taught about sunyata, or emptiness, was named for the nagas. It is said that he re-

ceived spiritual instruction from them in their undersea palace and
brought the teaching on emptiness from caves there. Garudas are
half giant eagle, half golden human, and are archenemies of ser-
pents. Both nagas and gurudas are portrayed by artists as companions or steeds for Hindu and Buddhist deities. Both have been used
as synonyms for the Buddha, representing the power of an enlightened being.

According to one legend, Nanda, king of the nagas, took the
heart of a guruda bird and made it into a luminous gem. The Buddha then transformed it into the cintamani jewel that grants all desires. In another legend, the mani jewel came from the brain of a
naga. In addition to granting wishes, it provides immunity from all
harm. One who possess it is unaffected by drinking poison and can
pass through fire unburned.

THE JEWEL IN US

These are not just curious legends from the past. Each aspect of
these stories points to a truth of our lives in this place and time. Is
there a jewel that can fulfill all our desires? Is there a jewel that can
give us protection from poison and fire? If it exists, where and how
can we find it?

That this gem was born from the heart and brain of gurudas and
nagas means that is birthed in the workings of our own pumping
and feeling heart and in the electrical circuits, machinations, and
speculations of our own mind. It is within us, not outside of us. It is
what we were before we were born, what we are now, and what we
will become after we die.

That it took the strength of great nagas, gurudas, and Buddhas to
bring the gem to light and call forth its brilliance means that we
have the potential within our small and pitiful self, if we call on the
power available within our huge Self, to plunge into the gore of our
dark and stinking guts and there find our true power and luminos-
ity. The jewel is our innate enlightened nature. It calls to itself and
helps itself emerge.

Master Wansong wrote a poem about a jewel:

The thread of the jewel passes nine bends.
The jade loom barely turns once.

This is from a legend about Confucius. Once the great sage was given the task of threading a jewel with nine curves in its bore. The penalty for failure was his life. He did not know how to accomplish this, but a mysterious girl he met in the mulberry bushes told him to think of a secret. The Chinese word for "secret" is close to the sound for the word "honey." The one word opened his mind and Confucius fastened a thread to an ant, luring it with honey into entering the jewel and negotiating the path with nine curves.

What is this jewel? This jewel is our life. This ant is also our life. We creep along a twisted path running up against barriers, turning and toiling on, blind to the jewel that surrounds us and kindly provides a path that is called "my life."

What is the thread? Also our life. Pulling that one straight thread of our life through nine or ninety-nine or ninety-nine thousand bends and twists, that pulling is the purpose for which we were born, to rescue Confucius, all the sages, the Shakyamuni Buddha from danger. Through our ignorance we grasp and push away, fight and kill. In doing so, we put in peril the lives of the great and mighty; the seen and unseen; medium, short, or small; our life; and the very life of the Buddha.

Because we are blind to the jewel and the path, we negotiate the twisted path of our life as best we can. Honey is used to lure us. What is that honey? It depends upon the person. Why do you practice? To pass koans? To become enlightened? To be special? To be in charge? To not hurt so much? Because it's fun? It doesn't matter. The Dharma accepts any motive. Any motive will do when your life is at risk.

The real honey has a subtle taste. It is the taste of peaceful abiding, clarity, and spaciousness. Once tasted, no substitute will be accepted.

The Zen poet Ryōkan wrote:

Leave off your mad rush for gold and jewels.
I've got something far more precious for you:
A bright pearl that sparkles more brilliantly than the sun and
    moon
And illuminates each and every eye.
Lose it and you'll wallow in a sea of pain;

Find it and you'll safely reach the other shore.
I'd freely present this treasure to anyone
But hardly anyone asks for it.

Zen Master Gensha taught, "The whole Universe in ten directions is one bright pearl, what use is understanding?" Zen Master Keizan added, "Although it is an ordinary jewel it does not come from outside but rather appears completely from the human mind. . . . If you use this jewel when you are ill, the illness is cured. If you wear this jewel when you are worried, the worry will dissipate on its own. All treasures appear from this mani jewel and it is said that no matter how much it is used, it is inexhaustible." Zen Master Dōgen adds, "Even though it seems to be continually changing the outward appearance of its turning and not turning, it is just the bright pearl. Those who surmise that 'I cannot be the bright pearl,' should not doubt that they are the pearl."

How can this one bright pearl, the jewel that Jizo carries, grant all desires? When we begin to see its light and then to see *by* its light, then all our desires—the poison of greed and the burning fires of lust—become pale and cool next to the kindling of the bright flame of the growing desire to awaken fully. As that one desire to draw closer and closer to the Source of all light and life grows greater we will be drawn, if we allow it, into brilliant heart of that jewel, which is our own heart. Dwelling in that heart there are no questions, no fevers, no for or against. There is only the ease and joy of all things perfect as they are. Do not doubt that you are the bright pearl!

chapter ten

THE *Six Rings* AND THE *Six Realms*

*I watch people in the world
Throw away their lives lusting after things,
Never able to satisfy their desires,
Falling into deep despair and torturing themselves.
Even if they get what they want,
How long will they be able to enjoy it?
'For one heavenly pleasure they suffer ten torments of hell.
Binding themselves more firmly to the grindstone.
Such people are like monkeys
Frantically grasping for the moon in the water
And then falling into a whirlpool.
How endlessly those caught up in the floating world suffer.*

RYŌKAN

THE BUDDHA TAUGHT THAT all living beings dwell in six different realms of existence. There are six rings on the staff carried by Jizo Bodhisattva, one for each of these six realms. The jingling of the rings, a constant sound whenever the pilgrim walks, is a reminder that we carry the six realms with us at all times. Jizo is a bodhisattva who has the ability to move freely through the six realms and assist those who are suffering. In Japan six statues of Jizo (Roku Jizo), one for each realm, often stand at the entrances to cemeteries. Their benign countenances bring ease to those who are anxious about the fate of a loved one who has died and entered that Great Unknown.

The origin of the six realms is "the five destinations," a teaching of the Buddha. The Buddha said that all life was in motion, ceaselessly moving among these five realms: hell, animal, hungry ghost, human, and gods. The sixth—the realm of the angry titans called *asuras*—was inserted between the human and god realms hundreds of years after the Buddha lived.

The Buddha described the experience in each realm through the simile of a hot, weary traveler. The hell realm, he said, is as painful as a traveler who has been scorched and exhausted by hot weather, is weary, hot, and thirsty and who falls into a deep charcoal pit full of glowing coals. Those in the animal realms are as miserable as a hot, exhausted man who falls into a deep cesspool filled with excrement. The realm of ghosts is like a tired man who is able to sit under a tree on rocky ground but in only a little shade.

The human realm, he said, is like the pleasant sensations experienced by a hot, weary traveler who can sit on smooth ground in

Four of six modern stone Jizos near Okayama.

deep shade. The god realm is extremely pleasant, like the experience of a man in a closed, windowless, and barred room in a mansion, lying on a couch spread with rugs, blankets, sheets, many crimson pillows, and a coverlet of deerskin.

Nirvana (release from the six realms), the Buddha said, is like the man who plunges into a pond with transparently clear, cool water, with smooth banks for getting in and out. In bathing and drinking the water, all his distress is relieved and he feels delight.

It is important to know about the six realms not only because they are the environment in which Jizo Bodhisattva travels and works, but also because we travel through each of the six realms on our spiritual quest. The six realms are the geography of our very life. It is not an odd and ancient Buddhist cosmology but a vivid and accurate description of the moment-to-moment experience we call "my life." It tells us why and how we and others suffer. It can guide us out of a blind groping in dark and twisted passageways toward the bright light and fresh air of freedom.

Each of these six realms, even the very pleasant existence called the realm of the gods, can be a trap. Notice that the Buddha described the room of the gods like a comfortable cell, but one that is closed and barred. There is only the appearance of freedom in the more pleasant realms, that of humans and gods. It is like wandering within a huge maze. Ultimately the experience in each realm is impermanent and unsatisfactory.

Buddhists do not believe in a higher authority that sentences a human to the realms of ceaseless suffering like the hungry ghost or hell realms. Nor do the six realms represent a ladder that we climb straight up to heaven. We move in a fluid, cyclic way from one realm to another, propelled by our actions, speech, thoughts, and their effects. The internal mechanism of our life's unwinding is the law of cause and effect. We will move endlessly among these realms, as long as our activity arises from ignorance.

Zen Master Hakuin once awakened a samurai to this truth. The samurai had come to ask for—or maybe demand—an explanation of heaven and hell. Hakuin taunted him, "What's the matter? Are you frightened of hell? A sniveling coward like you is not worth teaching!" The furious samurai swung his sword but Hakuin stepped aside and exclaimed, "Here open the gates of hell!" The samurai halted and then sheathed his sword. Hakuin said calmly, "Here open the gates of heaven."

The Buddha taught that nirvana exists above and separate from all of these six realms. In the same way that our action and reaction creates the "path and the way" to a hellish consequence, it is our own action that ultimately releases us from the realms of suffering and puts us on the path to nirvana. Only by destroying the things that stain and fetter the mind can a person realize the original clarity, freedom, and unbounded expanse of the True Mind that is our birthright.

Most beings are caught in transmigrating the six realms. Bodhisattvas are not. They have awakened, seen the emptiness of these realms, and are free of them. Jizo and Kannon are the bodhisattvas who are able to travel freely among the six realms. They have chosen to return to the six dream worlds, nightmarish and pleasant, to help others awaken. With clarity and compassion they see the suffering of each realm and the cause of that suffering. They are able to stand at the intersections between the realms and help those who are unable to move out of misery and unhappiness by their own power. Jizo Bodhisattva has taken a specific vow not to rest, to enter nirvana, until all those suffering in the hell realms have been rescued and brought to awakening.

Beings in the lower realms—hell, ghosts, and animals—obviously need assistance. We humans are sympathetic and are drawn to help those in the "lower" realms. We do work in prisons, with abused children, in war zones, and in animal shelters. But beings in the "higher" realms—the titans and gods—are in as much, if not more, need of help. Their pleasant living conditions disguise their suffering from themselves and others. Their very fame and wealth can cause other, less fortunate people to feel jealousy, which is the entry door into the titan realm, or to feel anger, which is the conduit into the hellish realms.

Ideally all beings will be assisted in moving into the human realm, for the human realm offers an almost unique possibility: that of undertaking a life of discipline and spiritual practice. Humans are not so overwhelmed by the unending torment of the hell or ghost realms that they are unable to practice, but they do suffer enough to want to find a way out. Unlike animals, they have enough wisdom to perceive the workings of cause and effect. They are not completely narcotized by the pleasures of the higher realms of existence. Human beings thus have the greatest potential to undertake a path leading out of endless transmigration and toward nirvana

To understand the work of Jizo Bodhisattva, we should know more about each realm. For each realm we will look at how Jizo Bodhisattva functions to help beings who are trapped there.

THE HUMAN REALM

The human realm can be seen in two ways. First, it can be seen as completely separate from the other five realms. From this point of view there are countless beings with bodies and minds who live in six distinct realms and experience their own particular kind of suffering. The other five realms of existence can coexist in time and place with human activity, but most humans have only a faint and occasional awareness of other beings such as ghosts or *devas* ("beings of light"). Human beings might have a better, but still dim, awareness of the animal domain, to the extent it interfaces with ours through our pets or domesticated animals.

The second way to see the human realm is that it contains all the other realms. The nonhuman realms are all aspects of our own awareness, states of mind and feelings that arise within us at different times. Our life consists of rapidly fluctuating experiences as human-animals, human-gods, human-ghosts, humans in hell, and human-jealous titans. From this perspective only the Buddhas and bodhisattvas are truly human, having realizing the purest and highest human potential. They are fully aware of the flux of thoughts in the mind, feelings in the heart, and sensations in the body, but they are not caused to suffer by them.

For example, in a single meditation period we can cycle through all the realms.

You are on your way to a meditation retreat in your new car. The sun is out and your favorite music is playing. Everything is perfect. The god realm. Someone sideswipes and nearly hits your car and you arrive and sit down to meditate feeling furious. An asura. Pretty soon you feel hungry. Your stomach growls. You dream of delicious food and, salivating, enter the animal realm. To pass the time you fantasize about how to spend the money when you win the lottery. A dip into the god realm. You could make much better use of the money than the old geezer farmer who won it last week. A jealous asura again. Winning the lottery would mean a Mercedes . . . the hungry ghost realm. The illusion fades as your knees begin to burn. You are in agony. When will the bell ring to end the pain? A (mild) hell realm. You begin to get annoyed with the people running the retreat but reason with yourself. The human realm. You undertake loving-kindness meditation toward the people who are leading the retreat. The human realm. It works. The knee pain disappears as you are filled with a blissful sensation of warmth radiating from your heart chakra. The heavenly realm. The dinner bell rings . . .

Actually the human realm is not merely a patchwork of other realms. It is unique. The Buddha spoke of the rare and precious opportunity of human birth. There are many billions of living beings. Of these very few are human. The Buddha admonished his disciples not to be fools and waste the rare opportunity of human birth. The difficulty in the other realms, he said, is that "There is no practicing of the Dhamma [Dharma] there, no practicing of what is righteous, no doing of what is wholesome, no performance of merit. There mutual devouring prevails and the slaughter of the weak."

As humans we have certain advantages over those in other realms. Our suffering is not as overwhelming and unremitting as in the lower realms. Thus we are able to look at our dissatisfaction and pain with some objectivity and look around for a way to decrease it. We have hope. We are able to summon some energy to practice. We have a modicum of wisdom. This consists of both a larger perspective on our life and its context, and a dim understanding of the operation of cause and effect.

With a little training we are able to step back, examine our states of mind objectively, and begin to learn to change them. We can catch glimpses of what drives our thoughts and actions and what the effects are, wholesome and unwholesome. We can perceive the struggling and suffering of the other five realms both externally as the lives of other beings, and inside us as states of mind. Eventually

Roku Jizo at Zenshu-ji Temple in Los Angeles.

we understand the need to practice. At that turning-moment, the very mind whose activity obscures the Truth and the path to it now becomes the very tool for liberation.

If we are more fortunate, "men and women of good families" as the Buddha said, we have the free time and resources to devote ourselves to practice. If we are truly fortunate, we encounter the Dharma and a clear-eyed teacher. If you are reading this book, you have fulfilled many of these conditions.

There is an opportunity in the human realm to encounter a great truth. It is that all that is, each life in every realm including your own human life right now as you read, is the One Mind's experience of itself. Please do not waste this rare opportunity.

The Hell Realms

Buddhist descriptions of hell are the same as those in every religion. Hell is characterized by great heat or great cold and by extreme physical pain, with no hope of escape. Hell is described as sitting in a blast furnace. To sit still is torture, to move is worse. This kind of hell is created by hot anger. It wants to move out, to attack people, to kill by searing. To sit still with hot anger is torture. It burns us inside. To give vent to hot anger seems like a relief, but it is ultimately worse, with even more painful consequences afterward.

The same is true of extreme cold. When we are very cold we pull inward. Our extremities, fingers, toes and ears, are horribly painful. We pull our attention away from the pain and shrink down to any place there is a little warmth, maybe in our belly, and we guard it. This is like cold anger. It numbs the pain by moving away, collapsing, and becoming guarded. It kills by ignoring; it's the "cold shoulder." There are also hells of pain described as piercing thorns or cutting knives. Attempts to escape bring worse pain, a doubling of the thicket of sharp blades.

In the *Sutra of the Past Vows of Earth Store Bodhisattva*, Jizo is asked to name the many hells and describe the path to those hells. Jizo lists hells with names like Flying Knives, Squeezing Mountains, Uninterrupted, Head Chopping, Quarreling, and Embracing Pillar. Within each of these there can be "hundreds of thousands of smaller hells, each with its own name." This means that each unwholesome act is unique in time and space, and every act committed by each one of hundreds of thousands of individuals has its own particular consequence.

Hells do not exist outside of our actions. Hells come into being at the time we act, as a direct consequence of what we do. It is also our own action that can free us from hells.

The Chinese Master Hsuan Hua explained that the hell called Embracing Pillar contains "a large hollow brass pillar full of fire." Those guilty of sexual misconduct fall into this hell and see the roasting pillar as a person. Men, for example, see it as a beautiful woman whom they rush to embrace, only to find themselves burned so badly that they cannot pull their seared flesh away from the pillar. After death they are revived by "a wind called the 'Clever Breeze' a wonderful Dharma . . . [they] then forget the painful consequences of their behavior, recalling only its pleasurable aspects. Driven by this memory, they rush to the pillar again, only to find the cycle repeated."

The hell of the Embracing Pillar is one I recognize from talking with women who are living with their third or fourth battering partner. After several years of being beaten and degraded they escape with their children to a shelter. Within a short time they are revived and return to embrace the same or a new version of the fiery relationship. This happens repeatedly, leaving the women and their children deeply scarred and, too often, dead.

Abused children have told me of life in the hell called Uninterrupted. For such natural childlike actions as wetting the bed, vomiting, or breaking a toy, they are burned with cigarettes, curling irons, hot plates, propane torches, or dunked in pots of boiling water. They are beaten with sticks, toilet brushes, electric cords, brooms, Ping-Pong paddles, belts, and coat hangers. Their hair is torn out; they are locked in dark closets. If they cry, they are beaten again or sodomized or bound and gagged with duct tape.

The Path to the Hell Realms

Hell realms are entered through indulging anger, allowing it to control our thoughts, speech, and action. When we are angry, we lose our humaneness and do not care whom we hurt or how we hurt them. We kick dogs, slap children, stab with verbal daggers, nurse old wounds, and plan revenge.

Jizo Bodhisattva's Activity in the Hell Realms

The staff of Jizo Bodhisattva is said to have such power that, if he strikes the iron doors of hell, they must open. What teaching provides such strength that, *if we use it*, it will surely free us from all hells? It is the teaching of karma, or action, and its consequences. As Kalu Rinpoche emphasized, "Of the 84,000 collected teachings of the Buddha the most essential is the understanding of the karmic process." It is also called retribution. The word *retribution* has extra, moralistic overtones to Western ears. It is, however, an impartial physical law, the action of cause and effect.

This law applies to all realms but is vividly described in the *Sutra of Earth Store Bodhisattva* in relationship to the hell realms. This description warns people about the implacable action of cause and effect and to encourage them to keep the precepts. Thus there are specific reparations in the hells for particular deeds. The retribution of flaying or "flesh from bone" is incurred by those who trap animals, especially young animals. Flaying hell refers both to the experience of physical pain like sharp knives cutting flesh from bone and also to the emotional pain of separation and loneliness when members of our family are cut off from each other by the sharp knife of anger. If a person beats step- or adopted children, their retribution is to be flogged in future existences. If a person makes fun of people who are ugly, the retribution is to become ugly.

How does the karma of retribution work? The first way is straightforward and easy to observe. For example, if you become angry your face becomes contorted. Even beautiful people become ugly, inside and out, by repeatedly giving vent to anger. The second mechanism is less obvious. We are very naive to think our bad actions can be hidden, that no one knows about them, and thus they won't have any consequences. It is delusion to think that when we die all of our poor or harmful actions will simply disappear.

If the physical elements of our body don't disappear but go on to make new living beings, why is the same not true of our emotional and psychological energy, our anger or our loving-kindness, our reactivity or our equanimity? Whatever we have set into motion with our words or actions will continue to act through cause and effect in the lives of new beings, will continue to affect the lives of our children, friends, and people not known to us, generation after generation. This is very important to consider. Retribution means that unwholesome acts bear unwholesome fruit and wholesome acts bear wholesome fruit.

The Buddha said that hell is extreme physical and emotional pain without hope of relief. The power of Jizo Bodhisattva, which is the power of sincere spiritual practice, can turn our physical and emotional pain around, make it work to knock on and open the gates of hell. It can lead us to freedom. For example, Zen masters have used hellish cold as a training tool. Daiun Harada Roshi had a temple with an unheated zendo in the snow country in Japan. He said the biting cold "drove people into their bellies." In this extreme cold the mind shrinks to the only place of warmth, a tiny warm spot in the center of the belly, the hara. When movement means pain, the mind becomes very focused. The usually huge sense of self also shrinks to one unmoving spot. From there it is only one sound, one touch away from the great death and the great rebirth.

One Zen student told me of enduring a childhood of physical and sexual abuse by her father, then falling into the hands of a misguided therapist who convinced her that she had many personalities. Pushed into exploring these personalities, she suffered for several years in hellish, demonic realms. Even fifteen minutes of meditation practice was very difficult for her, but her determination was as strong as her anguish, and she returned to practice again and again. One day she was driving on the freeway, immersed in her pain. She suddenly thought, "Who is suffering?" At that instant the suffering stood by itself and fell away. Now she is able to practice steadily, not completely free of suffering but out of its maw and firmly on the path.

Pain can also be used as a training tool. At her first retreat one student realized that she already had experienced meditation. She had learned it on her own in childhood when she suffered severe migraines. Holding mind and body absolutely still was the only way to be free of pain. This is also true of acute emotional pain, such as comes with a divorce or the death of a loved one. To move the mind even a bit into memories of the irretrievable past or shattered hopes for the future brings renewed waves of fresh pain. The only relief is in holding the mind still in the present moment. Out of this comes the first taste of that Great Peace that is our refuge.

At a ceremony of remembrance, a young mother spoke of finding this truth. A few weeks before she had gone into her seven-year-old son's room to waken him for school and found him dead. A virus had weakened his heart and he had died in his sleep. At first she was overwhelmed with grief, and kept playing the scene of finding him over and over in her mind. Then came a flood of thoughts about "what if?" "What if I had gone in his room earlier?" Then she was taken over by the torment of thoughts of what would never happen—his graduation, her grandchildren. If her mind strayed to memories of past times with her son or to future times without him, she was plunged into despair. The only place there was any relief from her intense suffering was when her mind was fully involved with the events of the present moment.

When we do not run away, cold is just cold, heat is just heat, and pain is only pain. This is where Jizo Bodhisattva works, pulling people from the agonizing fire of hell into the purifying fire of Dharma.

This is easy to say but hard to do. We spend a lot of energy trying to avoid even mild forms of discomfort, heat, or cold. What kind of person would deliberately choose to enter places of extreme misery, freezing and burning hells, as Jizo does?

We can name people who have, people like Albert Schweitzer and Mother Teresa. There are many we cannot name who also carry out the work of Jizo Bodhisattva. They are those who clean stool and maggots from the bedsores of a person dying with AIDS, who bandage a child's limbs amputated by land mines left from a war that ended before the child was born. They are those who welcome victims of family violence into foster homes and shelters at midnight, and those who offer water, food, and kindness to people who are starving in a famine thousands of miles distant.

What would compel someone to do this? What characteristics would such a person have? Two: no fear, great love.

In addition to these, Jizo Bodhisattva is said to have supreme optimism. She would have to be optimistic to go forward with a vow not to rest until every being is rescued from every hell. Jizo has thus become the patron of lost causes. In times of deep despair it is enough just to know that the energy of Jizo exists, that there is someone somewhere who does not believe that there are any lost causes and who will descend into the cesspool where you have fallen to give you help, whether you ask or not.

THE REALM OF THE HUNGRY GHOSTS

The hungry ghosts (called *preta* in Sanskrit) are one level above the agony of the hell realm. Their plight is to be constantly hungry and thirsty, tortured by unfulfilled desire. They are depicted in scrolls and paintings as emaciated beings with huge, swollen bellies. Their mouths are as small as the eye of a needle.

The hungry ghosts see rivers of water and heaps of food. They run to drink and eat, but when the water touches their mouths it becomes liquid fire. If they are able to stuff even a bit of food in their tiny mouths, it turns into a red-hot iron ball that sticks in the throat.

We experience this realm whenever our hunger is immense but we are unable to take in that which would be truly nourishing. The hungry ghost experience that is ubiquitous in the human realm is addiction. An addict is like an empty shell controlled by hunger. In the past I cared for infants born addicted to drugs. Their mothers

THE SIX RINGS AND THE SIX REALMS   177

were using combinations of cocaine, methamphetamine, heroin, methadone, and alcohol. They wanted to be good mothers, but their life energy was consumed by their habit. They sold food stamps the day they arrived in the mail for half their value in cocaine. Because crack and speed suppressed appetite, they did not feel hungry themselves so did not perceive their children as hungry and did not feed them. Their habits cost between twenty-five and three hundred dollars a day. To make this money they sold their possessions, stolen goods, their children, and themselves. In one study we did, several mothers were prostituting while visibly pregnant, and many were prostituting within a few weeks after giving birth.

Like the hungry ghosts, addicts see food and drink, alcohol and drugs, and run to it. But as soon as they use, they and everyone around them are further seared. Incarceration, job loss, divorce, drunk driving, AIDS all just inflict more pain.

In Pavlov's classic experiments with dogs, a bell rings and food appears. The dog salivates and eats. If you pair the bell with the food hundreds of times, soon the dog salivates when the bell sounds and no food appears. This is simple conditioning. Conditioning occurs with humans in relation to alcohol and drugs. The life energy of addicts is consumed in a ceaseless effort to end discomfort. Feelings of pain and anxiety are temporarily numbed by alcohol or drugs. If you don't drink and observe carefully others who are drinking, you can see that with the first sip of a drink there is a lessening of tension and fear in their bodies and faces. It becomes a conditioned response, stress—alcohol—relax.

A woman came to me during retreat worried about her increasing alcohol use. She was a nurse in rural Alaska. The frontier conditions demanded more than she had been trained to do. She might make a mistake, kill someone. Work became stressful. Each evening after work she would drink a shot of vodka. This had become a habit. One drink had turned into several. I asked her to go home and practice by looking carefully at her mind-state as the usual sequence occurred: driving home, opening the door, taking off her coat, going to the place the bottle was kept, picking up the bottle, pouring a drink, taking the first sip, etc. Could she pinpoint the exact moment the suffering lessened? She said, "Oh, I already know when. It's when I unscrew the top of the bottle."

We are the same as Pavlov's dogs. We are hungry for peace of body and mind. We find a something like alcohol that seems to shut off our neurotic mind, relaxes our muscles, and gives us a temporary ease. We become conditioned to relax when we taste alcohol. If we look carefully we find that we start to relax, as the student above was able to see, *before* we drink. We have become conditioned to the sight of the bottle, the motion of unscrewing the top, the smell of the alcohol.

This is actually quite wonderful, because it means that the mind can relax *without* the alcohol. It means we have the capacity to teach the mind itself to relax and be free. We have the ability to see through and change many of the states of mind that are painful. This is exactly what the Buddha taught about the mass of conditioning we call human life. It is also exactly what the Buddha taught about seeing through this mass and becoming free "by encompassing mind with mind." This means to encompass the crazed workings of the small frantic mind with the larger mind, the mind we call the "mind of the Buddha." When we begin to see this tangle of conditioning for what it is, we take the first step toward becoming an awakened being. It is the first step toward using the original unconditioned mind of Jizo Bodhisattva. It does not belong to Jizo alone—it is our own.

Not all of us have been addicted, but we have all experienced a restlessness that nothing seems to satisfy. We sit down to read, but the book isn't interesting enough. We make a cup of tea, but it doesn't taste very good. We flip the channels on the TV. Boring. There's nothing we like in the fridge. Maybe we could go shopping, but our closet and garage are full of junk. We try talking to a friend but don't really connect. Our eyes, ears, nose, tongue, body, and mind are hungry, but nothing is taken in. Everything seems dull, diluted, covered over with a film. This is the realm of hungry ghosts.

The Path into and out of the Hungry Ghost Realm

The pathway into the realm of hungry ghosts is desire, grasping, and greediness. It is the persistent feeling "If only I had X, I'd be content." As long as we believe the source of our happiness as *out there*, centered in some other person or thing, we will never be satisfied.

We will be in eternal pursuit and never experience more than momentary satisfaction.

Hungry ghosts who can swallow a bit of food find that it sticks like a red-hot iron ball in their throats. We can become human-hungry ghosts in relationship to our spiritual practice. We want so badly to experience a breakthrough, to be enlightened, that our very desire stands in our way. Although we must practice with determination and vigor, we have to let go of any idea of a particular outcome.

The pathway out of the hungry ghost realm is to stop pursuing, to sit still, to watch the naked process of grasping, and to not move to fulfill it. At first this is uncomfortable. We are used to feeling thirsty and immediately going to the sink or refrigerator to get something to drink. We seldom experience just thirst. I have seen students come into a meditation hall (not ours) loaded down with supplies. They make a nest of cushions surrounded by extra sweaters, breath mints, water bottles with built in straws! Are they afraid of experiencing sensations of thirst that might arise in an hour of meditation?

Jizo Bodhisattva's Activity in the Hungry Ghost Realm

The most effective teaching in the hungry ghost realm are the Four Noble Truths. There Jizo Bodhisattva teaches the intertwined truths of suffering and grasping, the cause of suffering. His peaceful presence shows those in torment the possibility of ending their suffering by following the Eightfold Path. Jizo knows the only food and drink that is always available, that satisfies any hunger and quenches the deepest thirst. This is the truth of Dharma.

When desire, driven by the thought of scarcity, is extinguished, then we see only abundance. Then our desire becomes the one desire of Jizo, to comfort those who suffer and help lead them to freedom.

THE ANIMAL REALM

The animal realm is characterized by ignorance, confusion, and habitual behavior patterns. Animals are driven by instinctual responses to basic biological needs. They spend their lives searching for food, fleeing danger, seeking shelter from bad weather, and reproducing.

They are enslaved by instinct and also by humans. They have difficulty adjusting to new situations outside of their genetic and conditioned programming. Our dog has never learned that the cars that speed by are dangerous. He sits happily in the middle of the road awaiting their approach with an interested expression. Only a lot of training or a painful accident will teach him not to.

Animals lack a certain kind of wisdom. They cannot see the wider perspective in which they live. They do not understand cause and effect. Because of this they are often bewildered or repeat behaviors that are not helpful to their lives. Our dog whines to go out at night to romp with the coyotes even though they once slashed his throat, necessitating surgery.

Humans fall into the animal realms through ignorance. Many people are barely able to provide the necessities for themselves and their families. They lose jobs and are evicted repeatedly, just scraping by without really understanding why. The life energy of many people is consumed by the relentless round of getting up, working, eating, defecating, TV watching, having sex, and going to bed. The preoccupations of food, sex, and shelter, with a little mind-numbing and often violent entertainment thrown in, occupy all of life.

In my work I have seen many children raised like animals. One family lived in an attic crawl space, urinating in the insulation and defecating in tin cans. The schizophrenic parents had sex in front of the children and with the children. I also have seen children who failed to grow and no medical reason could be found. They would begin to grow at age three or four, when they were tall enough to open the refrigerator and cupboards to rummage for food and to beg or steal food from neighbors. Abused and neglected children like these come into foster care behaving like feral animals. They hoard food, eat from garbage cans, drink from toilets, and do not know how to bathe, use toilet paper, or sleep on beds. They have no self-discipline and fight tooth and nail if their powerful instinctual drives are corralled.

My husband has found that many of the criminals he works with are caught in the animal realm. They do not understand the action of cause and effect. They are in jail because "the judge had it in for me." Why did they go before the judge? "Got in a fight." How did the fight start? "The other guy punched me first." Why did he punch you? "I propositioned his girlfriend." Do you like her? "Nah, I was too drunk to see straight."

They cannot link these events together—drinking, improper speech, anger, fighting, arrest, and imprisonment—let alone see their connection to the consequences for the future—an end to employment, friendship, marriage. Many come from chaotic and unpredictable families. A child in such a home is like a bewildered animal. Their experience is that a given action, such as asking an honest question, can result in apparently random effects, praise and kisses one time and slaps and insults the next. The child cannot understand the reason—that the parent was sober one time and drunk the next.

The Path into and out of the Animal Realm

Ignorance is the path to the animal realm. This ignorance could be willful, such as drinking to loosen our inhibitions and then have "license" to break other precepts—to lie, steal, or misuse sexuality. The ignorance could be imposed, as with children in addicted and neglectful families. When causes and effect seem randomly linked, we remain confused, fearful, and enslaved by patterns of instinctual behavior that are destructive to ourselves and others. Wisdom is the path out of this confusion.

The Work of Jizo Bodhisattva in the Animal Realm

Tibetan religious paintings often show Kshitigarbha carrying animals in his arms. Kalu Rinpoche says that we can help free animals by speaking about the Dharma to them. A bit of what is taught might be perceived and ultimately help them.

Our dog whines at the door of the meditation hall if he is not allowed in during retreats. Once inside, he sits quietly with everyone else. A visiting Tibetan teacher told us that he is part Lhasa Apso, a Tibetan temple dog. According to legend these dogs were once monastics that lapsed in their vows. They retain enough merit to live in temples where they might after death regain human existence so they could once again practice. I do not know if this is true. Our dog acts as if it is.

Certainly animals respond to our love for them. Many people are drawn to their innocence and can practice metta (loving-kindness) toward animals with more ease than toward human beings. Once when visiting Green Gulch Zen Center near San Francisco, I gave a talk on my work with abused children. Later a student approached somewhat shyly and told me that she understood the work I did. She had worked in an animal shelter, where her job was to euthanize the animals that no one claimed. She spoke movingly of the trust in the animals' eyes even as she carried them to their death. She talked quietly of her dread of Halloween, when animals that had been tortured, maimed, and skinned were brought in. With glistening, sorrowful eyes she said, "I came here because I had come to hate humans. I'll leave when I can be with people again." Hers was an intense practice, driven by an overwhelming experience of suffering in the animal realm and cruelty in the human realm, embodying the compassion of Jizo Bodhisattva.

To help humans caught in the animal realms the power of Jizo Bodhisattva works to raise the level of existence to a truly human one. It works to provide education and training in basic human-life skills to raise the standard of living. It gives compassionate medical care. It develops wisdom by teaching cause and effect. It helps people to see their unhealthy habit patterns and gives them tools of practice so they do not fall prey to them. Thus those who work in education, health care, social services, foster care, counseling, and religious work are manifesting as Jizo in the human-animal realm. It is our hope in this work to turn the energy of desire away from selfish animal needs and redirect it, to arouse desire in the spiritual heart to follow the spiritual path to deep awakening.

THE ASURA REALM

The realm above humans and below the gods is the home of the asuras. The inhabitants are described as jealous gods or angry gods, always fighting.

War is the human experience of the asura realm. There are more than fifty wars being waged on the earth at any time. Why do we fight with each other? Because we want something for ourselves and we have to get it away from someone else—territory, a lover, family honor, political or religious power. But these are all things that we made up. "My country," "my backyard," and "my airspace" are only concepts. The earth, grass blades, and clouds do not know who "owns" them, where France ends and Germany begins. We fight because we think that we need certain things in order to be safe. We fight because we see scarcity instead of abundance. Our minds invent ideas and then compel us to fight over them.

The Path into and out of the Asura Realm

The asura realm is entered through feelings of jealousy. At the core of jealousy is an idea that someone has something I should have. It could be a material possession like a house, a new car, or wealth. It could be assets such as beauty, youth, or talents we don't have or had once and lost. It could be good fortune, like winning at a casino. It could be a person we desire, like a child of our own, or a lover, or even an experience we never had—like a happy childhood.

Beneath jealousy is comparison. Someone has X and I do not. Beneath jealousy on a more subtle level is a feeling of entitlement. If someone has X and I want X, I deserve X.

It is a very interesting practice to become aware of this feeling of entitlement, which ironically is particularly strong in America. America is a land of jealous gods rather than a pure heavenly realm. In a curious way, jealousy seems to feed off abundance. On a trip to India I prepared myself to be distressed by the poverty and suffering I would see. Instead I was astounded to find the level of happiness and central sense of well-being was obviously greater there than in an American shopping mall or middle-class suburb. The difference was observable in the faces of Indian people all around me, from the thin dirty children begging and playing at the train station to the porters who staggered under enormous loads, then relaxed on their bundles, joking easily with each other as they awaited the next train. The difference was palpable in the gentle greeting of the wild-haired wandering ascetic awakening from sleep in a doorway in a frosty dawn in Dharamsala. Could it be that the less we have, the happier we are?

A study of happiness shows that once the basic need for food, clothing, and shelter are met, happiness is unrelated to material wealth. Actually you don't need a study to prove this. Any *National Enquirer* reader can tell you about the miseries of movie stars and millionaires in the United States. But we like studies. Especially with statistics. We just don't believe the study applies to us.

How much do TV and advertising support this feeling that everyone is entitled to everything they desire? How much does it fuel the
anger of "rising expectations" that leads to actions like one child
killing another to obtain a pair of coveted sports shoes? Or to a parent beating a child that won't stop crying? Or to our irritation with
a spouse who doesn't feel like making love tonight?

The epitome of the entitlement state of mind is the lottery mentality. We see someone win the lottery. What do we think? "Free
money! All my worries will be over." Actually studies of lottery win-
ners show the opposite to be true. Many people actually spend time
planning what they will do in the future when they win the lottery.
What a waste of time.

The state of mind "something for nothing" arises. Since the
chances of winning the lottery are so minuscule, people begin to
look around for another way to win a lot of money without putting
out much effort. Robbery, gambling, selling drugs—those will
work. Or combine the lottery mentality with the feeling, "If I am
suffering, then someone (else) must be responsible and therefore
must pay," and you file a lawsuit.

The path out of the imprisonment of jealousy is to realize impermanence and that good and bad are often temporary labels.
There is a story about this:

> Mr. Sai lived long ago in China. When his wife bore a healthy son
> the neighbors came to say, "How fortunate! A handsome son!" Mr.
> Sai smiled and said nothing. An epidemic swept through the land
> when the boy was ten, and he fell seriously ill. At last he recovered
> but was left with a crippled leg. "How terrible," said the neighbors,
> "to have a son who is deformed and will not be able to work hard
> or find a good wife." Mr. Sai said nothing, only smiled at the son
> he loved.
>
> The boy grew up and because of his handicap, had to learn to
> get around by riding a horse. He became an expert horseman, and
> won prizes in competitions. "How fortunate" said the neighbors,
> "to have such a talented son. Surely he will make you rich and
> have his pick of wives!" Mr. Sai only smiled and said nothing. One
> day when the young man was riding, the horse stumbled and fell.
> Mr. Sai's son was not injured, but the horse became lame and

could no longer be ridden in competition. Mr. Sai was too poor to buy another horse, but he would not have the lame horse put too death. "What a calamity!" said the neighbors. "Your only horse is now crippled and will not be able to win prizes or to work hard." Mr. Sai was silent, just smiling at the horse he loved.

War swept through the country. All the healthy young men and horses were conscripted into the army. The only farm left with a young man and a horse was Mr. Sai's. His son was able to harness the horse to a plow and grow enough food for Mr. Sai's family and the neighbors. "How lucky you are!" exclaimed the neighbors. Mr. Sai only smiled.

Jizo Bodhisattva's Teaching in the Asura Realm

What can Jizo Bodhisattva teach, in addition to the truth of impermanence, to free those in the asura realm? There are several specific practices that are effective antidotes to the poison of jealousy. These practices are loving-kindness (metta), sympathetic joy (mudita), awareness of abundance, and the bodhisattva practice of wishing enlightenment for all others before yourself.

The second type of asura realm, that of beings eternally at war, is entered through a taste for bloodletting. The path out of this realm is the practice of ahimsa, or nonharming.

THE HEAVENLY REALM

Life in the heavenly realm is always comfortable and pleasant. All desires are satisfied. The gods do not become ill during their very long lives.

It's like living in Southern California. I once led a retreat in Santa Barbara. Several blond, tanned, sleek students who attended told me, "It's very hard to practice here. The weather is always lovely, the surf's up, we're having fun." "It won't always be like this," I said. They replied, "We know it will change eventually. We should practice to prepare for that time, but it's too hard to get motivated."

Most Americans live with the abundance of the heavenly realm. We are really never hungry. We might complain that we're "starving" but we're not, not for food. We can choose among Chinese, Lebanese, Vietnamese, Mexican, Texas BBQ, and southern home cooking. We spend millions on cures for excess weight, but we won't face the simple truth: too many calories entering the mouth. We have good health, with a life span double that of our ancestors, but still we strive for immortality. We buy vitamin C, ginkgo, and hypericum, and choose among twenty-five kinds of olive oil.

If we wish to be entertained we can choose books, three hundred TV channels, movies, and thousands of videos. For education we have free schools and libraries plus the World Wide Web, which people could spend a lifetime exploring. We can travel by bike, car, van, truck, RV, ATV, or humvee; by bus, train, plane, and boat. Pretty much anywhere we want to go, we can. Are we happier than the Buddha and his itinerant monks and nuns? than the wandering Jizo?

A Polish student told me that Poles cannot imagine that Americans suffer. People in other countries see us as living in the heavenly realms. They want to live here. There's a great press of people at our borders, dying, sometimes literally, to cross over into this heavenly realm.

The BBC once sent a newsman to Sri Lanka, a Buddhist country for over two thousand years, for a special broadcast. He interviewed an old Singhalese woman in her small hut. "I come from London," he said grandly. "Have you ever been to London?" "No," she said. "I work for a television station. Have you ever seen London on television?" "No," she said. "In London there are lots of trains and buses, so you can go anywhere quite rapidly, and everyone has a television in their home," he announced. "You must have very bad karma," she said, shaking her head sadly. A Singhalese friend of mine who was watching this broadcast in America stood up at this point and cheered.

Unhappiness in the Heavenly Realm

Jizo Bodhisattva moves among *all* the realms, including the heavenly realm, to save beings. Why do we and other denizens of the heavenly realm, need saving? Why are we not happy?

There are several reasons. The first is because there's no contrast. It's only a lack of something that makes that thing delicious or warm or happy. We have to experience becoming dirty and sweaty and stinky with no way to wash for a week before we appreciate warm water and soap. Taking a bath becomes the heavenly realm—we feel so light, clean, and smooth. If there's no contrast, even the most wonderful things become boring. Chocolate mousse is heavenly, maybe through the first two helpings.

When there's no contrast we have to create it so we again can experience happiness and pleasure. We advertise "more" or "special." More flavor! Limited editions! The most luxurious! Rare! More excitement! Sometimes we try to create our own contrast by purposefully depriving ourselves. We go camping or to a meditation retreat. By depriving ourselves we appreciate again the simplest things—a warm fire, cool water in a brook, the breeze moving leaves of grass.

The second reason that there is dissatisfaction in the heavenly realm is that there are no hardships, no deprivations. It is in encountering difficulties and going through them that we feel worthwhile as human beings. We want to be challenged, tested, and to come through. The deva realm, the realm of the gods, is no test of our true substance. Anyone can live there and be calm and beneficent.

Part of the sense of accomplishment that comes from doing a long retreat is accepting and rising to the challenge. Sitting quietly side by side on our cushions in misery and joy, a camaraderie develops, even among strangers, as we work hard together in that revealing silence.

A student once said sesshin is like the boot camp of Zen practice. True. Until you have sat down for five or seven days, watched what the mind is doing, and done battle with the ego with its millions of tricks, you've barely begun the practice of the Buddha.

There's a third reason why the gods are dissatisfied. The sutras tell us that everything is fine for hundreds of years in the heavenly realms until one day the gods look in a mirror and see one gray hair! Then they begin to clutch at what they have and to be anxious for the future. Thus begins the slide into the hell realms. The highest realm becomes the lowest and heaven turns into hell with the realization of impermanence.

The *Earth Store Bodhisattva Sutra* describes this and the help available through Jizo (Earth Store) Bodhisattva:

The Buddha told the Bodhisattva "Contemplator of the World's Sounds," "In the world of the present and future there will be gods whose heavenly merit has ended, who manifest the five signs of decay and who are about to fall into the evil paths. When these signs appear, those gods whether male or female, see Earth Store Bodhisattva's image, hear his name, gaze at him, or bow once to him, they will increase their heavenly blessings, receive great happiness and never again fall into the retribution of the three evil paths."

Master Hsuan Hua lists the signs whose appearance heralds the imminent fall of a god. The five major signs are:

1. The ever-fresh flower headdresses of the gods begin to wilt.
2. The permanently clean clothes of the gods become soiled.
3. The gods never sweat, but when signs of their decay occur, they perspire under their arms.
4. The normally fragrant bodies of the gods begin to stink when the signs of decay appear.
5. The gods normally sit still and composed as if in samadhi. When the signs of decay appear they begin to fidget.

Familiar? We sit in sesshin "as if in samadhi," feeling a blissful heavenly state of mind. Along comes an anxious thought and we "begin to fidget." Oops.

There are additional minor signs:

1. The subtle voices of the gods become coarse.
2. The shining light of their bodies fades.
3. Their bodies usually repel water like glass. When the signs of decay appear they become soaked by rain.
4. They become unable to renounce certain states of existence and become strongly attached to them.
5. They become weak and devoid of energy. At this time their eyes, which normally remain fairly steady, begin to flit about.

These are the signs of human illness and old age that will happen to all of us even in the heavenly realm called the United States. The rounded curves, the sculpted bodies begin to sag. Our voices crack. The light of our bodies will begin to fade. Skin loses its luster, nails their natural shine, eyes grow dim with cataracts. We are no longer impervious to rain, cold, or germs. If we use mouthwash, deodorant, perfume, and aftershave we might smell good right up until the moment we die. But within a few hours the body begins to stink. The nature of any body, even a god's body, is to disintegrate and die. One day something happens to us—a gray hair, a young person dismissing us as an "old fogey"—and we realize this truth. The movie's star begins to fall.

The Path into and out of the Heavenly Realm

How do people end up in the heavenly realm? The first part of the path to the heavenly realm is fortunate circumstances. How were we born in a wealthy country? How did we end up intelligent enough to read and understand this book? Not, as we subtly and arrogantly assume, primarily under our own power. Rather this fortune came to us as a result of choices made by people many generations before we were born, choices such as whether or not to migrate, whom to marry, how to eat, when to wage war, and whether education is important. This is the second part of the path to the heavenly realms, good choices. At certain crossroads we and others have made choices that had a favorable outcome.

The path out of the heavenly realm is fear and grasping. We fear, quite correctly, that our good fortune will reverse. We try to ignore this or grab onto something to prevent those inevitable changes.

Jizo Bodhisattva's Teaching in the Heavenly Realm

As Jizo Bodhisattva moves through the heavenly realm, what can he teach the languid, well-fed, beautiful inhabitants to save them from future suffering? Impermanence. The gods actually know this truth, but they push it away, like the students in Santa Barbara. The sick and dying are kept out of sight. Only the beautiful people live in our movies and magazines. Jizo Bodhisattva knows that if we deny and fear impermanence we are doomed to fall out of the heavenly realm. We will descend into bitterness over our aging, anger over our death. Only if we are able to look at impermanence square on and enter its flow will we be saved.

Jizo Bodhisattva stands at the crossroads where four paths lead out of the heavenly realm. Three are the "evil paths" in the *Earth Store Sutra*. One, anger and aversion, leads to hellish existence.

The next, greed and grasping, leads to the domain of the hungry ghosts. The third, ignoring, leads to the animal realm. The figure of Jizo, a monk, points out the fourth and least-traveled path—the path of practice, the path to freedom. Can we do what the sutra asks, see his image, bow once to him, and then choose his path?

The next chapter will unfold Kshitigarbha as the Earth Store Bodhisattva. We look to the *Sutra on the Past Vow of Earth Store Bodhisattva* to understand more about the origin, vow, and functioning of Earth Store Bodhisattva. Then we can consider in a deliberate way what our own origins, vows, and true life-function are.

chapter eleven

Earth Store Bodhisattva

The colors of the mountains,
The sound of the valley streams
Just the body and voice of
My Shakyamuni Buddha.

DŌGEN ZENJI

THE ORIGINS OF EARTH STORE BODHISATTVA

The original name of Jizo Bodhisattva was Kshitigarbha. This Sanskrit name comes from *ksiti* (earth) and *gharba* (womb). It has been translated as Earth Store Bodhisattva, Earth Womb Bodhisattva, or the Bodhisattva of the Mysteries of the Earth. The name may have its origins in the Indian legend of the earth as witness to the Buddha's enlightenment. This is one version:

> When Siddhartha, the future Buddha, sat upon his meditation seat, vowing not to move until he was enlightened, Mara the Evil One was distressed. He sent armies of terrifying beings to attack the Buddha, who remained unafraid and unmoved. The light radiating from the Buddha shivered the swords and dented the battle axes. As arrows and weapons fell to the ground they turned into flowers. Mara, dismayed, questioned how he could be defeated by the Buddha. He asked his fleeing troops to bear witness that he, Mara, has been kind and generous. They respond that he has. Mara then asks about the Buddha,
> "And he, what proof has he given of his generosity? What sacrifices has he made? Who will bear witness to his kindness?"

Whereupon a voice came out of the earth, and it said, "I will bear witness to his generosity." Mara was struck dumb with astonishment. The voice continued: "Yes, I, the Earth, I, the mother of all beings, will bear witness to his generosity. A hundred times, a thousand times, in the course of his previous existences, his hands, his eyes, his head, his whole body have been at the service of others. And in the course of this existence, which will be the last, he will destroy old age, sickness and death. As he excels you in strength, Mara, even so does he surpass you in generosity." And the Evil One saw a woman of great beauty emerge from the earth, up to her waist. She bowed before the hero, and clasping her hands, she said: "Oh most holy of men, I bear witness to your generosity." Then she disappeared. And Mara, the Evil One, wept because he had been defeated.

In the legend above the "woman of great beauty" is Prithivi, the Hindu goddess of the earth, a probable precursor in India to the Buddhist bodhisattva called Kshitigarbha. A number of other connections between Kshitigarbha and the earth have developed over time. As Mahayana Buddhism spread to China, each of its bodhisattvas developed an association with one of the five elements: Avalokiteshvara with water, Samantabhadra with fire, Manjushri with air or space, and Kshitigarbha with the earth. In China Kshitigarbha was also designated the overlord of the lower regions of hell, deep in the earth. In Japan Jizo Bodhisattva is thought to descend regularly into hell to rescue the treasure buried there. This treasure is suffering human beings who, if dug out of samsara and set upon the path to liberation, will eventually become Buddhas. In Japan, Jizo also has a more literal relationship to the earth. He watches over the fields from his many shrines among the rice paddies and sometimes ventures out at night to give secret help with planting. The annual Jizo festival in Japan is a time to celebrate the first harvest of fruits given by the earth to support human life.

Chinese beliefs about the origins of Earth Store Bodhisattva are recounted in the *Sutra of the Past Vows of Earth Store Bodhisattva*. This sutra is the oldest sutra about Kshitigarbha that has survived and is recited and venerated today. While some sources say that it was translated from Sanskrit into Chinese in the seventh century by

Jizo Bodhisattva sitting
on a turnip in the rain,
by Mayumi Oda.

Sikshananda, an Indian monk from Khotan, most scholars believe the sutra was composed in China several centuries later.

Sutra is a Sanskrit word meaning "thread." A sutra is a collection of essential teachings, "lovely to hear," that are strung together just as flowers and leaves are strung to make a beautiful garland. The original Indian sutras were collections of the teachings of the Buddha. Written on palm leaves, they were threaded together to make books.

The *Sutra of the Past Vows of Earth Store Bodhisattva* (referred to hereafter as the *Earth Store Bodhisattva Sutra*) provides us with more information than any other sutra about Kshitigarbha. It tells of the origins of this bodhisattva and of his many divisions, which are called "transformation bodies." It describes various hell realms and tells of Kshitigarbha's promise to the Buddha to work unceasingly to save those who would be left in these hells, still caught in suffering, after the death of the Tathagata. The sutra answers certain questions posed by the Buddha's mother and others who are in heaven to hear the Buddha teach. The sutra also describes several practices that people can do to access the energy of Kshitigarbha and cultivate his qualities. What follows is a brief summary of the *Earth Store Bodhisattva Sutra*. Passages from the sutra appear in italics.

The sutra tells of four people—a boy, a king, and two young women—who practiced in such a sincere and continuous manner that eventually they all became Earth Store Bodhisattva. The first was a young man who was overwhelmed by the beauty of a radiant Buddha. He asked what one must do to gain such a wondrous and perfect body. The Buddha said, "If you wish to attain such a body, for many eons you should work to liberate all living beings who suffer." The boy became inspired to make and carry out this vow, thus becoming Jizo Bodhisattva. He will not go on to become a Buddha until all beings have been freed from their unhappiness.

The next account in the sutra is of two friends who were rulers of neighboring countries. These kings were good-hearted and kept the precepts themselves, but many of their subjects fell into evil actions. The two kings worked together to find expedient means to enlighten their citizens. Through diligent practice, the first ruler became a Buddha. The second became Earth Store Bodhisattva.

In two much longer stories the sutra then describes the feminine origins of Earth Store Bodhisattva. Both stories are about devout daughters who were afraid that their mothers, who had recently died, had gone to hell because of previous misdeeds. One mother had been a glutton. As she was especially fond of fish, turtles, and their eggs, she had taken many thousands of lives. The other mother had slandered Buddhism and its monks. Their daughters, called Bright Eyes and Sacred Daughter, sold their possessions to make offerings of food and Buddha images, and prayed for their mothers to be released from suffering. During meditation Sacred Daughter saw her mother's fate, drowning in a huge sea teeming with millions of men and women who were being torn apart by cruel and horrible beasts. The two daughters were told that due to their steadfast practice, their mothers had been released from this and worse hells. Even though their mothers were released, the girls could not forget the tormented state of all the other people trapped in the hell realms. Through their efforts to help their own mothers they had come to know the power of the sincere spiritual practice of even one person. Thus they vowed to continue to practice unceasingly until the very last being who was in the hell realms was liberated. By the power of their vows and their devotion, both girls were transformed into Earth Store Bodhisattva.

THE DIVISION BODIES OF
EARTH STORE BODHISATTVA

Jizo Bodhisattva does not have only these four human forms. The *Earth Store Bodhisattva Sutra* relates that just before his death the Buddha ascended to heaven to preach to his mother, who died soon after his birth and thus was unable to hear the Dharma. Hundreds of thousands of division bodies (manifestations) of Earth Store Bodhisattva then arrived from innumerable worlds wherever suffering existed. Each bodhisattva in this enlightened crowd brought flowers and incense for the Buddha. Suddenly the multitude of bodies assembled into a single body to listen to the Buddha teach.

The sutra tells us that the many aspects of Jizo Bodhisattva are not limited to human forms or origins. In order to teach and transform "obstinate living beings," Kshitigarbha is able to divide into hundreds of thousands of millions of bodies.

One thousand jizo wood sculptures by Enkyu. In 1690, after 38 years of work, Enkyu completed a vow to carve 100,000 images of Buddhas and bodhisattvas.

Perhaps I appear in a male body, or that of a woman, or in the body of a god, or dragon, or that of a spirit or ghost. Or I may appear as mountains, forests, streams and springs, as rivers, lakes, fountains, or wells, in order to benefit people. All of these may save beings. Or I may appear in the body of a heavenly king, a brahma king, a wheel-turning king, a layman, the king of a country, a prime minister, an official, a monk, a nun, . . . in order to teach and rescue beings. It is not only the body of a Buddha that appears before them.

What are the division bodies of Earth Store Bodhisattva? How are they given birth? The phrase *division bodies*, also called *transformation bodies*, refers to the thousands of millions of ways in which Earth Store Bodhisattva transforms in order to fulfill his/her vow, which is to "cross over" all beings trapped in hellish realms. These division bodies do not exist independently. They arise in response to need. When someone is suffering and cries out even silently for help, a transformation body is born because of that request. How many transformation bodies are there? As many beings as there are right now who are in distress and asking for help, that is, right now, the number of transformation bodies.

This has important implications. First, if we are in need of spiritual help, we should ask for it. Our asking is the cause for the arising of division bodies. If we don't ask, not only are we stuck in our own pride, but we are blocking the arising of bodhisattvas like Jizo.

We all have had the experience of being transformed by becoming aware of someone's vulnerability and suffering. We are often not aware of their plight until they ask for help. Consider this difference. If a friend or partner snaps, "Turn off the TV! You never do a lick of work around here!", we might be transformed, but not into a bodhisattva, into a demon! If they say instead, "My mother just called to say she's coming over and the house is a mess. Please, could you help me clean for awhile?", we might transform into a bodhisattva.

When we attack someone we risk creating demon bodies. When we ask for help we can give birth to the heart and mind of a bodhisattva in someone else. We are the very cause for the creation of bodhisattvas and their offerings of incense and flowers, and also fruit, soup, cookies, pulled up weeds, and clean floors.

This is an aspect of sangha, the co-creation of enlightened beings. Perhaps we are practicing with the idea that we would like to be a bodhisattva. However, if we only practice by ourselves we are blocking our own transformation into bodhisattvas. This is because we are keeping ourselves isolated from those who might ask for help in ways that might be difficult. Also we are blocking the transformation of others who could respond to us with compassion if we were willing to be vulnerable, to ask for, and to accept their help. Sangha, the community, means not to hoard our spiritual practice. Sangha means the human being-bodies, the raw material out of which bodhisattvas are created. The needs of those sangha bodies are the means by which this creation occurs. When we see others who enter the path and begin to enjoy its fruits, our hearts should jump with joy. The path of practice bears fruit not in isolation but in interaction with others.

The sutras talk about lifetimes of practice together in which we appear and interact in all possible roles. We all have been or will be birthed and cared for by all other beings. We are all aspects of the One Great Life that continually appears and disappears according to cause and effect. What we call one lifetime is a constant flickering, now student, now teacher, now parent, now child, now male, now female, now born, now dying.

Nothing is continuous. Everything is part of that great flickering of light and darkness. Even our awareness is not continuous. It too is impermanent. Many people think that the purpose of Buddhist practice is to be completely aware at all times. This is a misapprehension. Awareness is also subject to cause and effect. We are not trying to hold onto a particular state, but to be responsive to the needs of the ever-changing moment.

This is an aspect of the division bodies of Kshitigarbha. When we can rest quietly in the huge humming dynamo of the energy of all existence, we are completely available, as Jizo Bodhisattva is, to respond to each need that comes forward. With nothing extra in the way, the response is mathematically appropriate to that need. After the response occurs, no traces are left. The amount of energy that is available for this kind of functioning is beyond our comprehension. So too is the mysterious precision of the response to each situation. When we have released ourselves as the center of the universe, then we are released to fulfill our function to heal the suffering of the human world. Then each moment of our life is a division body, arising in response to the need that appears before us.

This is why we say "emptiness." Emptiness means that nothing is fixed. At its core everything is fluid, potential. What we seek has nothing to do with any kind of permanence, security, continuity or final state to be reached. If it did it would become static and die. It would not then be the "deathless" that the Buddha spoke about. If it did become static, it could not be transformed into the myriad bodies of Earth Store Bodhisattva or even into our own particular body.

We are familiar with this assembling of the myriad division bodies into one great body. This is our zazen. When we can rest with body still and mind open, all the division bodies assemble in one place, right here. That is who we all are, division bodies of the One. That is what each grass blade, each yellow or red or brown tree leaf is, one of ten thousand million division bodies of the one body. It is this assemblage that makes up our life.

In response to our suffering, Jizo Bodhisattva transforms into many forms: a man, a woman, a god, a king, or a stream. This means that whatever we will pay attention to that can relieve our suffering, Jizo Bodhisattva will transform into. A man who has had a difficult mother might be better able to hear the Dharma from a male teacher. A woman who was abused by her father in childhood might only be able to be open and inspired by a woman teacher. A Vietnam veteran might distrust all humans and find peace only living alone in the creases and folds of the huge mountain torso and forest pelt of the Earth Store Bodhisattva body. In any of us a turbid, peevish state of mind can arise. We can go to the sanctuary of a forest to breathe in the fresh air exhaled by the damp-earth and flowing-stream transformation bodies. Jizo transforms into whatever resuscitation equipment the parts of the One Body require to find relief from distress.

One person might listen to the Dharma spoken by a splendid king. Others might be open only to a monk, or a spirit that appears in a vision, or a person now dead who appears in a vivid dream with a message. Maybe we will only listen carefully to a teacher who can startle us by reading minds or making watches appear out of thin air, or who manifests as a ten-foot golden Buddha.

We can ask who has appeared to liberate us. But a more important question is, whom have we been born to liberate? For we are all division bodies born in response to urgent need, to heal the human world. Can we be awakened enough to hear those who call to *us*, to know where our place of healing activity is—home, temple, school, lab, store, shop, garden or office? For suffering has to be actively and repeatedly abandoned, in every situation in which it manifests. It does not disappear completely in one magic instant as we sit in the meditation hall.

In the sutra the ten thousand million forms of Jizo return to a single form. This did not just happen in the past, it happens all the time. Right now where is that form? That one form is the storehouse of all forms of human benevolence, supreme optimism, and unflagging effort to save all beings. Do you know where to find it?

The Vow of Earth Store Bodhisattva

The four people in the sutra who eventually became Earth Store Bodhisattva were able to do so because of the power of their vows. Each had a different motive. The young boy wanted a beautiful shining golden body like the Buddha. The kings wished to help their subjects. The young daughters were compelled by the sight of their mothers' intense pain. When we began spiritual practice our motives were like the boy's. We wanted to be healthy, to reduce stress, to become enlightened. Our motives were, in retrospect, self-centered.

That's okay. The Dharma accepts any motive. The fire of practice will burn out the impurities eventually. In fact, it is not until we truly begin practice that we realize how self-centered we are and how much harm we have caused. We vow to do better. The body of selfishness divides, giving rise to a body of practice.

Once we have gained some benefit from practice we, like the two kings, want to help others. Our self-focused vision has expanded and we become aware of how those we care for—our parents, friends, and children—are suffering. Only great love—like the love expressed as the filial piety of the two daughters in the sutra—can motivate us to exert ourselves strenuously on behalf of another person. The ante is upped. Practice becomes more and more essential.

The consequences of not practicing become more dire, affecting not only us but all those we love. Body of practice buds off a body of unselfishness.

> *She saw hundreds of thousands and millions of men and women rising and sinking in the water, being mauled and devoured by beasts . . . sharp sword-like teeth protruded from their mouths . . . myriad horrifying shapes at which none would dare look. The [Sacred Daughter] was calm and fearless because of the power of remembering the Buddha.*

As we work to help a few, the capacity of our hearts and minds expands. We become aware, like the Sacred Daughter, of all the beings in the churning sea of samsara. Our televisions transport us to the churning sea of suffering: a child blown apart by a land mine from a forgotten war, the parents of a mentally ill child who has shot teachers and classmates, the wife of a man who has jumped from a bridge. It is common at this point for people who are opening to the truth of the immensity of human suffering to become very distressed if that misery overwhelms them and they cannot "remember the Buddha."

Many students encounter this deep distress at a certain point in their practice. Often they come to an interview during a retreat weeping and trying not to weep, afraid that if they enter the grief they will not be able to stop crying, ever. They want to know what is wrong. Nothing is wrong. The floor has collapsed out of the small compartment called "my personal room of suffering" and they have fallen, or at least dipped, into the sea of the suffering of all beings. They are hearing with the ears of the bodhisattva Avalokiteshvara, she who hears the cries of the world and responds, and their response is to cry with her eyes, her tears. These tears fill her vase and are transformed into the life-giving elixir of immortality that pours out of her vase to heal the world. This transformation does not occur by itself. It is a distillation that occurs in the huge cauldron of spiritual life cooked over the fire of intense practice. It distills out of us whatever prevents us from functioning as the transformation bodies of Avalokiteshvara and Earth Store Bodhisattva.

In the sutra the millions of division bodies unite to form the one body of Earth Store Bodhisattva. Weeping with pity for those who suffer, he tells the Buddha not to worry about the seemingly impossible task of saving all suffering beings. He renews his vow to divide his body as often and in as many places as necessary to save all beings in these terrible realms and to work for endless *kalpas* (eons) to liberate anyone who had done even a dust mote's worth of good.

The Buddha says that he is worried about what will happen to human beings after he dies. He compares humans, who are tossed about throughout time by their desires and actions, to fish swimming in a long stream through nets. They are caught in the net, struggle, and perhaps escape briefly, but because of their ignorance and confusion they are inevitably trapped again. The Buddha thanks Earth Store Bodhisattva for his strong and ancient vow and his willingness to undertake this task "to heal the human world."

Our Vows

Jizo Bodhisattva has vowed to cross all living beings out of places of suffering. He is called the king of vows because he has promised to work unceasingly in the time between the death of the last Buddha, Shakyamuni, until the next Buddha appears in the world to teach. Hearing about this great vow we should ask, do I also have a vow?

"Vow" means an aspiration that is not limited or obscured by the details of the energy movement of any one lifetime, or anyone's lifetime, but is able to act through them. It propels us forward on the path even when we become discouraged. The vow operates not only within our life but through those beings and circumstances that flow toward us and challenge us.

It is important to clarify our vow and state it daily. Until we know our life direction all decisions are difficult and we are anxious, thinking endlessly about what to do with our life. Once we know our life direction and can state it in a vow, all other decisions are simplified. For example, if our vow is to awaken ourselves and also others, then in a given situation we can ask, will this action, this thought, these spoken words, help in that awakening or not? If not, then don't carry them out. Many of our chants contain vows. We have recited the Four Great Bodhisattva Vows or the Three Refuges hundreds of times. Even if we do not fully understand these vows, we have given voice to them. It is too late to take them back. They are our life.

This sutra tells us that we are human beings, we are men and women, we are division bodies of the One Body of Compassion. We are Earth Store Bodhisattva; we are becoming Earth Store Bodhisattva. "Are" means one of the countless division bodies called forth by need. "Becoming" means to clear away all that obscures our full experience of this One That Is Many. This occurs through the power of atonement, our vows, and our wholehearted practice.

WHY DOESN'T EARTH STORE BODHISATTVA BECOME DISCOURAGED?

In the sutra King Yama asks Earth Store Bodhisattva how he can work continuously using hundreds of thousands of expedient means to cross over hundreds of thousands of beings and not show the least fatigue or weariness. He also asks, if Earth Store Bodhisattva has worked in this tireless way for so long using all his powers, why do living beings continue to fall back into suffering? Earth Store Bodhisattva replies that living beings are stubborn and obstinate, difficult to tame. They have bad habits that make their life a revolving door in and out of abodes of suffering. Kshitigarbha does not become discouraged because he sees erring human beings as bewildered travelers who have lost the way home.

ARE THERE ANY BENEFITS TO THE SUFFERING WE CALL HELLS?

> To cruel stepparents Earth Store Bodhisattva speaks of the retribution of being flogged in future lives; to those who net and trap young animals he speaks of the retribution of separation of flesh from bone; . . . to those who defile the pure conduct of others and purposely slander the Sangha he speaks of an eternity in the animal realm; to those who scald, burn, behead, cut or otherwise harm animals he speaks of repayment in kind.

When Shakyamuni Buddha spoke about hell he said simply that it is physical and mental misery that we have no means to escape from. What of the terrifying descriptions of the kinds of retribution and endless realms of suffering in hell such as appear in the *Earth*

Store Bodhisattva Sutra? These were added after the time of the Buddha, designed to make people aware of the implacable and inexorable nature of cause and effect, action and reaction. Cause and effect should not be underestimated. Its workings are marvelous, the fabric woven and rewoven moment by moment on the jade loom of our lives. Cause and effect operate like all the laws of physics. If we can *truly see* that there is only one body with many manifestations, we will understand how everything works.

We all pay lip service to karma. But if we actually experienced it fully—that whatever we do to hurt someone would be returned immediately to us several fold—how quickly would we change how we act? Pain is a demanding and efficient teacher.

I have seen hundreds of people impelled into practice by acute suffering such as the death of a partner or friend. Very few remain in practice when the suffering eases a bit. My most vivid spiritual lessons have emerged in times of distress and unhappiness. At those times I was paying close attention. It has taken me many years to learn to practice steadily regardless of my mood, whether I feel sick, happy, or tired, or how much time I think I do or don't have for practice. Our suffering bears fruit if it compels us into and returns us to spiritual practice.

> *At that time the World Honored One stretched forth his golden-colored arm and rubbed the crown of all the division bodies of Earth Store Bodhisattva and said, "I teach and transform obstinate living beings such as these within the evil worlds of the five turbidities, causing their minds to be regulated and subdued, to renounce the deviant and return to the proper.*

The Buddha rubs the heads of those destined for enlightenment. It is a prediction of Buddhahood. He then tells of the job of Buddhas and bodhisattvas, to help people who are unhappy because of their agitated and turbid minds. "Turbidity" refers to a condition of murkiness or lack of clarity that occurs when things, like mud and water, are mixed together. Our ordinary minds are turbid. That is the state we call small mind. We could also call it turbid mind.

Sesshin, the name for an intensive silent retreat in Zen practice, literally means to settle the mind. Our minds often run like a hamster in a wheel, around and around in the same circle of worries.

Zazen is the way to rest the mind so that the restless swirling activity that creates turbidity gradually ceases. In sesshin there is a change in our state of mind. It undergoes a transition from cloudy and agitated mind to simple, calmer mind activity, to a more powerful one-pointed mind, and finally to clear mind. When the mind settles, like mud to the bottom of a pond, we can perceive the characteristics of pure transparent Mind separate from the dark, heavy, murky aspects of depression, anxiety, and self-obsession.

This is why the Zen tradition emphasizes seated meditation. We don't add much to it because each thing that is added gives the mind something to grab on to and embellish—usually at length. Zazen by itself will eventually do the settling. Just like a glass of muddy water, if we can just sit still long enough the turbidity will clear. But to just sit with no expectation, no entertainment, is very hard to do. Zazen acts slowly because it acts deeply and completely. To keep from becoming impatient and giving up on practice we embellish this slow process with chanting, eating meditation, Dharma talks, and sanzen. We are distracted a bit while zazen does its work, purifying karma and dissolving obstructions.

IS THERE A WAY OUT OF SUFFERING?

If there were no way out of suffering there would be no reason to continue to live. Buddhism is sometimes said to be pessimistic because the first truth of the Buddha is that suffering exists. But the Buddha also taught the way out of suffering. The first step on the path consists of looking suffering square in the eye and investigating it. When we do this we find what the Buddha found, that we suffer because:

1. We are human, with bodies that become ill, deteriorate, and die.
2. We don't like the way things are (= aversion or anger).
3. We like the way things are and we don't want them to change (= clinging or desire).
4. We try to deny the truth of cause and effect and impermanence (= ignorance).

These four reasons seem simple but are quite profound. If we could accept impermanence completely and live within its stream, we would find ease and contentment. If we could drop our clinging to a self- and personality-centered view, we could come into our birthright—an inheritance of joy and wisdom.

There are many beliefs about the treasures stored in the body of the Earth. Some people believe that the treasures are limited and some day will be used up. Others believe that the treasures are unlimited, self-renewing, and cannot be used up. Some people believe that the treasure belongs to one human or group of humans.

We have similar beliefs about our own life. It is a treasure that is limited and one day will be used up. It is also a treasure that is unlimited, self-renewing, and inexhaustible. Our life belongs only to us or it belongs to all. This is what the Buddha called "a wilderness of views."

As Jizo Bodhisattva descends into the realms of hell to rescue the treasure, the potential Buddhas, who are trapped there, so we make our way through the thicket of views, probe the realms of anger, desire, and delusion hidden in our own minds and hearts, in order to rescue the treasure that we call our Buddha nature. Only when we advance beyond all opinions and views can we enter the spacious treasury of true reality. Once this treasure house has opened, its wealth is available for us to use at will. Its use will bring benefit to all. This is the reason we practice.

Practicing WITH *Jizo* Bodhisattva

 The Buddha said, "Manjushri, the awesome spirit and vows of this Bodhisattva are beyond thought. If good men or women in the future hear this Bodhisattva's name, praise him, regard and worship him, make offerings to him, or if they draw, carve, cast, sculpt or lacquer his image, they will be born among the Heaven of the Thirty-Three one hundred times, and will never again fall into the Evil paths. "

SUTRA OF THE PAST VOW OF
EARTH STORE BODHISATTVA

RECITING THE NAME OF JIZO

The Chinese *Sutra of the Past Vows of Earth Store Bodhisattva* and the Japanese *Sutra on the Bodhisattva Enmei Jizo* tell of a number of ways to practice with Jizo Bodhisattva. The simplest is recitation of the name of Jizo or of the Jizo Dharani. In the sutra the Buddha asks Jizo Bodhisattva to help people who make the effort of even calling his name.

> *Earth Store Bodhisattva, in the future there will be people who are headed for suffering because of the unwholesome deeds they have done or people who are on the verge, at the gates of doing unwholesome acts. If these people recite the name of one Buddha or Bodhisattva or a single sentence from a sutra, please manifest your unlimited body, smash the hells they are about to enter and help them arrive at the place of boundless joy.*

The practice of reciting the name is done by chanting the name of Jizo either aloud or silently as many as ten thousand times in a day. You can use a mala, or rosary, saying the name once as each bead passes between the fingers. Any of Jizo Bodhisattva's names can be used. Traditionally the name is prefaced with the Sanskrit word *Namo*, which means "Praise to," "I take refuge in," "Homage to," or "Becoming one with . . ." Here are examples of how the name can be recited:

Namo Earth Store Bodhisattva
or
Namo Kshitigarbha Bodhisattva
or
I take refuge in Jizo Bodhisattva
or
Homage to Jizo Bosatsu, King of All Vows

RECITING THE JIZO DHARANI

Reciting the name of Jizo is a form of mantra or dharani practice. A mantra or dharani is a group of syllables whose recitation brings spiritual benefit. A dharani is usually longer than a mantra. The dharani for Jizo Bodhisattva in Japanese is:

OM-KA-KA-KABI-SAN-MA-EI-SOHA-KA

In Sanskrit it is:

OM-HA-HA-HA-VIS-MA-YE-SVA-HA

Om is a mantra by itself and a common opening word in many longer mantras. To chant "Om" invokes our awareness of the presence of absolute perfection within the relative world of our everyday life activity. *Sohaka* (Sanskrit, *svaha*) is a common ending phrase meaning "so be it," "may it endure," or "may good arise from this!" The syllables between om and sohaka (or svaha) invoke Jizo Bodhisattva. The entire mantra thus helps us stop and become aware of the perfection of this moment, asks that the energies of Jizo Bodhisattva enter our lives, and ends with a confident benediction. The Jizo dharani is short enough to memorize easily. It can be chanted three, seven, or nine times, or recited continuously in times of greater distress and need. Vary the speed of the chanting until you find the pace that works best to slow and calm the mind. During seated meditation you can say the Jizo mantra or dharani silently, one time with each out breath. Rest in the quiet mind during the in breath.

Ka is a germ or seed syllable (Sanskrit, *bija*; Japanese, *shuji*) containing the power of a whole mantra or deity. The Sanskrit character "Ka" represents Kshitigarbha in esoteric Buddhism. In the Japanese esoteric sect of Shingon, the Sanskrit letter "A," a symbol of the ultimate reality we emerge from and return to, is written on thin wooden plaques marking graves. When a child dies, "Ka" is written on the top of the plaque, invoking Kshitigarbha's protection for the helpless little one who has left this life.

How can reciting the name of Jizo or the Jizo dharani bring spiritual benefit and help free us from hells we are about to enter? A mantra inducts us into meditative state. If the mind is busy with discursive thought, reciting a mantra continuously and with attention can clear the mind. A mantra stops the action of the mind at the first *nen*, the first movement of thought. In the first nen the mind is in the present moment. As soon as thoughts branch out into the second nen, third nen, and so on, we are ruminating over the past and anxious for the future. A mantra holds the mind in the present moment where it finds rest.

A mantra that is not an English word (or a word in any language you understand) is the best. The difference becomes clear if you

Jizo's seed symbol KA.

meditate on the word "sad" saying it silently on each out breath for about twenty breaths. Then change to the syllable "Om" for about twenty breaths. The intellectual mind links a word it knows like "sad" with a chain of old memories and emotions that sweep us away from now and here. The mind tries to grapple with the unknown word of a mantra and cannot, so it relaxes while staying alert for possible meaning. A mantra thumbtacks the mind to this place of life, the present moment.

A mantra or dharani can be especially effective in times of emotional distress. When a calamity has occurred—we lose a job, a lover leaves, a parent or child dies—the mind becomes distraught and obsessed. In our fear and grief the mind becomes a wailing, chaotic thing at a time when we most need to rest and have clarity. This is when a mantra can help. The Buddha gave a series of prescriptions for the unquiet mind including distracting it, substituting something more wholesome for it to think on, or, finally, crushing the thoughts. Chanting a holy name or a mantra can do all of these. Chanted quietly internally it distracts and calms, chanted out loud and powerfully it can crush thought.

If the mantra is chanted aloud, the musical tone resonates in the body. The syllable Ah is said to be the sound of the fundamental energy of all created things. The musical note "A" on the Western scale is said to be the fundamental tone of this resonance, with harmonics unfolding in an array around it.

When the name of Jizo Bodhisattva or the dharani is recited wholeheartedly, the sound vibrations interact with the body/heart/mind to unfold certain expanded states of awareness. As we experience these states we become aware, even faintly, of the vast clear consciousness of beings we call Buddhas and bodhisattvas. We are inspired to continue to practice until our awareness opens into theirs.

MAKING A VOW

Shakyamuni Buddha said, "Earth Store, I now carefully entrust the multitudes of men and gods of the future to you. If they plant good roots in the Buddha Dharma, be they as little as a hair, dust

mote, grain of sand or drop of water, please use your spiritual pow-
ers and virtues to protect them so that they gradually cultivate the
unsurpassed way and do not retreat from it."

Kshitigarbha knelt down with clasped hands and spoke to
Shakyamuni Buddha, "Honored of the World, please do not be
worried. If good men and women in the future have even a single
thought of respect for the Buddha's teachings, I shall use hundreds
of thousands of expedient devices to lead them out of the suffering
of constant Birth and Death to liberation. Those who have heard
of good deeds and practiced them I will help to proceed to Bud-
dhahood without falling back."

The *Earth Store Sutra* tells of ordinary human beings becoming
bodhisattvas through the power of their vows. My teachers talked
often about the importance of making vows. It took me many years
to understand that vows are at the core of practice, actually are the
"nuclear" core of the energy pile that is our life. An interviewer
once asked Maezumi Roshi if Buddhists believed in something like
a soul that continued after death. Maezumi Roshi said, "No. It is the
vow that continues." A vow is like a seal that imprints itself on the
wet clay of another emerging life, but it is more than a passive seal.
It has a propelling energy. It propels us into the search for an end to
suffering and into finding ways to help others. Finally, when all the
various schemes we have developed to do those things fail, it propels us into practice.

All Buddhist practices involve vows. At the Zen Center we chant
the Four Great Bodhisattva Vows every day:

Beings are numberless, I vow to free them.
Desires are inexhaustible, I vow to put an end to them.
Dharma gates are boundless, I vow to enter them.
Buddha's way is unsurpassable, I vow to embody it.

Over the years we have chanted vows like these hundreds, thousands of times. It does not matter if the vows were made when we
were half-asleep or if we didn't quite understand them. We have
made these promises and now the jig is up, the promissory note is
due. This explains the common feeling people have. "I don't know

why I practice, I just have to." "Something is compelling me to do this practice." The ongoing vow operates below the conscious mind.

It is very important to shape and say our vows. Maezumi Roshi recommended starting each day with vows. There are many possible vows. They can be a simple. "I vow to do what I can to relieve suffering." "I vow to do what needs to be done to awaken fully, even if I'm afraid at times." "I vow to open my mind and hands and let go of what needs to be dropped for me and others to be free." Vows can be formal and part of a ritual. They can be simple and spontaneous. What is important is to vow. At that point the things that are needed for the vow to be fulfilled begin to flow toward us.

Jizo Bodhisattva is called the King of Vows. When we call upon the power of Jizo we are calling upon the power in each one of us that is always urging us in the direction of fulfilling our life vow or purpose. For all of us the fundamental vow is actually the same, to uncover and embody our innate wisdom and compassion. For each of us the specific situation that helps us with the uncovering and the embodying is different. It could be having a difficult child, caring for an elderly parent, working an extra job to earn money for retreats, or driving a city bus in a poor part of the city. When we are in the midst of these specifics, we often lose track of our larger purpose. We get angry or impatient and feel like we are failing. This is the time to call upon Jizo Bodhisattva.

CALLING UPON JIZO BODHISATTVA

The *Earth Store Bodhisattva Sutra* tells of the benefits of calling on Jizo for help.

> *There are people who have insufficient clothing and food, who are sick and fall into bad luck, whose families quarrel, whose relatives are scattered, whose sleep is poor because of nightmares. If they hear the name or see an image of Earth Store Bodhisattva and recite his name with sincerity and respect ten thousand times, these problems will disappear. Their needs will be supplied and they will become peaceful and happy even in their dreams.*
>
> *If men or women must enter mountain forests, cross over rivers, or seas, or travel on dangerous roads in order to earn a living, or*

Jizo of the Night, who watches over those who cry out and suffer alone in the dark.
Print by the author.

because of the public good, or because of urgent matters of life and death, they should first recite the name of Earth Store Bodhisattva a full ten thousand times. The ghosts and spirits of the ground they pass over will surround and protect them as they walk, stand, sit, and lie down.

Reciting the name of Jizo or the Jizo dharani is putting forth a request for help—help in attaining that great awareness that creates bodhisattvas from ordinary humans. However, if it is true that our own thoughts, speech, and actions can either keep us trapped in the maze of the six realms or can place us on the path that leads out of that maze, where is there a place for Jizo Bodhisattva? Is salvation only a pull-myself-up-by-my-own-bootstraps-and-sheer-force-of-will operation or is there "another," unseen by our ordinary eyes, that we can call on for help?

Our experience of reality is very confined. Evidence of this is all around us. For example, we cannot hear many sounds dogs respond to and we cannot see the infrared patterns on flowers that provide information to birds and moths. In the air all around us is an invisible energy flow filled with pictures, sounds, and other information. If we have the right receiving equipment we can perceive these as "real" things such as radar signals, television soap tragedies, radio news programs, and cellular phone calls between lovers or to 911 for emergency help. It is obvious that there is a great deal of hidden information, many unnoticed forces and unseen existences around us all the time.

There is a story from the time of the Buddha about this. Mogallana, one of the Buddha's chief disciples, descended from Vulture Peak for alms rounds. At a certain place in the road he smiled for no apparent reason. His companion monk was puzzled and asked the reason. Mogallana told him he would explain what had happened when they were in the presence of the Buddha. When they had rejoined the Buddha, the monk again asked Mogallana the reason for his smile. Mogallana said he had seen miserable ghosts flying through the air. They had many forms: a skeleton, a lump of flesh, a man eating dung, a man pierced by his hair which was made of needles. He had smiled in wonder at being able to see the working of karma that created these experiences. The other monks accused

Mogallana of claiming "further powers," that is, of being more enlightened than he was, but the Buddha verified that what Mogallana had seen was indeed true and was therefore not cause for either
jealousy or blame.

If there are unseen energies and beings around us, if some of
these are able to assist us in our spiritual quest, and if we do not call
on them for aid, is that not the height of pride, the kind of hubris that
characterizes the realm of the gods and leads to their downfall? Buddhists in Japan talk of *jinriki*, "self power," and *tanriki*, "other power"
or "power from the other side." This "other side" is not outside of our
self; it is just currently hidden from us by our clouded perception,
just as the beings and karmic forces the Buddha and Mogallana saw
were hidden from the perception of the other monks. When this
other side is concealed, we have to call upon it in faith. Its hidden
nature helps to develop and strengthen our faith-mind. We are calling to—and thus calling forth—Jizo Bodhisattva.

A dedication for our chants says, "When this request is sent
forth it is perceived and subtly answered." That a response comes
is not a matter of belief. It is simply a matter of physics, of cause
and effect. It is the "subtly answered" part that is tricky. Sometimes
the answer is so subtle we miss it if we're not alert, and sometimes it seems to come from a source with a warm but wicked
sense of humor.

We are told that Jizo responds to those who call upon her with
single-minded devotion. Because we cannot know all of the causes
that are producing a certain effect, and because we do not usually
know what barrier within ourselves or others is preventing a certain
effect, we call on Jizo with a simple and humble faith. Jizo is said to
open people's hearts to be able to see their wrongdoing and its
cause. This faith is simple because we ourselves are simple; we are
just one tiny birth-and-death interval manifesting from the eternal
Whole. This faith is humble because we are immensely fortunate.
As we open more fully to the great Whole so also opens our awe and
gratitude to be manifesting as the very body-mind of the Whole.

As we call upon Jizo we may envision what this bodhisattva
might look like. How would great wisdom and compassion appear
when embodied in a human body? How do our own body, mind,
and heart appear when wisdom and compassion manifest fully?

Making Offerings to Jizo Bodhisattva

Wholeheartedly make offerings to Earth Store Bodhisattva using scented flowers, incense, food, drink, clothing, colored silks, banners with sacred texts, money, jewels, . . . lighting oil lamps, reciting the holy sutras . . .

Another practice recommended in the *Earth Store Bodhisattva Sutra* is making offerings. We are used to buying and reserving the best things for ourselves. We spend time and money on favorite foods, on clothing that we think makes us look attractive, on jewelry or expensive watches, and in fixing up our homes. This fundamentally selfish orientation begins early, as part of an ancient survival drive. We watch our mother carefully as she cuts a cake. Who will get the biggest piece? My mother solved this by making one girl cut, the other choose the first piece. A difficult choice: should I follow my instincts and choose the biggest piece or demonstrate my unselfish nature for all to see by taking the smaller? This selfish stance dissolves only when we really love someone. Our in-turned energy flows outward; their happiness comes first. We are glad to give them a gift—the biggest piece.

Making an offering is an active practice that helps us open that me-first center. The Zen cook makes an offering of food to the Buddha on the altar before each meal. After a meal is prepared, small amounts of each dish are placed in three miniature eating bowls on a ceremonial tray. The cook makes three full prostrations to the offering, then takes it to the zendo where the meditators are seated with their own eating bowls opened. The cook thus offers the first portion of all food to be eaten to the Buddha on the altar.

This practice of offering signifies our willingness to share what we have, both material goods and spiritual benefit, with all who are in need. It is a three-times-a-day reminder of generosity. The offering transforms us into a host, one who welcomes the Buddhas and bodhisattvas into our home each day with an altar table set with fresh food, clear water, flowers, and candlelight. It reminds us to be generous, to be willing to share what we have with the teeming hungry ghosts who populate even—maybe even more so—this richest of countries. The food is offered to the Buddhas, bodhisattvas, hungry ghosts first, before we have taken even one bite. This indicates what our priorities are: first, our spiritual practice and helping others; second, our own basic needs.

The traditional offerings described in the sutra are offerings to the five senses. Flowers and incense are lovely to smell. Candlelight and jewels delight the eye. Music or chanting is a practice of the ears. Food and drink appeal to the tongue. Bowing is a practice of the whole body touching the earth. The mind is open and quiet. When we open our senses in this way we are offering up our whole selves. Everything we call "dead" is given back life.

The pause created by the food offering and the meal chants before we "dig in" helps us remember where things come from. Where do the food, drink, and eating bowls come from? What about the clothes, the metal, the glass, and the jewels we wear, even the money we donate? They all come from and ultimately return to the earth—as do we. We are reminded that everything we have including the body and mind we call "mine" is actually borrowed. Borrowed from the domain—the treasury house—of Earth Store Bodhisattva. This is the practice of being a guest.

The traditional offerings are offerings of each of the five elements. They are pure water, jewels from the earth, music from the movement of air, flowers representing wood, and candlelight or oil lamps as fire. These offerings, given one at a time, remind us that we are a very temporary assemblage of the same elements. They continuously offer themselves to form our life. We offer a small part back to indicate that we recognize this and are grateful.

If you have a Jizo image in your home, you can do the practice of making offerings. This is the practice of being a host, of seeing every being as a guest. You offer your guest fresh flowers, a candle, a cup of clean water, and fruit. You can make an offering of a small portion of the food from the evening meal, bowing before your honored guest on the altar, before you begin eating yourself.

MAKING IMAGES OF JIZO BODHISATTVA

In the *Sutra of the Past Vows of Earth Store Bodhisattva,* an earth spirit named Firm and Solid speaks to the Buddha. He says that he has worshiped all the innumerable bodhisattvas but regards Earth Store Bodhisattva as having the weightiest vow because the vow has no end. The earth spirit says,

*A tiny Jizo made sponta-
neously from a silkworm
cocoon by a seven-year-old
Japanese boy when his fa-
ther died suddenly of a
heart attack. The blotch
over the heart is red.*

*World Honored One, looking at beings living in the present and
future I see people making shrines of earth, stone, bamboo, or
wood. They place within the shrines an image of Earth Store Bodhisattva, either carved, painted, or made of gold, silver, copper or
iron. Then they burn incense and make offerings, worship and
praise him. By doing these things they will receive ten kinds of advantages and benefits.*

The earth spirit vows to use all his spiritual powers to protect
these people day and night from floods, fire, theft, calamity, and
accidents.

The stories in the *Earth Store Bodhisattva Sutra* of those who became Earth Store Bodhisattva are stories of everyday men and
women who were moved by human suffering and vowed to do what
they could to help. That Jizo Bodhisattva and the Buddha himself
were human is wonderfully inspiring. It inspires us not to become
overwhelmed or defeated by difficulties that arise, but to use whatever transformation body we have been endowed with and the tools
in our very hands to help chip away whatever prevents us from manifesting the qualities of Jizo.

To make an image of Jizo Bodhisattva is to affirm that such a being could exist, a being composed of generosity, benevolence, optimism, determination, and fearlessness. In the work of portraying this image in paint, clay, stone, or metal, we call out and magnify those qualities nascent in ourselves.

Once I read a true story of a young man named David who was cast as Jesus in a movie. He was not a Christian, but he felt the weight of the responsibility of portraying a man whose simple short life had changed the world. He decided to become Jesus as completely as possible, not taking off the costume or the way of being for the several months the movie was in production. He did not mingle with other cast members during breaks but remained alone and quiet. After he had immersed himself in the role of Jesus for a few weeks, strange things began to happen. Others in the cast began to come to him with their problems. He found, with the qualities he had assumed to portray Jesus, he was able to see these people with a new and genuine love. His compassion and wisdom caused more people to come to him for guidance even after the filming of the movie ended. For weeks afterward he found himself living as Jesus, helping people as Jesus did. He said, "I forgot that I was David and thought that I was Jesus. Afterward I had to forget that I was Jesus and remember that I was David."

We all have this problem. We are immersed in the movie called "my life," written, produced, narrated by, and starring—me. We have forgotten that we are the Buddha and live instead as unhappy men and women. If we can step out of the movie even once, even briefly, the spell will be broken and we will begin to remember who we really are. Then all those around us will also become free.

When I began to make images of Jizo Bodhisattva I discovered that the face was most important. I saw that people chose the statues they wanted by picking them up and scrutinizing the faces, so I finished each one carefully with attention to their expressions. As orders began coming in, I couldn't keep up. I asked students for help working on the Jizos during a sesshin. Afterward I looked at the little clay Jizos and was astounded. Their faces had all been changed! Some now had long pointed noses, some had fatter cheeks, some had thin wide lips. When I saw one Jizo with its mouth screwed up to the side exactly like one woman's characteristic expression, I realized what had happened. As each person worked on the Jizo's face, he or she had unconsciously adjusted it to look like him- or herself. My husband was skeptical about this discovery until the next interesting event occurred.

I had made a few small Jizo statues and sent them to Japan for Harada Roshi to give as gifts. Months thereafter we went to Japan for several weeks of Zen training. Harada Roshi had asked the lay-woman who did the temple sewing to come measure my husband and me for new kimonos since the indigo on our new robes had rubbed off, dyeing our old kimonos—and our hands—blue. As we sat waiting in a small tearoom there was a tap on the shoji screen next to me. I slid the screen open and found myself face-to-face with a middle-aged Japanese woman. She froze, then exclaimed in Japanese, "I know you! Haven't I met you before?" I demurred, saying I had never met her. She looked flustered at her rude and very un-Japanese outburst, then came in and sat down. She studied my face surreptitiously. In a few minutes she burst out once more, "Surely I have seen you somewhere!" then colored again with embarrassment. As Roshi whisked tea the conversation went on. Suddenly she smiled and exclaimed, "I know where I've seen you before! Your face is on my little Jizo!"

In doing this practice of making an image of Jizo you can use any medium—paint, clay, wood, photo, papier-mâché. It can be as transient as a hundred images of Jizo outlined in the sand at the beach with a stick and wiped away by the incoming tide. It can be as solid as a statue carved of stone. Some people make a vow to undertake the making of a hundred or ten thousand Jizo images. The images can be given away to those in need, placed on a Jizo altar, or left to stand guard in the forest.

This is the practice of making images of Jizo Bodhisattva. As we make Jizo ourselves, we make ourselves into Jizo.

TRADITIONAL TIMES AND SITUATIONS FOR PRACTICE WITH JIZO BODHISATTVA

The traditional time for veneration of Ti-tsang in China and Jizo Bodhisattva in Japan is the twenty-fourth day of the seventh lunar month. In modern times this is celebrated in either July or August in different areas of Japan. This often coincides with the early autumn festival of the dead called Ullambana (Obon in Japan). On the birthday of Jizo, the thirtieth day of the seventh month, the festival of the dead comes to an end and hell is closed. Jizo then asks the Ten Kings of Hell for forgiveness of those who repent of their misdeeds. This is a particular time to remember those who have died and to confess and make amends for past misdeeds.

Sickness and Death

The *Earth Store Bodhisattva Sutra* tells of specific situations when practice with Earth Store Bodhisattva is helpful.

> *Since all beings have such [bad] habits their parents or relatives should create merit for them when they are on the verge of dying in order to assist them on the road ahead. This may be done by hanging banners and canopies, lighting lamps, reciting the holy sutras or making offerings before images of Bodhisattvas or sages. It includes recitation of the names of Buddhas and Bodhisattvas . . . in such a way that the recitation of each name passes by the ear of the dying one and is heard in his fundamental consciousness.*

The sutra recommends that something of value belonging to the one who is ill, such as clothing, jewels, gardens, or houses, should be offered at the temple. The sick person should be told that this is being done on their behalf.

> *Men or women may be bedridden with a long illness and in spite of their wishes be unable either to get well or to die. In this instance this sutra should be recited once in a loud voice before the Buddhas and Bodhisattvas and possessions which the sick one loves, such as clothing, jewels, gardens or houses should be offered, saying before the sick person, "Before this sutra and image I give all these items on behalf of this sick person."*

In addition to reciting the names of the Buddhas the sutra recommends chanting the name of Kshitigarbha one thousand times a day for as many as one hundred days or chanting the entire sutra itself once a day for three, seven, or forty-nine days. The sutra proscribes blood sacrifices, recommending that vegetarian food be prepared and offered to the Buddha and to the monks. The practices of chanting and making offerings are continued during the dying process and in the forty-nine days after death. This is a time when consciousness is in transition and there may be benefit from spiritual effort directed toward the person who has died.

Japanese Buddhists observe forty-nine days of mourning after a person's death. This practice seems to have evolved out of the cosmology of the Chinese *Ten Kings' Sutra*. The forty-nine days are divided into seven separate seven-day periods of transition. At the end of each seven-day interval the person is said to come before the Buddhas and bodhisattvas. With their help the person will be able to make progress toward becoming a Buddha and entering the realm of enlightened beings. Relatives and friends who wish to help the deceased along this path are encouraged to use the entire forty-nine days as a time for daily meditation and religious services. In Shingon practice a different deity is petitioned at the end of each seven-day interval. Jizo Bodhisattva (Kshitigarbha) is the deity for the fifth seventh day, that is, the thirty-fifth day after death. On the night preceding the thirty-fifth day, offerings should be made to Jizo with recitation of the Jizo dharani.

Birth

> If there are [those] who have newborn sons or daughters they should recite this inconceivable sutra and recite the Bodhisattva's name a full ten thousand times within seven days before the child's birth. If that newly born child was to have had a disastrous life he will be liberated from it and will be peaceful, happy, easily raised and long lived.

Expectant parents can set up a Jizo altar and recite the Jizo dharani for the benefit of the unborn child. We know that after birth infants are able to recognize voices they have heard in utero. How beneficial for them to hear, very early in embodied life, the sounds of good music or of spiritual practice.

Travel

> Good men and women of the future who must enter mountain forests, cross over rivers, seas and great waters, or pass through dangerous roads for the sake of earning their own livelihood, for pub-

lic affairs, matters of life and death, or other urgent business, should first recite the name of Earth Store Bodhisattva a full ten thousand times. The ghosts and spirits of the ground they pass over will always surround and protect them in their walking, standing, sitting and lying down. The peace and happiness of those persons will constantly be guarded, so that even if they encounter tigers, wolves, lions or other harmful evil creatures, the beasts will be unable to hurt them.

We may not be afraid of encountering lions, but we are not free of fear as we travel. The mind conjures up freeway snipers, people who drop rocks from overpasses, muggers at stoplights, black ice, drunk drivers, hijackers, and airline crashes. Anxiety makes us suffer. It does not make us safe. Reciting the Jizo dharani when we are afraid can help keep us safe by making the mind relaxed and alert and the heart open and at ease. Many people take a small statue of Jizo with them when they travel. They can be carried in a small traveling altar that can be tucked in a suitcase and set up in a hotel or guest room.

Difficulty Remembering the Sutra

The *Earth Store Bodhisattva Sutra* recommends that those with memory problems place a bowl of clear water in front of an image of Jizo for one night and day, then face south and drink the water. *As the water is about to enter their mouth they should be particularly sincere and earnest.* Then they must keep the precepts for seven to twenty-one days afterward, abstaining from lying, killing, sexual activity, eating meat or rich foods, and from alcohol. This will endow them with the ability to understand and remember the sutra.

How might this work? Certainly alcohol befuddles the mind. Eating too much or indulging in too much sex makes us dull, sleepy. When we tell one lie, it somehow gives birth to another and soon our mind is tense, occupied with trying to remember to whom we told what and with anxiety over the lie being found out. Leading a disciplined life and keeping the precepts supports a mind that is wise and able to remember. One student decided to undertake the discipline of not watching videos or television. At the end of a week he was overjoyed. He said, "I got my life back!" He had gained an extra two to four hours of time each day, some of which he devoted to meditation. In just a few days his mind became more lucid and stable.

PRACTICING WITH THE QUALITIES OF EARTH STORE BODHISATTVA

Earth Store Bodhisattva is described as having a number of wonderful qualities. These include compassion and benevolence, supreme optimism, lack of fear, an irreversible vow, unflagging determination, taking full responsibility, equanimity, and active engagement in everyday life. These are aspects of the earth, and as Earth Store Bodhisattva is rooted deeply and continuously in the earth, these qualities are naturally present. If we are, even unknowingly, division bodies of Earth Store Bodhisattva, these are our own innate qualities. There are specific Buddhist practices that help us develop these nascent qualities and to let go of whatever impedes their emergence and free functioning.

Equanimity

A Shingon text says, "Kshitagarbha Bodhisattva does not get angry or give up even though he may be trampled upon and stepped on as if he were the earth." This image comes from the instructions of the Buddha to his eighteen-year-old son, Rahula.

> *Rahula, develop meditation that is like the earth; for when you develop meditation that is like the earth, arisen agreeable and disagreeable contacts will not invade your mind and remain. Just as people throw clean things and dirty things, excrement, urine, spittle, pus, and blood on the earth, and the earth is not horrified, humiliated and disgusted because of that, so too, Rahula, develop meditation that is like the earth; for when you develop meditation that is like the earth, arisen agreeable and disagreeable contacts will not invade your mind and remain.*

The word equanimity comes from the Latin *aequo animo*, meaning an "even mind." This even, balanced mind is one of the effects we hope for in practice. The earth bears all kinds of action with equanimity. Earth has such a huge awareness-body that all the open mining pits and nuclear explosions are less than a mosquito landing on its skin and drilling in.

The practice associated with this quality is the meditation on the earth taught to Rahula. If we could develop a continuous awareness of the earth beneath us, we would need no other practice. We already have great faith in the Earth Store body. Every time we take a step, we trust that the earth will be under our feet. Expanding that faith into consciousness of the perpetual presence and support of the earth, we develop equanimity.

The *Earth Store Bodhisattva Sutra* says, "All the grasses, woods, sands, stones, paddy fields, hemp, bamboo, reeds, grains, rice and gems come forth from the ground." Meditate upon the parts of your body from the hairs on the head to the toenails. Include everything, teeth, saliva, bones, urine, feces, muscles, blood—can you find anything that does not come from the earth? Truly we are born from and nourished by the earth womb.

Benevolence

Benevolence means a disposition to do good. We might understand it best as parental mind. Those who are not parents still have parental heart-mind. Even people who do not get along well with other humans often are caring and careful with animals, children, or even plants. What are the qualities of small children and animals that evoke benevolence in us? They are innocence, purity, and vulnerability. Earth Store Bodhisattva is benevolent because she sees all beings in this way.

We are innocent because our wrongdoing comes from wrong understanding, born of the confusion of turbid minds. We are pure because at our core we have a pure bright and open heart. We are vulnerable to greed, anger, and ignorance, to the machinations of small mind, to "bad habits," to becoming "obstinate," and to clinging to improper behavior. We are vulnerable because our life is fragile as a ball of foam floating on a stream.

One practice to cultivate the benevolence of Earth Store Bodhisattva is to envision a baby Buddha in each person's heart. Our proper relationship toward a baby it is that of a parent. We can be patient when we see small children who are stubborn, rude, have bad habits, or throw temper tantrums. The emergence of these baby Buddhas requires us not to be distracted by their clever disguises or odd antics, but to love and guide them as they grow.

No Fear

How is Kshitagarbha able to have no fear? We sometimes have bad dreams. Perhaps I have a dream that I have been shot in the leg. In the dream I am crying and afraid. I awaken and am no longer afraid. Why? A dream body can't be harmed. A dream cannot hurt the real body. The brief dream of our lives, even if nightmarish, cannot hurt the Real Body.

Practices to cultivate no fear are the meditations on the five elements, on death, and on impermanence. Earth Store Bodhisattva is unafraid because he knows that our fear is, like a dream, only a state of mind. What we are afraid will be harmed is a collection of five elements that will soon fall apart and return to the great earth body it emerged from. He is no more afraid of this than of the disappearance of a mirage or a play of shadows on moving water. Flux cannot hurt flux, impermanence cannot hurt impermanence.

Fully Responsible

Earth Store Bodhisattva has taken full responsibility for "carrying across" all beings who suffer. We are also fully responsible, for our own practice and for our eventual release from suffering. It is not the sangha's fault or the teacher's fault if we do not have equanimity, wisdom, and loving-kindness.

We are fully responsible for creating our own hell, hot, sterile, futile, an endless source of suffering. We are responsible for freeing ourself and others from it, and entering that place that is cool, quenched, fertile, gentle, an endless source of renewal. We have to be very careful, however, not to become confused about what responsibility means. It does not mean that if bad or difficult things occur such as catching a cold or having someone we love become ill and die, that we are at fault and should feel guilty. It means that we are responsible for how we react to these circumstances that cause and effect brings to us. Yatsutani Roshi gave the example of someone who is put in prison and can choose to use the time there either to become a more cunning criminal or to begin a serious spiritual practice. Our place of choice and action is in the present. It is our responsibility, our privilege, and our joy to bring ourselves out of ignorance and reactivity, to dig into our own earth and uncover our own hidden potential.

Engaged in Life

In Japan Jizo Bodhisattva is found everywhere. This means that Jizo is never far from someone who needs help. Of all the bodhisattvas, Jizo is felt to be accessible, even interested in the problems of daily human life.

We are all engaged in life. We can't help it. We are alive. But how much more alive and happy we feel when our body and mind are fully engaged. A practice to cultivate this factor is to meditate with the flow of impermanence. With each breath we step into the next moment awake and curious. When resistance arises we ride the out breath and move through. For example, if there is resistance to getting up in the morning, lie still and become aware of the movement of breath in and out. Ride the movement of the out breath up and out of bed.

We can surrender our life as Jizo has done and live it fully. It requires giving up our neurotic preoccupation with the collection of five elements and mind-events we call our life. When we are not the center, then we are unhindered, free to be engaged to heal the human world in whatever way is appropriate. We could go on a medical relief mission. We could send money. We could help homeless people in our own city. We could intensify our practice to clarify what our place of assistance is and how to function better in it. All are needed. All our lives are the division bodies of Earth Store Bodhisattva, given life for the purpose of healing the human world.

Unquenchable Optimism

Many people lose their initial joy and optimism in practice after a few years. They become depressed and worried because they cannot tell if they are making spiritual progress. This is because the changes due to practice are deep, below the level of operation of the conscious mind. The more objective observers of the fruit of practice are those on the outside, those impacted by how we speak, think, and act. The second reason you cannot measure progress is that it is actually antiprogress. It is not the process of gaining something the self can measure, compare, and feel proud of, but rather of letting go of that which relentlessly judges, criticizes, makes up ways to compete, and wants always to win.

Optimism can be cultivated if we meditate upon the qualities of enlightenment and know that they are already present in us, working their way out to full expression. We cannot know the time scale in which this will occur. We can only optimize the conditions for the birth of the baby Buddha within.

KOANS ABOUT JIZO

Here are several koans about Jizo Bodhisattva that were used by Zen masters during the Kamakura era in Japan. They are from a collection called the *Warrior Koans*, named for the fierce men and women of the samurai class for whose training the koans were devised. Zen students would ponder the koan night and day until they had a breakthrough. The master checked the authenticity and depth of their realization using testing questions, as few of which are included here.

Koans are studied under the guidance of a qualified Zen teacher. The essence of koan practice is to absorb yourself so thoroughly in the koan that you become it, it is an event in your own life. Then the realization that occurred in the koan also opens for you.

Jizo Stands Up

> The image in the great hall at Kenchō-ji was a wooden Jizo seated on a lotus throne. The samurai Mamiya Munekatsu confined himself to the hall for 21 days, vowing to make Jizo stand up. He continuously recited the Jizo mantra, "OM KA KA KABI SAN MAEI SOHA KA!" On the last night he was running around the hall like a mad man, shouting, "Holy Jizo, stand up!"
>
> At two o'clock in the morning the monk on night watch rounds struck a single blow on the sounding board in front of the hall. Munekatsu suddenly had a realization, and cried, "Holy Jizo, it's not he that stands up, and it's not he that sits down. He has a life that is neither standing nor sitting."

Testing question: What is the life of Jizo apart from standing or sitting?

The Very First Jizo

> The samurai Koresada entered the main hall at Kenchō-ji and prayed to the Jizo of a Thousand Forms there. Then he asked the monk in charge of the hall, "Of these thousand forms of Jizo, which is the very first Jizo?" The monk said, "In the mind of the man before me are a thousand thoughts and ten thousand fantasies. Which of these is the very first?"
>
> The samurai was silent. The monk then said, "Of the thousand forms of Jizo, the very first Jizo is the Buddha-lord who is always using those thousand forms." The warrior asked, "Who is this Buddha-lord?" The monk suddenly caught him and twisted his nose. The samurai's mind immediately opened.

Testing question: Which is the very first Jizo out of the thousand forms of Jizo?

Honored Jizo

> A general asked the priest of Jōmyō-ji temple to borrow an ink drawing of Honored Jizo to use as a protective charm with his battle armor. The priest exclaimed, "Honored General!" "Yes?" "Who is it that said, 'Yes?' Honored Jizo is there. Do not go seeking for another!" The general had a realization.

Testing question: When you paint a picture of Jizo, does it happen that you become Jizo or does Jizo become you?

What Are the Benefits of Practicing with Earth Store Bodhisattva?

The Buddha praises Earth Store Bodhisattva's activity and tells of the benefits and blessings that will be experienced by those who revere her, chant her name, or make images of Kshitigarbha. These benefits encompass all common human desires including long life, good health, beautiful features, prosperity, good sleep, sharp mental faculties and memory, an extension of these benefits to family members in the past and future, freedom from accidents and natural disaster, and harmony and happiness in the family.

> *The Buddha told Empty Space Treasury Bodhisattva, "Listen attentively, listen attentively, I shall enumerate them and describe them to you. If there are good men or women in the future who see Earth Store Bodhisattva's image, or who hear this sutra or read and recite it; who use incense, flowers, food and drink, clothing, or gems as offerings; or if they praise, gaze upon, and worship him, they will benefit in twenty-eight ways:*

1. *Gods and dragons will be mindful of them and protect them,*
2. *The fruits of their goodness will increase daily,*
3. *They will accumulate superior causes of sagehood,*
4. *They will not retreat from Bodhi [being awakened],*
5. *Their food and drink will be abundant,*
6. *Epidemics will not touch them,*
7. *They will not encounter disasters of fire and water,*
8. *They will not have any difficulties with thieves or armed robbers,*
9. *They will be respected by all who see them,*
10. *They will be aided by ghosts and spirits,*
11. *Women will be reborn as men,*
12. *If born as women they will be daughters of kings and ministers,*
13. *They will have handsome features,*
14. *They will often be born in the heavens,*
15. *They may be emperors or kings,*
16. *They will know their past lives,*
17. *They will attain whatever they seek,*
18. *Their families will be happy,*
19. *All disasters will be eradicated,*
20. *They will be eternally apart from bad karmic paths,*
21. *They will always arrive at their destinations,*
22. *At night their dreams will be peaceful and happy,*
23. *Their deceased ancestors will leave suffering behind,*
24. *And they will receive the blessings from their former lives to aid their rebirth,*

25. *They will be praised by the sages,*
26. *They will be intelligent and they will have sharp features,*
27. *They will have magnanimous, kind, and sympathetic hearts,*
28. *They will ultimately realize Buddhahood.*

There are some benefits listed here that sound desirable but also some that might sound odd. Many are things we take for granted in America in the twenty-first century: to have abundant food and drink, to be intelligent and have sharp senses, to arrive at our destinations, and to be freed from epidemics, floods, and fires. None of these could be counted on ten centuries ago when this sutra was written. A quarter or a third of the population could be wiped out in one epidemic of plague, measles, smallpox, or influenza. Those who did survive could be blind, deaf, or mentally damaged. Starvation was one summer's drought away. Fire devastated cities like Kyoto and London repeatedly. Travel was perilous and arrival at a destination uncertain.

Benefits eleven and twelve might cause a reaction among modern women. But we shouldn't take these as chauvinistic. In many cultures and times to be born as a woman meant life in servitude. If you did not have a man to protect you—a father, husband, or adult son—you had no place to live, no means of support, were a target for rape and likely to starve. Only a female in a wealthy family would be guaranteed food, shelter, safety, and enough leisure time for spiritual endeavors. This list of favorable conditions points to a body, heart, and mind that are relatively free from fear, ill health, constant anxiety, and constant work. They are conditions favorable to practice.

The *Earth Store Bodhisattva Sutra* states many times the potential rewards from worship of Earth Store Bodhisattva. This is not just a method for guaranteeing perpetuation of the sutra and veneration of Jizo, but it verifies a common experience. If we practice wholeheartedly, things will happen that will open up means and ways for wider and deeper practice. Rather than the experience of "we are practicing," the practice begins to practice us. The way of the bodhisattva manifests through each transformed and undivided life.

MULTIPLYING THE MERIT

The spiritual benefit of practices with Earth Store Bodhisattva can be multiplied by the process called dedicating or transferring the merit. We do this during a day of retreat, chanting, "We dedicate this merit to all those who are ill . . ." or in our vows, "For the sake of all suffering sentient beings we vow . . ." This means that we are not taking any benefit from the practice to ourselves alone, but are giving it away to benefit others. As this good passes through the chain of cause and effect, it is multiplied. It can be imagined in this simple way: If you smile at a post office or grocery clerk, his spirits may lift. He may be more kind and helpful to fifty people he sees that day. Those fifty people may in turn affect positively several hundred others. Good actions and bad actions multiply rapidly in this way. The *Earth Store Bodhisattva Sutra* commends generosity to the poor, the aged, to those who are ill, and to women giving birth. It recommends the practices of repairing temples that are old or destroyed, restoring old sutras, and donating to monks, temples, or to Buddhas.

Some of the practices recommended by the sutra may seem, and indeed might be, self-serving, designed to perpetuate the sutra itself, the worship of Kshitigarbha, and to ensure donations to monks and temples. As the sutra says, Kshitigarbha can help those who perform even a good deed as small as a mote of dust. Good is always the seed for more good.

chapter thirteen

A *Simple Ceremony* of *Remembrance*

for *Children Who Have Died*

THE PRACTICE WITH JIZO Bodhisattva that is finding a place in the liturgy and yearly cycle of ceremonies at many Zen centers in America is the ceremony of remembrance for children who have died. Guidelines for this ceremony were developed by Zen teacher Yvonne Jikai Rand, who studied the Jizo tradition in Japan and carefully adapted it to practice in the West. The liturgy is derived from a ceremony she and Robert Aitken Roshi created and also contains elements from ceremonies conducted by Maezumi Roshi. I have altered the language somewhat to make it more accessible to the non-Buddhists who attend our ceremonies. The marks for the bells and percussion instruments that are traditionally used in chanting the sutras and dharanis have not been included here as they vary somewhat among practice centers.

GENERAL GUIDELINES

Location

The ceremony usually is held in a remembrance garden, a place where Jizo statues can remain and remembrance tokens can remain undisturbed as they weather and fade away. Ideally the garden can be visited by families who wish to return and meditate there at a later time.

Who Attends

Only people who are participating in the ceremony may attend. Observers like reporters are not allowed unless they participate fully. They should not be taking notes. Those who staff the ceremony must also participate—that is, make remembrances for a child who has died. Participants may not know one another, and the privacy of grief for the most sensitive participant is respected. Thus taking photos is not allowed during the ceremony.

Staffing the Ceremony

Because the ceremony is related to a funeral or memorial service, we have an ordained priest direct the ceremony here, as we do in Japan. We find it is best to have two people staff the ceremony jointly. Although rare, occasionally a participant becomes emotionally overwhelmed and needs help. The assistant can provide this while the priest remains with the rest of the group. The priest should have the experience and training necessary to maintain a ceremonial space or vessel that can contain a large amount of grief.

Preparations for the Ceremony

Preparations for the ceremony are held indoors, in a room where people can be quiet and comfortable together, where they can grieve, where intrusions will not occur. Any supplies for sewing or constructing remembrances, tissues, brochures from relevant organizations, and for a tea after the ceremony should be set out ahead of time so participants can be greeted and made welcome as they arrive.

Introducing the Ceremony

A brief explanation should be given of what will occur during the time of preparation and during the ceremony. This includes the reason for maintaining silence except for simple (and optional) statements by participants about whom they are there to remember.

A brief history of Jizo Bodhisattva and the mizuko ceremony of remembrance for children can be given.

Preparing Remembrances

About an hour is spent making small garments or simple toys for the
children. If people finish early they can sit quietly in the room or
walk outside. A bell signals people to gather for the actual ceremony. Everyone walks together to the garden or forest location for
the ceremony.

The Service

The service consists of several chants followed by a dedication that
includes the names of the children being remembered. The leader
can choose chants and a dedication that are appropriate to their own
tradition. They may wish to reword chants to make them more accessible to participants who are not Buddhists. At some time during
the service the participants offer incense and place the remembrance tokens they have made on or around the Jizo statues in the
garden. A closing dedication or poem ends the ceremony. Participants can be invited for a quiet tea or to walk around the grounds
until they are ready to leave on their own. This helps people to make
the transition out of the ceremony in their own way and time.

A Ceremony of Remembrance for Children who Have Died

Officiant:
Because of the ceaseless action of cause and effect, reality appears
    in all its many forms.
To know this fully liberates all those who suffer.
All beings appear just as we all do, from the One, and pass away as
    we all do, after a few flickering moments or years of life, back to
    our Original Unborn Nature.

Truly our lives are waves on the vast ocean of True Nature, which
    is not born and does not pass away.

In gathering today we remember children who have died and express our love and support for their parents, family, and friends. Here these children are in complete repose, at one with the mystery that is our own birth and death, our own no-birth and no-death.

All recite together:

THE HEART OF PERFECT WISDOM SUTRA

The Bodhisattva of Compassion, from the depths of Prajna Wisdom,
Clearly saw the emptiness of all the five conditions,
Thus completely relieving misfortune and pain.
Know then:
Form is no other than emptiness,
Emptiness no other than form.
Form is exactly emptiness, emptiness exactly form.
Sensation, conception, discrimination, awareness are likewise like this.

All creations are forms of emptiness, not born, not destroyed,
Not stained, not pure, without loss, without gain.
So in emptiness there is no form, no sensation, conception, discrimination, awareness,
No eye, ear, nose, tongue, body, mind
No color, sound, smell, taste, touch, phenomena,
No realm of sight, no realm of consciousness,
No ignorance and no end to ignorance . . .
No old age and death, and no end to old age and death,
No suffering, no cause of suffering, no extinguishing, no path
No wisdom and no gain,
No gain and thus the Bodhisattva lives Prajna Wisdom
With no hindrance in the mind,
No hindrance, therefore no fear.
Far beyond deluded thoughts, this is nirvana.

All past, present, and future Awakened Ones live Prajna wisdom,
And therefore embody perfect enlightenment.

Therefore know that Prajna wisdom is the great mantra, the best
mantra, the unsurpassable mantra.
It completely cures all pain—this is the truth, not a lie.
So set forth this mantra and say:
Gaté! Gaté! Paragaté! Para-sam-gaté! Bodhis-vaha!
Heart of Perfect Wisdom!

All recite together:
ENMEI JUKU KANNON GYO (SUTRA OF COMPASSION)
KANZEON NAMU BUTSU YO
BUTSU U IN YO BUTSU U EN
BUPPO SO EN JO RAKU GA JO
CHO NEN KANZEON BO NEN KANZEON
NEN NEN JU SHIN KI
NEN NEN FU RI SHIN

All recite together nine times:
THE JIZO DHARANI
OM KA KA KABI SAN MA EI SOHA KA.

Officiant:
Eternal Nature pervades the whole Universe
Existing right here now.
In chanting the Heart of Perfect Wisdom sutra, the Enmei Jukku
Kannon Gyo, and the Jizo Dharani we dedicate our love and
prayerful thoughts to:

(List names of children)

And to all beings in the six realms.
May penetrating light dispel the darkness of ignorance
Let all karma be wiped out and the mind-flower bloom in eternal
spring
May we all practice, realize, and manifest the enlightened way
together.

Optional:
(Poem or the story of Kisagotami)

All recite together:

CLOSING DEDICATION

All Enlightened Beings throughout space and time,
All Honored Ones, Bodhisattvas, Mahasattvas,
Wisdom beyond wisdom,
Maha Prajna Paramita.

Appendix

ZEN MASTER BASSUI

A collection of the talks of Zen Master Bassui (1327–87) contains a dialogue with a monk who asked questions about the nature of Jizo Bodhisattva.

QUESTIONER: "In the sutra of Jizo Bodhisattva it is written: 'The bodhisattva rises early each day and enters various meditations and various hells to free ordinary people from their suffering in the Buddhaless era.' If these words mean that this is his skillful means for beings immersed in the six realms, those who whole-heartedly appeal to this bodhisattva will not fall into evil paths. But why would they seek enlightenment? People would simply appeal for Jizo's guidance. What do you think of this reasoning?"

BASSUI: "What's your purpose in asking this question?"

QUESTIONER: "For the sake of understanding the great matter of life and death."

BASSUI: "Then why don't you ask the bodhisattva Jizo?"

QUESTIONER: "I have only heard his name and seen his picture and statue. I have never seen his real body. How can I ask him?"

BASSUI: "If he can't teach you of the great matter of life and death now, he is not the right teacher for the world today. If he isn't a good teacher for this present world, how can he guide you after you leave it? If this is the case, then the words 'he guides them through this world and the next' are deluded speech. If you say it is deluded speech, you are slandering the sutra. But if you say it is true, it doesn't conform with what you said earlier. How then could you hope to rely on salvation by the bodhisattva? The words of the sutra are unmistakably clear. Error derives from the reader. As the sutra states that he rises early in the morning and enters various meditative states, could anyone be in any of the many hells when Jizo already abides in the state of meditation? If he were in hell, he could not be in a state of meditation. If he were in meditation he could not be in hell. How could he be in various meditative states and various hells at the same time?"

QUESTIONER: "I only understand the words from the sutra. The reality behind those words is not clear."

BASSUI: "Jizo stands for the mind-nature of ordinary people. Ji (the character for earth) is the foundation of the mind. Zo (the character for storehouse) is the storehouse of Buddha nature. It is in this Buddha nature that all the virtue of ordinary people is contained. Hence it is called the storehouse of the Tathagata. When the mind is deluded, as many ignorant thoughts as sands of the Ganges arise; when enlightened, this mind gives birth to infinite wonderful meanings. Being the source of good and evil, this mind is called earth (Ji). The earth gives birth to trees and grasses, hence it is used as an example here. Nature, the place where all the jeweled Dharmas return, is referred to as the storehouse (zo). That is why Jizo (earth-storehouse) is another name for mind-nature. Originally mind and nature were not separate. They were the one center where ordinary people in the six realms observed and perceived, and where they were masters of the six senses. It is here that they were teachers of those in the six realms. Since the four activities (walking, standing, sitting, and lying) of Buddhas and ordinary people throughout the day and night are the wonderful work of this mind-nature, it is referred to in the sutra as 'each day.' As for 'early morning,' it refers to the period before the distinction between black and white. Early morning means original nature—where there is no division between Buddhas and ordinary people.

"Ordinary people, not realizing their mind-nature, transmigrate in the six realms, encountering hardships imposed upon hell-dwellers. When they see into their own nature, good and evil thoughts all return to their roots. This is what is referred to as entering various meditative states. When you destroy the thinking process, eliminating the karmic activities of consciousness completely, your nature will be purified and you will enter the Dharma where the ten directions merge into one and the heavens and hells all become the Pure Land. Hence it is said that Jizo enters various hells. This is what is meant by the saying, 'Exhausting words and thoughts, there is no place that can't be penetrated.' Ordinary people are people with analytical thoughts. When you investigate your original nature thoroughly, thoughts will be under control and this nature of yours will be purified. There are neither Buddhas nor ordinary people within the realm of this purified nature—hence the expression 'saving ordinary people in the Buddhaless world.' Your own nature is truly a permanent part of you; it remains unchanged through eternity; and from the past up to the present it has lacked nothing to prevent you from applying yourself to save others. This is what is referred to as 'guiding them in this world and the next.'

"Now, hearing the teaching expressed in this way, what is it that is always acting? If you truly understand this, you are at that instant Jizo Bodhisattva. If on the other hand, you do not understand it at all, then Jizo becomes you. Hence the sutra says: 'Good believers in the Dharma: Because the benevolent bodhisattva has a clear and tranquil mind, he is called the Kannon Holding the Jewel of Suchness and Dharma Wheel. Because nothing can obstruct his mind, he is called the Bodhisattva of Universal Compassion. Because his mind is not subject to birth and death, he is called the Bodhisattva of

Long Life. Because his mind cannot be destroyed, he is called Jizo Bodhisattva (Bodhisattva of the Storehouse of Earth). Because his mind has no limits, he is called the Great Bodhisattva. Because his mind has no form, he is called the Maha Bodhisattva. If you can believe in this bodhisattva mind and receive it, you will be one with it and never lose it. . . .

"So you should realize that all the names of the bodhisattvas are just different names for the nature of the mind. As an expedient in the World Honored One's sermons, he defined things using certain names. With these names he pointed to the truth. Ordinary people, unaware of this truth, become attached to the names and, in the hope of attaining Buddhahood, seek the Buddha and Dharma outside their minds. It's like cooking sand in the hope of producing rice.

"In ancient times there was a certain bodhisattva. Though he had not yet attained enlightenment he had developed a compassionate mind. He spent his time building bridges across the Yangtze and Yellow rivers and building roads for ordinary people to come and go. To carry on this work he carried earth and mud on his back until he realized that his nature—that is to say, his very own Buddha nature—was the earth and he became emancipated. For this reason the World Honored One named him the Bodhisattva of the Storehouse of Earth. The vast mind of compassion of this bodhisattva was used as a metaphor to show that the true nature of the Dharma body of ordinary people is everywhere and to teach of the many creations that come from it. How can the virtuous work of any bodhisattva be compared to the magnificent perfection of this wonderful Dharma of mind? Ordinary people, being rather dull-witted, delude themselves and mistake these metaphors for facts. When you truly understand your own mind, you will realize for the first time that the sermons of all the Buddhas are nothing more than metaphors to point to the minds of ordinary people."

ZEN MASTER HAKUIN

The autobiography of Zen Master Hakuin (1686-1768) contains a story about Jizo Bodhisattva entitled "National Master Musō's Solitary Retreat."

THERE WAS ANOTHER OLD PRIEST living in those parts who went by the name of Tarumaru Sokai. Another half-baked, muddleheaded member of the Unborn tribe. One day he dropped by the temple and gave the following Dharma talk to the brotherhood:

YEARS AGO, THE NATIONAL Master Muso decided to spend the summer retreat alone in a mountain hut to devote himself to a practice regimen of rigorous austerity. He climbed the slopes of Mount Kentoku in the province of Kai, empty-handed except for a single skewer of dried persimmons, and took up residence in the tiny hut. He pledged firmly that, instead of the two normal meals each day, he would eat nothing but a single dried persimmon.

A young monk about fourteen or fifteen years of age, suddenly appeared out of nowhere, addressed Musō, and asked to be permitted to stay at the hut and serve as Musō's attendant during the summer retreat.

"What an uncommon request to hear from a boy of your years in this day," Musō said admiringly. "But you don't know that I plan to live here on only one dried persimmon each day. I'm afraid there won't be anything for you to eat."

"Share half your persimmon with me, then," the boy said. Musō, taken somewhat aback, didn't know what to answer. As he was mulling a response, the boy continued: "I'll serve you all summer. On only half a dried persimmon a day. What is there for you to consider, master?"

Musō reflected, "Even though he says that, he can't possibly stick out the whole summer on a few bits of dried persimmon. He'll be around a day or two, then he'll run off." With this in mind, Musō told the boy he could stay.

One month passed. Two months. Not only did the admirable young monk show no inclination to run off, he performed all his duties scrupulously, never slacking his efforts from first to last, whether he was engaged in his day-to-day chores or reading and chanting sutras. Neither did he seem the least bit bothered by the lack of nourishment. He swept. He drew water. He worked hard and well.

On the morning of the final day of the retreat, Musō summoned the young monk. "You have done an excellent job," he told him. "The valuable support you have given me all summer long has helped immensely in allowing me to focus on my practice. I know this isn't much of a gift, but I want you to have it as a token of my appreciation for the service you have rendered this summer."

So saying, Musō lifted the surplice [kesa] from around his shoulders and handed it to the boy. The boy accepted it, raising it up three times in veneration, and put it over his own shoulders.

"Master," he said, "as you leave this morning, you will come to a small hamlet at the foot of the mountain. To the left of the path you will see a house, recently built. The owner is a kinsman of mine. I'm going to hurry on ahead and ask him to have some food ready for your midday meal. You can take your time going down."

The boy made a parting bow, pressing his forehead to the earth, and sped off down the mountain path. He covered the ground almost as though he were flying.

Musō, aided by a bamboo staff, proceeded feebly, step by step, down the mountainside. It was nearly noon when he reached the hamlet. As he came to the newly built farmhouse the boy had described to him, a man emerged from the entrance. He hurried to where Musō stood, pressed his head to the ground in a deep bow, and said: "I'm very glad, and very relieved, to see you, master. I had expected you earlier and was just about to go up the mountain and start looking for you. Please, come into my house."

Musō asked where the young monk was.

"I was wondering that myself," the farmer replied. "He was here just a moment ago."

Stepping outside to see if he could catch sight of the boy, the farmer spotted one of his neighbors coming to the door.

"The strangest thing just happened," said the man. "I saw a young monk—he couldn't have been more than thirteen or fourteen—fly straight through the latticework of the doors on the shrine over there. I couldn't believe my eyes. No human could have done that! I went over to the shrine and pushed apart some loose planks to look inside. There was no sign of anyone in there. I don't know what to make of it."

Musō's host listened in amazement. He went over to the shrine to have a look for himself. Opening the doors, he went inside and carefully searched the interior of the hall from wall to wall. Seeing nothing out of the ordinary, he was about to leave when something caught his eye. "How odd," he thought. That three foot statue of Jizo Bodhisattva standing serenely in the corner there is wearing the very same damask surplice I saw on that young monk just a few hours ago. It's so eerie it frightens me."

In the meantime Musō, learning what had happened, rushed over to the shrine. He entered, took one look at the statue of Jizo, and immediately placed his palms together before him in homage. Then, overcome with tears, he dropped to the floor in a deep bow. Villagers who were clustering around the doorway began sobbing, too, and followed Musō's example by prostrating themselves in veneration, the scene impressed indelibly on their minds.

When Musō was finally able to suppress his tears, he exclaimed, "I cannot believe what has happened. My old surplice. I had worn it for years. I gave it to the young monk just this morning to reward him for his help during my retreat. Look at the Bodhisattva's face! And the rest of his appearance. The mirror image of that young boy monk! There is not the slightest difference.

"How unworthy I have been! I didn't have any idea he was Jizo Bodhisattva. But even so, I still didn't grant him so much as a bow. I made him work very hard all summer long. How frightening that I remained completely unaware of the Buddha's unknown working."

A great wave of excitement now spread through the village. "It was Jizo Bodhisattva!" villagers exclaimed in wonder and admiration. "The young monk we saw this summer up on the mountain following the master around was really this Jizo Bodhisattva."

People from places all over the district, some from as far as five leagues distant—young and old, men and women, priests and laity, all social ranks—began filing into the shrine. An unbroken stream of pilgrims that continued without cease for eight or nine days. All who came promptly expressed their respect and undying devotion for

National Master Musō. It is a story that has been handed down from generation to generation on the lips of village elders far and wide.

As Tarumaru finished telling his story, the monks were all wringing the tears from their sleeves. "What a splendid story." "What a splendid story . . . " they mumbled over and over.

But I thought to myself: "What those village elders admired and revered, what all those pilgrims came to worship—that's not what I'm after. I value Musō's deep faith and steadfastness of purpose. I envy his pure, unswerving dedication to the Way. I want to do as he did, find a pure, consecrated spot, quiet and secluded, where no one ever comes. I don't think I'm quite up to a daily ration of a morsel or two of dried persimmon, but if I could get a fistful of rice to boil up into a daily bowl of gruel, I'd like to spend a summer finding out how strong my dedication to the Way really is."

Zen Master Ryōkan

Zen Master Taigu Ryōkan (1758-1831) was a poor monk who lived in a simple hut in Japan's snow country. He spent his days begging for his meals, and was often accompanied by children, with whom he played games and wrestled. His poetry is much loved.

This poem is said to have been written to Ryōkan's prized Buddha statue, a small stone image of the bodhisattva Jizo, which, according to legend, Ryōkan used as a pillow when he napped. The statue, known as the "Pillow Jizo," is still preserved at the Ryōkan Museum in Izumozaki.

> *We sit face to face, and you don't say a word*
> *Yet your silence reveals the timeless essence of things*
> *Open books lie strewn about the floor*
> *And just beyond the bamboo shade*
>   *a gentle rain soaks the flowering plum*

Shukumon Kera was a village chief and friend of the poet. Ryōkan was particularly fond of the Lotus Sutra and copied it by hand as a gift for Shukumon. The chief buried this copy on the grounds of his home, under a statue of Jizo Bodhisattva. This ritual, traditionally done as a means of preserving the Dharma, also had the purpose of protecting the Kera family tutelary deities and assuring guidance for Shukumon after death.

Once Ryōkan was caught in a rainstorm. He took shelter with a Jizo, under the straw rain hat that had been placed on the statue. A passerby recognized Ryōkan and took him home, then pressed the famous poet for some calligraphy. Ryōkan wrote out a children's song about the alphabet.

Jizo-sama and the Straw Hats

This story of Ryōkan and Jizo's hat is related to a beloved traditional Japanese tale about Jizo.

ONCE THERE WAS A POOR elderly couple who lived a simple and contented life by making traditional straw hats. During a particularly bitter winter they found that they had no more rice or any other kind of food. They had just enough straw in their storeroom to fashion five hats. The old man took the hats to the market, where he walked and sang the virtue of his wares all day, but not a single hat was sold. As he returned home in the dusk, a snowstorm arose. As he trudged along in the wind and thick and swirling snow he almost missed seeing the Six Jizos at the crossroads that marked the path to his hut. He uttered a prayer of thanks for their guidance and then noticed that the Jizos were standing bareheaded in the snow. He took his five new straw hats and placed them on their heads. On the sixth Jizo he put his own old battered hat.

When he arrived home, his old wife greeted him happily, thinking that he had returned with food for a New Year's dinner, for it was New Year's eve. The old man was worried that his wife would be upset, but when he told her that he had no food nor money, and that he had not sold any hats but instead had given them away to the Six Jizos, she kissed him. She said that she had loved him all these years for just this, his generosity and kind nature. They drank some tea to warm themselves and went to sleep.

The next morning the couple opened the door of their cottage to welcome the first day of the New Year. Outside the door they found several sacks and big baskets filled with food and firewood. Who could have brought these unexpected gifts? In the new fallen snow they saw many small footprints. The tracks led them down the path to the six Jizo statues who stood at the crossroads, straw hats upon their heads, silently smiling.

Zen Master Soko Morinaga

Soko Morinaga Roshi was a modern Rinzai Zen Master and successor of Zuigan Roshi.

Jizo Bodhisattva and Children

Today we had an eye-opening ceremony for Jizo Bodhisattva. In Japan Jizo is considered to be a protector of children. On scrolls we often see Jizo with several children clinging to him, standing on the banks of the River Sai. Here children who have died very young must come and pile stones as offerings saying, "This one is for my father, the next for my mother." No sooner have they done this than blue and black devils come to demolish the piles of stones. When the devils disappear the children return to begin piling up stones again.

When my mother told me this story it touched me deeply and moved me almost to tears. When I was a child I was a very picky eater and [in] poor health. My mother often told me stories of Jizo Bodhisattva in order to encourage me to eat. She would tell me that children have to eat a lot to build a health body and live a long life. To die earlier than one's parents is totally against filial duty.

Isn't it interesting that the way Jizo protects children is just to shelter them under his sleeve? He doesn't send the devils away in order to make it easier for the children. If Jizo is so compassionate and is the King of Vows, why doesn't he wipe out the devils so the children can pile stones with ease? The real compassion of Jizo is to raise children who patiently pile stones without saying "I give up" even if devils endlessly demolish their piles of stones. Jizo protects those who courageously try again and again.

I am afraid that we have made a big mistake in raising our children. The big misunderstanding is about the devil named hardship. Many years ago our grandparents thought hardship was very important for building character, saying "The young should struggle with adversity." But after we were defeated in World War II, the idea spread that we should avoid hardship as much as possible, viewing it as unlucky to have excessive hardship. As it is troublesome to open the door, we have invented the automatic door opener. In the kitchen alone we have developed the electric stove, saving all the trouble of cooking with charcoal. Now we have the dishwasher, lemon squeezer, food chopper, mix master. People began to think that time and labor saving was equal to happiness. We used to use grandmother's worn out kimonos for diapers, and washed them one-by-one. Now people use paper diapers and throw them away after one use. Children used to take lunches to school in a box wrapped in cloth. They struggled to learn to tie a bow knot, a vertical knot and a horizontal knot. But nobody does such troublesome business anymore. They don't even tie shoes or sharpen pencils. Everything is made easy.

In this way people have begun to think that if they take all the troublesome things from children's lives they will live a life without hardship. If today's parents were Jizo Bodhisattva they would kill all the devils and make a machine to pile up the stones for the children. But, with all hardship removed, have children become happy?

We have to recognize that we are not born to live without hardship. We cannot enjoy true freedom until we go through hardship. When you play the piano you work hard and are corrected many times by your teacher. Sometimes you might be discouraged but if you continue patiently gradually your skill improves and you can play well. The devils at the River Sai might be called the partners of Jizo Bodhisattva. They contribute their half to his virtuous action. Hardship and effort always accompany us to insure our happiness and help us avoid misfortune. If we accept our hardships with a gentle mind, believing in the Buddha Way and praying quietly before him, our hardships will give us happiness. Jizo shelters the children from the devils but he also sends them out to pile the stones up once more. This is the very Buddha, the essence of religion.

Transmission of the Light

Nagarjuna and the Cintamani Jewel

The Transmission of the Light, a record of enlightenment stories of the ancestors in the Zen lineage, contains a story and verse about the cintamani jewel.

THE FOURTEENTH ANCESTOR WAS the Venerable Nagarjuna. Once the thirteenth ancestor Kapimala paid a visit to a Naga king and was given a wish-fulfilling jewel. His student Nagarjuna asked about it, "This jewel is the most precious in the world. Does it have a form or not?" Kapimala replied, "You only understand having form and not having form, but you do not understand that this jewel neither has form nor is without form. Furthermore you do not yet know that this jewel is not a jewel." Hearing this Nagarjuna was deeply enlightened.

Its solitary light, marvelously vast, is never darkened;
The wish-fulfilling mani jewel shines, illuminating everything.

A Hymn to Jizo Bodhisattva

Several hymns to Jizo Bodhisattva have been attributed to the Buddhist priest Kuya (903-72). They describe the scene at the bank of the River Sai.

This is a tale that comes not from this world,
But is the story of the Riverbank of Sai
By the road on the edge of Death Mountain.
Hear it and you will know its sorrow.
Little children of two, three, four,
Five—all under ten years of age—
Are gathered at the Riverbank of Sai
Longing for their fathers and mothers;
Their "I want you" cries are uttered
From voices in another world.
Their sorrow bites, penetrates

And the activity of these infants
Consists of gathering river stones
And of making merit stupas out of them;
The first storey is for their fathers
And the second for their mothers,
And the third makes merit for siblings
Who are at home in the land of the living;
This stupa-building is their game
During the day, but when the sun sets
A demon from hell appears, saying
"Hey! Your parents back in the world
Aren't busy doing memorial rites for you.
Their day-in, day-out grieving has in it
Much that's cruel, sad, and wretched.
The source of your suffering down here is
That sorrow of your parents up there.
So don't hold any grudges against me!"
With that the demon wields his black
Iron pole and smashes the children's
Little stupas to smithereens.
Just then the much-revered Jizo
Makes an awe-inspiring entrance, telling
The children, "Your lives were short;
Now you've come into the realm of darkness
Very far away from the world you left.
Take me, trust me always—as your father
And as your mother in this realm."
With that he wraps the little ones
Inside the folds of his priest's robes
Showing a wondrous compassion.
Those who can't yet walk are helped
By him to grasp his stick with bells on top.
He draws them close to his own comforting,
Merciful skin, hugging and stroking them,
Showing a wondrous compassion.
Praise be to Life-sustaining
Bodhisattva Jizo!"

Jizo the Sky Is Crying

by John Wentz

This poem was written on the passing of John B., an infant with multiple congenital anomalies and who was considered to be blind. It was written by a medical worker who had cared for this special little person. There were three days of showers after John died. This poem can be used in mizuko services.

Your face so serene, beggar's staff in your right hand,
wish-fulfilling jewel in your left,
my brother, please escort him,
give him to comfort, as today the sky is crying.

One of my special people, he never caused harm.
Over the years he came to know my touch.
He allowed me to pick up his fragile body,
bloated with fluids, little movement in his arms and legs.

They told me, "Don't go too near him,
he will convulse in seizures and fracture.
He must always stay in bed.
You know, he can neither see nor hear.
Let the nurses take care of him."

But I brought him along anyway,
The doctor said to go ahead and try.
Each day I lifted him, placing him on his belly
for a little ease in breathing.
Softly I would tap the fluids loose.
He became accustomed to my ways.

One day I sat him up in front of me, John supporting John.
His swollen body held in my arms adjusted its balance.
and he breathed a little deeper.
He pursed his mouth, swallowed and grimaced.

Each day he sat for shorter periods.
We faced a mirror, I behind him, watching his little signs.
One day he tracked me as I went to tend another special one.
As I returned he smiled—he could see!
That day I held him longer.

Another day his belly shook with laughter, frail arms extended,
rolls of flesh like a Chinese Buddha.
Looking at us in the mirror, he shook from the marrow.
Ahhhh—ha, ha, ha. Ahhhhhh.

Jizo, guide my friend to the Buddha's Western Paradise play-
   ground.
He wants to run and play at last. When I come,
I will play tag with him, and hold him in my arms once more.
Mind him for me, gentle Jizo.

References by Chapter

PREFACE

Nanamoli, Bikkhu, and Bikkhu Bodhi, trans. *Majjhima Nikaya.* Sutta 19:6. Boston: Wisdom Publications, 1995.

Vajirarama, Narada Thera, trans. *Dhammapada: Pali Text and Translation with Stories in Brief and Notes.* New Delhi: Sagar Publications, 1972.

CHAPTER ONE: JIZO IN AMERICA

DeVisser, M. W. *The Bodhisattva Ti-tsang (Jizo) in China and Japan.* Berlin: Oesterheld Verlag, 1914.

White, Helen C. *Tudor Book of Saints and Martyrs.* Madison: The University of Wisconsin Press, 1963.

CHAPTER TWO: JIZO IN JAPAN

Agency of Cultural Affairs. *Japanese Religion: A Survey.* New York: Kodansha International, 1972.

Arai, Abbot Yusei. *Shingon Esoteric Buddhism: A Handbook for Followers.* Fresno: Shingon International Buddhist Institute, 1997.

Dykstra, Yoshiko Kurata. "Jizo, the Most Merciful: Tales from Jizo Bosatsu Reigenki." *Monumenta Nipponica*, 33: 2. Tokyo: Sophia University, 1978. 179-200.

Kitagawa, Joseph M. *Religion in Japanese History.* New York: Columbia University Press, 1966.

Sakuma, Ryu. "Gyōgi," *Shapers of Japanese Buddhism.* Ed. Yusen Kashiwahara and Koyu Sonoda. Kyoto: Kyosei Publishing Company, 1994.

Wilson, William Scott, trans. *The Buddha's Sutra on the Bodhisattva, Enmei Jizo*. Self published. (available from Gentle Jizos — see Sources for Jizo Images)

Yamada, Patricia. "The Worship of Jizo." *Kyoto Journal* 2, Spring, 1987: 22-26.

Yamada, Patricia. "A Friend in Need: The Bodhisattva Jizo," *Japanese Religions* (Kyoto) 16 (1991): 76-92.

CHAPTER THREE: THE WATER BABY JIZO

Brooks, Ann Page. "Mizuko Kuyo and Japanese Buddhism," *Japanese Journal of Religious Studies* (Nagoya, Japan: Nanzan Institute for Religion and Culture) 8 (1981): 119-47.

Hardacre, Helen. *Marketing the Menacing Fetus in Japan*. Berkeley: University of California Press, 1997.

LaFleur, William R. *Liquid Life: Abortion and Buddhism in Japan*. Princeton, NJ: Princeton University Press, 1992.

Miura, Archbishop Domyo. *The Forgotten Child*. Trans. Jim Cuthbert. Oxon, UK: Aidan Ellis Publishing Ltd., 1983.

Nitta, Mitsuko. "Mizuko Kuyo and Foreign Scholars," *Bulletin of the Faculty of Sociology* (Shiga, Japan: Ryukoku University) 14 (1999): 59-67.

Nyanaponika, Thera, and Hellmuth Hecker. *Great Disciples of the Buddha*. Boston: Wisdom Publications, 1997.

Smith, Bardwell. "Buddhism and Abortion in Contemporary Japan: Mizuko Kuyo and the Confrontation with Death," *Japanese Journal of Religious Studies* 5 (1988): 3-22.

Vajirarama, Narada Thera, trans. *Dhammapada: Pali Text and Translation with Stories in Brief and Notes*. New Delhi: Sagar Publications, 1972. 107-108.

Yuasa, Nobuyuki, trans. *Matsuo Bashō: The Narrow Road to the Deep North and Other Travel Sketches*. London: Penguin Books, 1966.

Chapter Four: Jizo Bodhisattva, Protector of Children

Hall, Manly P. "Jizoji: House of the Comforter," *Buddhism and Psychotherapy* (Los Angeles: Philosophical Research Society, 1967): 225-249.

Hoff, Benjamin, ed. *The Singing Creek Where the Willow Grows: The Rediscovered Diary of Opal Whitely.* New York: Warner Books, 1986.

Mitchell, Stephen, trans. *Tao Te Ching.* New York: Harper Collins Publishers, 1988.

Morinaga, Soko. *Jizo Bodhisattva and the Children.* Trans. Giko Shimazaki with Susan Postal. Available through Gentle Jizos, see Sources for Jizo Images, page 273.

Yamada, Patricia. "Jizo and the Festivals of August," *Kansai Time Out* (Kobe, Japan) 54 (August 1981).

Chapter Five: The Stone Woman Dances

Bays, Jan Chozen. "What the Buddha Taught about Sexual Harassment," *Tricycle: The Buddhist Review* 8 (1998): 55-59.

Deal, William E. "Buddhism and the State in Early Japan," *Buddhism in Practice.* Ed. Donald Lopez. Princeton, NJ: Princeton University Press, 1995.

Glassman, Hank. "The Nude Jizō at Denkō-ji: Notes on Women's Salvation in Kamakura Buddhism," *Engendering Faith: Women and Buddhism in Pre-Modern Japan.* Ed. Barbara Ruch. Ann Arbor: University of Michigan Center for Japanese Studies, 2001.

Horner, I. B., trans. *The Book of the Discipline,* 10: 1. 1938; reprint, London: Pali Text Society, 1982.

Leighton, Daniel Taigen, *Bodhisattva Archetypes.* New York: Penguin, Putnam, 1998.

Murcott, Susan. *The First Buddhist Women: Translations and Commentary on the* Therigatha. Berkeley, CA: Parallax Press, 1991.

Murdoch, James. *A History of Japan: From the Origins to the Arrival of the Portuguese in 1542 A.D.* London: Kegan Paul, Trench, Trubner and Co., Ltd., 1925.

Tsai, Kathryn Ann, trans. *Lives of the Nuns: Biographies of Chinese*

Buddhist Nuns from the Fourth to Sixth Centuries. Honolulu: University of Hawaii Press, 1994.

CHAPTER SIX: THE PILGRIMAGE OF JIZO BODHISATTVA

App, Urs, "St. Francis Xavier's Discovery of Japanese Buddhism," *The Eastern Buddhist* 31 (1998): 40-71.

Boheng, Wu, and Cai Zhuozhi. *One Hundred Buddhas in Chinese Buddhism.* Singapore: Asiapac Books, 1997.

Dore, Henry, S. J. *Researches into Chinese Superstitions,* trans. from the French with historical and explanatory notes by M. Kennedy, S.J. Shanghai: T'usewei Printing Press, 1922. VII:i-vii, 235-302.

Eliade, Mircea, ed. *The Encyclopedia of Religion.* New York: MacMillan Publishing Company, 1987.

Frederic, Louis. *Flammarion Iconographic Guides: Buddhism.* Paris: Flammarion, 1995.

Getty, Alice. *The Gods of Northern Buddhism.* New Delhi: Munshiram Manoharlal Publishers, 1978.

Johnson, Reginald F. *Buddhist China.* San Francisco: Chinese Materials Center, 1976.

Mkhas-Grub-Rje. *Introduction to the Buddhist Tantric Systems.* Trans. F. D. Lessing and Alex Wayman. Delhi, India: Motilal Banarsidass Publishers, 1978.

Nanamoli, Bikkhu. *The Life of the Buddha According to the Pali Canon.* Kandy, Sri Lanka: Buddhist Publication Society, 1972. 263-264.

Saunders, E. Dale. *Mudra: A Study of Symbolic Gestures in Japanese Buddhist Sculpture.* London: Routledge & Kegan Paul Ltd., 1960.

Teiser, Stephen F. *The Ghost Festival in Medieval China.* Princeton, NJ: Princeton University Press, 1988.

────── *The Scripture on the Ten Kings and the Making of Purgatory in Medieval Chinese Buddhism.* Honolulu: University of Hawai'i Press, 1999.

ten Grotenhuis, Elizabeth. *Japanese Mandalas.* Honolulu: University of Hawai'i Press, 1999.

Yamada, Patricia. "Through Space and Time: Iconography of the

Bodhisattva Jizo." Lecture presented at Department of East Asian Studies, University of Arizona, October 1991.

CHAPTER SEVEN: JIZO BODHISATTVA AND THE PATH OF PILGRIMAGE

Nanamoli, Bikkhu, and Bikkhu Bodhi, trans. *Majjhima Nikaya: The Middle Length Discourses of the Buddha.* Boston: Wisdom Publications, 1995.

Rahula, Walpola. *What the Buddha Taught.* New York: Grove Press, 1959.

Sekida, Katsuki, trans. *Two Zen Classics: Mumonkan and Hekigan-roku.* New York: Weatherhill, 1977.

Suzuki, Shunryu. *Zen Mind, Beginner's Mind.* New York: Weatherhill, 1970.

Walshe, Maurice. *The Long Discourses of the Buddha: A Translation of the Digha Nikaya.* Boston: Wisdom Publications, 1987.

CHAPTER EIGHT: THE RING STAFF

Aitken, Robert, trans. *The Gateless Barrier: The Wu-Men Kuan (Mumonkan).* San Francisco: North Point Press, 1990.

Blyth, R. H. *Mumonkan,* vol. 4 of *Zen and Zen Classics.* Tokyo: Hokuseido Press, 1966.

Prip-Moller, J. *Chinese Buddhist Monasteries: Their Plan and Function as a Setting for Buddhist Monastic Life.* Hong Kong: Hong Kong University Press, 1937. 83-85.

Shibayama, Zenkei. *Zen Comments on the Mumonkan.* New York: The New American Library, Inc., 1975.

Yamada, Koun. *Gateless Gate.* Los Angeles: Center Publications, 1979.

CHAPTER NINE: THE CINTAMANI JEWEL

Cook, Francis H. trans. *The Record of Transmitting the Light: Zen Master Keizan's Denkoroku.* Los Angeles: Center Publications, 1991. 82-83.

Hofstadter, D. R. *Godel, Escher, Bach: An Eternal Golden Braid.* New York: Basic Books, 1979.

Nishijima, G. and C. Cross, trans. *Ikka-no-myoju (One Bright Pearl)*, in *Master Dōgen's Shobogenzo*. Surrey, England: Windbell Publications, 1994. 39-44.

Stevens, John, trans. *Dewdrops on a Lotus Leaf: Zen Poems of Ryōkan*. Boston: Shambala, 1993.

CHAPTER TEN: THE SIX RINGS AND THE SIX REALMS

Hsun Hua, trans. and commentary. *Sutra of the Past Vows of Earth Store Bodhisattva*. New York: Buddhist Text Translation Society and The Institute for Advanced Studies of World Religions, Publishers, 1974.

Kalu Rinpoche. *Luminous Mind: The Way of the Buddha*. Boston: Wisdom Publications, 1997.

Khema, Ayya. *When the Iron Eagle Flies: Buddhism for the West*. London: Arkana, 1991.

Salzberg, Sharon. *Lovingkindness: The Revolutionary Art of Happiness*. Boston: Shambhala, 1995.

Stevens, John. *Three Zen Masters: Ikkyu, Hakuin, Ryōkan*. Tokyo: Kodansha, 1993.

CHAPTER ELEVEN: EARTH STORE BODHISATTVA

Herold, A. Ferdinand. *The Life of the Buddha*. Tokyo: Charles E. Tuttle Company, 1954.

Hui, Pitt Chin, trans. *Bilingual Sutra on the Original Vows and Attainment of Merits of Kshitigarbha Bodhisattva*. World Fellowship of Buddhists, Singapore Regional Centre. Hong Kong Buddhist Book Distributor, 1976.

CHAPTER TWELVE: PRACTICING WITH JIZO BODHISATTVA

Leggett, Trevor. *The Warrior Koans: Early Zen in Japan*. London: Arkana, 1985. 34-38, 74-76, 116-118.

Chapter Thirteen: A Simple Ceremony of Remembrance for Children who Have Died

Aitken, Robert. *The Mind of Clover: Essays in Zen Buddhist Ethics*. San Francisco: North Point Press, 1984. 21-23, 175-6.

Poems

Cook, Francis H. trans. *The Record of Transmitting the Light*. Los Angeles: Center Publications, 1991

Heine, Steven, trans. *The Zen Poetry of Dōgen: Verses from the Mountain of Eternal Peace*. Boston: Tuttle Publishing, 1997.

Stevens, John, trans. *One Robe, One Bowl: The Zen Poetry of Ryōkan*. New York: Weatherhill, 1977.

——, trans. *Dewdrops on a Lotus Leaf: Zen Poems of Ryōkan*. Boston: Shambhala Publications, 1993.

Wentz, John. "Jizo the Sky Is Crying." Unpublished. Used by courtesy of the author.

Appendix

Abe, Ryuchi, and Peter Haskel, trans. *Great Fool: Zen Master Ryokan*. Honolulu: University of Hawai'i Press, 1996. 122.

Braverman, Arthur, trans. *Mud and Water: A Collection of Talks by the Zen Master Bassui*. San Francisco: North Point Press, 1989. 23-26.

Cook, Francis H. *The Record of Transmitting the Light: Zen Master Keizan's Denkoroku*. Los Angeles: Center Publications, 1991.

LaFleur, William R. *Liquid life: Abortion and Buddhism in Japan*. Princeton University Press: Princeton, 1992. 63-64.

Morinaga, Soko. "Jizo Bodhisattva and Children." Translated by Giko Shimazaki with Susan Postal.

Waddell, Norman, trans. *Wild Ivy: The Spiritual Autobiography of Zen Master Hakuin*. Boston: Shambhala, 1999. 57-60.

Glossary

BHIKSHU/BHIKSHUNI: (ALSO SPELLED BHIKKHU) a monk/nun, a person who has been ordained into a monastic life of poverty, celibacy and obedience to the rules set down by the Buddha in the Vinaya. Jizo is the only bodhisattva portrayed as a bhikkhu, with shaved head and monk's robe.

BODHISATTVA: an "enlightenment being," a person who vows not to enter the freedom from suffering called nirvana, but instead works with the wisdom and compassion he/she has gained through spiritual practice to free all others who suffer. Avalokitesvara or Kannon Bodhisattva is the embodiment of compassion. Often shown as a companion to Jizo Bodhisattva, she also is able to move freely among the six realms to aid those who cannot free themselves under their own power. Jizo is sometimes portrayed as the other bodhisattvas usually are, in royal garments and jeweled ornaments.

BUDDHA: literally "awakened one." See also Three Treasures. Shakyamuni Buddha is the completely enlightened being who lived during our historical era. Amida Buddha is the Buddha who has the power to bring believers to paradise if they believe and call upon him, particularly at the time of death. Maitreya Buddha is the Buddha who will come in the future. Jizo Bodhisattva has vowed to save all beings in the interval between the appearance on earth of Shakyamuni Buddha and Maitreya Buddha.

CINTAMANI JEWEL: a jewel carried by Jizo that represents the light that banishes fear, the light of the Dharma truth.

DEVA: literally "light- or shining-being", a being who is mortal and, living in a realm higher than the human realm, may be not at all or only barely visible to humans.

DHARANI: longer than a mantra, a dharani may also induce a particular state of mind and/or contain a particular teaching in an abbreviated form. The most abbreviated form or seed syllable of the Jizo mantra is KA.

DHARMA: See the Three Treasures.

EARTH MEDITATION: one of the meditations on the four great elements that the Buddha taught to his son Rahula. Rahula had been ordained at the age of seven. When he was eighteen he realized that he was handsome like his father. The Buddha detected his adolescent son's emerging pride and prescribed the four-element meditation to help him let go of attachment to his body as a self or as a possession of the self. In this case the meditation on earth helps develop impartiality and imperturbability. These are the qualities of Kshitigarbha or Jizo Bodhisattva.

EIGHTFOLD PATH: the eight aspects of spiritual practice which, if practiced sincerely and continuously, will become correct or "right" and lead to release from suffering. They consist of (1) right understanding, (2) right thought, (3) right speech, (4) right action, (5) right livelihood, (6) right effort, (7) right mindfulness, (8) right concentration.

FOUR NOBLE TRUTHS: the first and foundational teachings of the Buddha. They are (1) a fundamental aspect of life is the experience of dissatisfaction or suffering, (2) the cause of this suffering is clinging, ignoring or pushing away, (3) there is a way to lessen and ultimately end this suffering, (4) there is a path of practice to accomplish this (see Eightfold path).

IHAI: wooden memorial plaque inscribed with the name of the deceased. An ihai for a child may have the seed syllable for Jizo written at the top.

KESA: patchwork robe (surplice) worn by an ordained Buddhist.

KSHITIGARBHA: Sanskrit for earth store or earth womb. *Kshiti* (Ji- in Japanese, Ti- in Chinese, Ji- in Korean) means "earth," and -*garbha* (-zo, -tsang, -jang) means "storehouse," "treasury" or "womb."

MAHAYANA: a school of Buddhism that arose in the first century C.E. It stresses practicing not only to liberate the individual, but also to free all who suffer. Jizo Bodhisattva emerged from the Mahayana.

MANDALA: a symbolic representation of the structure and forces of the universe, used to teach and as a focus for meditation. Jizo Bodhisattva is one of the eight great bodhisattvas often depicted in mandalas.

METTA: loving-kindness, one of the four divine states of dwelling that can be cultivated through practice. The other three are karuna or compassion, mudita or appreciative joy, and upekkha or equanimity.

MIZUKO: "water baby," a child who has died before or shortly after birth. The mizuko kuyo is a memorial ceremony for these children.

NIRVANA: literally "extinction." The goal of Buddhist practice, an indescribable "state" revealed by the cessation of suffering.

OBON: Japanese harvest festival. From the Sanskrit word *ullambana*, the ceremony is said to have originated with Moggalana, a disciple of the Buddha. Moggalana's mother had died and he had a vision of her as a hungry ghost. He asked his teacher what he could do to relieve his mother's suffering. The Buddha recommended preparing a feast and offering it to the other monks on behalf of his mother. The Jizo festival is usually held at the end of Obon so that Jizo can guide and comfort distressed spirits who come to the feast.

SAMSARA: literally "journeying," the cycle of suffering, birth and death that will perpetuate itself endlessly until nirvana is revealed through practice. Jizo is the guardian of those who journey, both in physical and spiritual realms.

SANGHA: See the Three Treasures.

SANZEN: individual instruction from a Zen master, usually held in a private room. Also called dokusan.

SUTRA: literally "thread." A sutra is a collection of essential words or teachings, "lovely to hear," that are strung together as flowers and leaves are strung to make a garland. The original Indian sutras were collections of the teachings of the Buddha. They were written on palm leaves which were threaded together to make books. The Sutra of the Past Vows of Earth Store Bodhisattva is the most popular sutra about Kshitigarbha in China, and the Enmei Jizo Kyo is the most popular in Japan.

SHARIRA: relics, sometimes appearing as jewels, left when the body of an enlightened one is cremated. They may be collected and placed in a pagoda or shrine for veneration.

SESSHIN: literally "to settle the heart/mind." A silent Zen retreat, three to seven days in length.

SIX REALMS OF EXISTENCE: the realms through which all existence cycles, including those of hell (pain), hungry ghosts (desire), animals (ignorance), humans (rare opportunity to practice), asuras (jealousy and fighting) and gods (temporary pleasure). The six rings on Jizo's staff represent these realms.

TATHAGATA: "thus come one," an enlightened being.

THERAVADA: "teachings of the elders," the school of Buddhism found in Southeast Asia and closest to the original teachings of the Buddha. See MAHAYANA and VAJRAYANA

THREE REFUGES: taking refuge in the Three Treasures.

THREE TREASURES: also called the triple refuge, three jewels, triple jewel. The first treasure is the Buddha. This refers to both the historical Buddha who lived, became awakened, and taught in India, and also to the inherent perfection that dwells in all existence, which is revealed through spiritual practice. The second treasure is the Dharma, the law underlying all existence. Dharma can refer both to the teachings of the historical Buddha and also to all forms of existence, for anything can teach us about our mutual and original essence. The third treasure is the Sangha, which refers both to the community of people, lay and ordained, who practice the way taught by the Buddha, and also to the harmony in all things that is revealed when we practice and become awakened. Jizo may be shown carrying three jewels representing the Three Treasures.

TWELVE-LINKED CHAIN OF ARISING: a teaching of the Buddha that nothing is permanent or exists in isolation. The staff carried by Jizo may have twelve rings representing the twelve factors that give rise to a cycle of existence that is conditioned, relative, and interdependent.

VAJRAYANA: an esoteric school of Buddhism that arose in about 500 C.E. and spread to the countries of northern Asia. It emphasizes devotion to the teacher (guru) and the practice of rituals and mantras.

ZEN: literally "concentration." A spiritual practice based upon silent, seated meditation.

ZAZEN: seated meditation.

For further definitions and information, please consult *The Encyclopedia of Eastern Philosophy and Religion*, published by Shambhala Publications.

Acknowledgments

GRATITUDE TO MY BELOVED hermit friend, Donald Meyer, who loved books and whose death gift supported me as I wrote this book.

Gratitude to those at Tuttle Publications who made the vision manifest: Michael Kerber, Jan Johnson, Ben Gleason, Robyn Heisey, and PJ Tierney.

Gratitude to those who have given support, encouragement and advice. These include Robert Aitken Roshi, Ajahn Amaro Bhikkhu, Gyokuko and Kyogen Carlson, Daniel Taigen Leighton, Bob Ryan, Gary and Carol Koda Snyder, and all my students.

Gratitude to those who have reviewed or added to the book, including Jean Blomquist, Pat Boland and Reverend Heng Sure. Gratitude to those who contributed original artwork and poetry or helped in obtaining permissions: John Braverman, Lou Hartman, Tetsuo Kurihara, Wendy Egyoku Nakao, Reverend and Mrs. Nishiyama at Denko-ji, Mayumi Oda, Mikyo Ogushi, Susan Jion Postal, David Schneider, Kaz Tanahashi, and Philip Whalen.

Gratitude to those who have generously shared what they know about Jizo Bodhisattva, translated texts I could not read, found references I had overlooked and helped me with a Jizo pilgrimage. These include Laren Hogen Bays, Lenny Rozan Gerson, Hank Glassman, Ruben and Maria Habito, the stonemason Maekawa Ichiro, Scott Miller, Gary Snyder, David Wilson, William Scott Wilson, Mrs. Yamazaki and her grandson. Unfailing help came from the living intercultural bridge Tom Yuho Kirchner and the kind family outside the Myoshin-ji gate, Mr. and Mrs. Yunsei Yamaguchi.

Gratitude to Jillian Jiyu Romm for helping with the Jizo Ceremonies at Larch Mountain Zen Center.

Gratitude to the others who especially love Jizo and who have helped nurture this book in many ways: Yvonne Rand, Jack Van Allen, and Patricia Yamada.

Gratitude to my parents who began me on the path, my children and my husband who have continued to teach me so well. Lastly to my teachers who have given the greatest gift, the gift of the wonderful Dharma: Taizan Maezumi Roshi and Shodo Harada Roshi. Nine bows.

Index

Permissions

About the Author

JAN CHOZEN BAYS was born to pacifist parents on the day the atomic bomb was dropped on the city of Nagasaki. In childhood she lived in Chicago, Alabama, upstate New York, and Korea. After graduating from Swarthmore College in 1966, she taught biology and English in Malawi, Africa. She graduated from the School of Medicine at the University of California at San Diego in 1972.

Chozen began Zen practice in 1973 under Taizan Maezumi Roshi at the Zen Center of Los Angeles. She and her family moved to ZCLA in 1978 to allow for more intensive Zen study. Chozen took lay precepts in 1975 and received priest's ordination in 1979. Four years later she received Dharma transmission from Maezumi Roshi. She has served since 1986 as teacher for the Zen Community of Oregon in Portland and for the residential program at Larch Mountain Zen Center.

Chozen is also a pediatrician specializing in the area of child abuse. She has published a number of articles and chapters on the medical evaluation of child abuse and conditions mistaken for abuse. She has three grown children and enjoys playing marimba and making Jizo images in clay and glass.

Sources for Jizo Images

GENTLE JIZOS
P.O. Box 368, Clatskanie, OR 97016
(503) 728-0654
e-mail: zenworks@zendust.org
www.jizo.org

Ceramic images of Jizo from 2" to 8" tall, for gifts, and home or children's altars.

Cement images of Jizo from 18" tall, for outdoor use in gardens, with jewel and ring staff, available with receptacle for ashes. Jizo windows and nightlights for altars. Cards for giving with Jizo images and special occasions.

Sales support the Jizo Mountain Temple and Great Vow Zen Monastery.

DHARMACRAFTS
405 Waltham Street
Lexington, MA 02421
(800) 794-9862
www.Dharmacrafts.com

Various statues of Jizo made of wood, ceramic, or cast metal.

SAMMA AJIVA
   Distributed by Garden of Dreams
   1201 Bridgeway, Sausalito, CA 94965
   (800) 554-5048
   www.samma-ajiva.com

   Cement and plaster Jizo images from 2" to 24" tall, for the garden or
      altar. The faces are especially nice, some with a Western flavor.
   Sales support traditional village carvers in Indonesia.

KIRSTEN GALLERY
   5320 Roosevelt Way NE
   Seattle, WA 98105
   (206) 522-2011
   www.kirstengallery.com

   Original prints and cards. Both antique and modern statues of Jizo.

This information is current as of printing.